DIARY OF A BLACK JEWISH MESSIAH

T0324268

STANFORD STUDIES IN JEWISH HISTORY AND CULTURE

Edited by David Biale and Sarah Abrevaya Stein

DIARY OF A BLACK JEWISH MESSIAH

The Sixteenth-Century Journey of David Reubeni

through Africa, the Middle East, and Europe

ALAN VERSKIN

STANFORD UNIVERSITY PRESS

Stanford, California

Stanford University Press
Stanford, California

Printed in the United States of America on acid-free, archival-quality paper

Library of Congress Cataloging-in-Publication Data
Names: Reuveni, David, active 16th century, author. | Verskin, Alan, translator, writer of introduction.
Title: Diary of a black Jewish messiah : the sixteenth century journey of David Reubeni through Africa, the Middle East, and Europe / [translated by] Alan Verskin.
Other titles: Sipur Dayid ha-Re'uveni. English | Stanford studies in Jewish history and culture.
Description: Stanford, California : Stanford University Press, 2023. | Series: Stanford studies in Jewish history and culture | Translation of: Sipur Dayid ha-Re'uveni. | Includes bibliographical references and index.
Identifiers: LCCN 2022016420 (print) | LCCN 2022016421 (ebook) | ISBN 9781503634428 (cloth) | ISBN 9781503634435 (paperback) | ISBN 9781503634442 (ebook)
Subjects: LCSH: Reuveni, David, active 16th century. | Pseudo-Messiahs—Biography.
Classification: LCC BM752 .R4813 2023 (print) | LCC BM752 (ebook) | DDC 296.8/2092 [B]—dc23/eng/20220608
LC record available at https://lccn.loc.gov/2022016420
LC ebook record available at https://lccn.loc.gov/2022016421

Typeset by Elliott Beard in Baskerville 10.5/15
Cover design: Jason Anscomb
Cover image: Library of Congress, Genoese World Map 1457

For my parents-in-law,
Jerry and Sharon Muller

מי כמוך באלמים יי מי כמוך רואה בעלבון בניך ושותק

Who is like You among the mute, O Lord? Who is like You, who—even when seeing the humiliation heaped upon Your children—keeps silent?

Mekhilta de-Rabbi Yishmael (5th–6th century CE)

Cast aside the conventional view that the Messiah will suddenly sound a blast on the great trumpet and cause all the inhabitants of the earth to tremble. On the contrary, the Redemption will begin by awakening support among the philanthropists and by gaining the consent of the nations to the gathering of some of the scattered of Israel into the Holy Land.

R. Zvi Hirsch Kalischer, *Seeking Zion* (1862)

Help yourselves and God will help you!

Leon Pinsker, *Auto-Emancipation* (1882)

CONTENTS

Acknowledgments   xi

Note on the Translation   xiii

Map 1. The World of David Reubeni   xv

Map 2. The World of David Reubeni   xvi

Introduction   1

1   Africa   31

2   Egypt and the Holy Land   43

3   Italy   58

4   Portugal   87

5   Spain   154

Appendix
Solomon Cohen's Addendum   163

Notes   167

Index   185

ACKNOWLEDGMENTS

The path leading to my interest in David Reubeni is a long one. My teachers Nicholas Terpstra and Susan Schreiner drew me into the world of Renaissance studies. Mercedes García-Arenal's work has been inspirational. Her book *A Man of Three Worlds: Samuel Pallache, a Moroccan Jew in Catholic and Protestant Europe* showed me the potential for research that crossed religious and geographical boundaries. In 2016, she kindly invited me to a conference on forced conversion that drew my attention to its extensive ramifications and led me to focus on David Reubeni. I have been fortunate to get to know William Miles, the foremost expert on the Jews of contemporary Africa. His enthusiasm for research into Jews of color has been infectious. Many years ago, Yaron Ayalon cautioned me against using the term "false messiah." To do so, he argued, is to make an epistemological claim that historians should not make. I have studiously followed this advice. I would also like to thank Juan Miño for his help with Portuguese texts.

I am grateful to Margo Irvin at Stanford University Press for her enthusiasm for this book and for all her efforts in shepherding me through the process of publication. Cindy Lim and Tiffany Mok gave me invaluable help as this project neared completion, and Elspeth MacHattie meticulously copyedited the manuscript. I also thank the anonymous reviewers for their valuable feedback.

The History Department at the University of Rhode Island has been a wonderful place to work and I am deeply grateful to all my colleagues. This book has benefited from the tireless efforts of two of that department's chairs, Rod Mather and Robert Widell, who have gone out of their way to provide me with time to engage in research. Leslie Dancy, our department office manager, has generously helped me with copying research materials. At the URI library, Amanda Izenstark has provided me with access to vital library resources, and Tawanda Maceia has made this project possible by going to great lengths to procure books and articles through interlibrary loan. I would also like to thank my students, both undergraduate and graduate, who took my travel literature seminar and contributed to my thinking on the topic. I gratefully acknowledge the support of the URI Center for the Humanities and the Office of Research Development.

This book was written over the course of the pandemic. I would like to thank some of the people who helped to make the experience less isolating: Donny Cotton, Mehmet Darakcıoglu, Meyer Goldstein, Larry Katz, Marsha and Alvan Kaunfer, John Landry, Mordechai Levy-Eichel, Morty Miller, Michael Satlow, Mark Sinyor, Noah Tetenbaum, and Mark Wagner. I would also like to thank all those people who posted their research or primary sources online and thereby made this project possible.

My father, Milton Verskin, has read over this entire manuscript and provided me with valuable feedback. My wife, Sara, has provided me with expert advice and translation assistance. I am grateful for Hannah's and Maya's fascination with Reubeni's diary. They even read several chapters of it with me in the original Hebrew. Their brother, Daniel, has provided welcome breaks of running and Ping-Pong and stimulating ethical debates.

This book is dedicated to my parents-in-law, Jerry and Sharon Muller. While scholarly life is so often portrayed as inimical to family life, they introduced me to the opposite model. From the very first, they warmly welcomed me into their family. Their dinner table is a model of what open and inclusive, intergenerational intellectual inquiry should be. To hear them speak of their own pursuits is a pleasure, and to have them as a sounding board for my thoughts is a privilege. I thank them for this and for so many other things.

Alan Verskin
Providence, Rhode Island

NOTE ON THE TRANSLATION

David Reubeni's diary was written in a Hebrew that, we can assume, was intended to represent the native Hebrew spoken in his invented Jewish kingdom in Arabia. It is indeed a fresh Hebrew, quite unlike the flowery prose that usually characterizes Jewish literary writings of the Renaissance. It is also a Hebrew like no other. Hebrew writings of this period can often be mined for clues regarding the language that their authors spoke in their daily lives. Reubeni's grammar and usage, however, is so idiosyncratic and anarchic that philologists have come to no consensus as to what language he and his authorial collaborators might have originally spoken, and guesses range from Yiddish to Arabic, from Slavic languages to Romance ones.

To add to the difficulties of translation, only a single manuscript of the diary survived into the modern period and that manuscript was lost before the era of photographic reproduction. The result was that the scholars who produced the first printed editions of the diary had to rely on a nineteenth-century facsimile of the manuscript made by hand with tracing paper. That facsimile manuscript often appears to be corrupt or missing text, and it is unclear whether these lapses ought to be assigned to the author or to the scribe. There are frequent repetitions, jumbled sentences, and awkward switching between first, second, and third person. While the text's general meaning is usually clear, determining the specifics frequently requires considerable creative interpretation on the part of the translator. I have noted some, but not all, of the instances in which I have made such interpretive choices, since a more comprehensive accounting would have required the publication of a second volume consisting only of notes.

These difficulties aside, I will also note that an intermediate student of Hebrew interested in consulting the original text will have little difficulty reading it and understanding the gist of Reubeni's meaning. Reubeni's vocabulary is not large. His conversational, down-to-earth, make-do approach to communication in Hebrew both lends authenticity to his message and is the perfect complement to his talent as a consummate improviser. Thus, in my translation, I have attempted to replicate Reubeni's direct, intimate, unpretentious, but self-assured, literary register.

Scholarly readers will notice that I have omitted diacritics from transliterated terms. I have done so to make the text more accessible to a popular audience and to those reading on a variety of electronic formats. Researchers who are moved to delve further into this material are welcome to contact me about these specifics. As for personal names derived from the Bible, I have rendered them in ways that will likely be familiar to contemporary English-speaking audiences, just as the names Reubeni used were familiar to his contemporaries.

This translation is based on Aaron Aescoly's 1940 critical edition of Reubeni's diary, and the numbers in the margins of my translation refer to the page numbers of that edition.

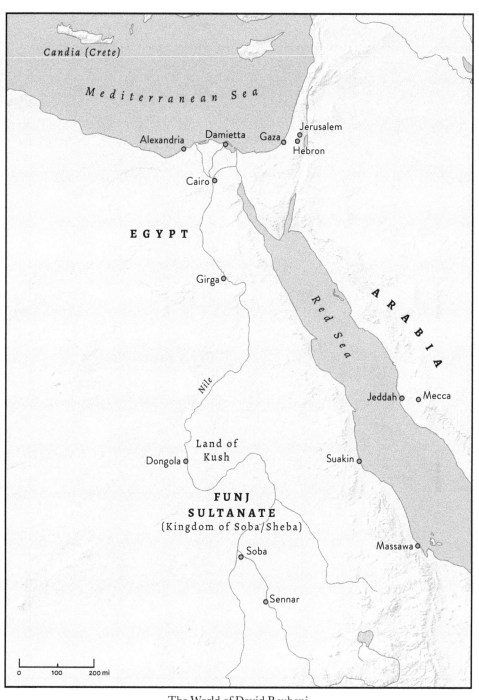

Candia (Crete)

Mediterranean Sea

Alexandria Damietta Gaza Jerusalem
                                    Hebron

Cairo

EGYPT

Girga

Red Sea

A R A B I A

Nile

Jeddah Mecca

Land of
Kush

Dongola

Suakin

**FUNJ
SULTANATE**
(Kingdom of Soba/Sheba)

Soba

Massawa

Sennar

0   100   200 mi

The World of David Reubeni

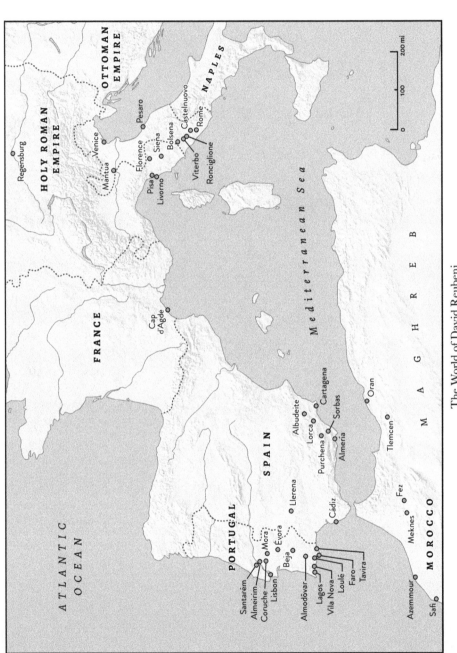

The World of David Reubeni

DIARY OF A BLACK JEWISH MESSIAH

INTRODUCTION

"I am not the Messiah," said David Reubeni, "I am a greater sinner before God than any one of you. I have killed many people. In a single day, I once killed forty enemies. I am not a sage or a kabbalist, neither am I *a prophet nor the son of a prophet*. I am merely an army commander."[1] Short and thin, with skin "as black as a Nubian"[2] and a body covered in scars, Reubeni claimed to be the commander of a powerful Jewish army and the brother of a Jewish king who ruled over three hundred thousand Jews in the Arabian desert of Habor, all descendants of the lost Israelite tribes of Gad, Manasseh, and Reuben (hence his name).[3] Despite speaking only Hebrew and Arabic, he successfully forged relationships with Christian rulers, including the Holy Roman Emperor, Charles V, the King of Portugal, João III, and Pope Clement VII, by dangling the possibility of an alliance against the Ottomans in exchange for weapons and experts in their manufacture. He gained Jewish followers, including many forced converts to Christianity (conversos), who practiced Judaism in secret to avoid persecution, with the promise that his army would liberate them from oppression by force, deliver them to the Holy Land, and restore their pride and autonomy. Many Jews embraced him as the Messiah, despite his denials, and he attracted the patronage and support of some of Europe's wealthiest Jews and rabbinic elites. A mysterious figure who guarded his secrets closely, he traveled through Africa, the Middle East, and Europe before being halted by the Inquisition and burned at the stake in 1538 for preaching Judaism to Christians. He left us his diary, detailing the hustle and daily grind of a charismatic showman—a showman whose promise of a reunion between far-flung peoples, of allyship, conquest, and power, appealed to the giddy optimism, credulity, and fear that gripped the Mediterranean world in the age of exploration.

Africa and the Middle East

Reubeni's diary begins in the year 1521 with him leaving Arabia, charged by his brother, King Joseph, and the seventy elders to seek an audience with the pope. From the Red Sea port of Jeddah, he proceeded by ship to the Sudan and then gradually made his way up the Nile. We have no external confirmation of his journeys in either Africa or the Middle East. Some scholars have argued that he did not visit Africa, because the details he provides on the people he met are comparatively sparser in the African section of his diary. Further, some of his descriptions seem to pander to a European audience that viewed Africa as an exotic locale. Reubeni thus tells of narrow escapes, cannibalistic tribes, and his encounters with enslaved women. Others, however, argue that Reubeni likely did visit Africa because he includes some reliable geographical details that could not have been culled from literary sources.[4]

In Africa, Reubeni reports, he disguised himself as a Muslim *sayyid* (descendant of Muhammad) and was widely embraced by Muslims as a holy man. He tells of his close relationship with Amara Dunqas, the founder of the Funj Sultanate, with whom he traveled around the region for ten months.[5] Amara treated him as an honored guest until their relations soured when another *sayyid*, angling for the monarch's attention, spread rumors that Reubeni was Jewish and he was compelled to leave.

Reubeni's next stop was Cairo, where, despite still being disguised as a Muslim, he made overtures to the Jewish community, all of which were rebuffed. He reported meeting Abraham de Castro, the Chief of the Mint and the most powerful Jew in Cairo.[6] Despite Reubeni's sharing his "secret" with him, Abraham was unmoved, and refused to host Reubeni, on the grounds that it would compromise both Abraham's own safety and that of all the Jews of the city.[7] Reubeni's valuables were then stolen by the unscrupulous Muslim host he ended up with after being turned away by Abraham de Castro, and despite the efforts of a friendly Turkish Muslim official, he was unable to recover them. This incident was no doubt included in Reubeni's description of his travels to explain to a European audience why, despite being the ambassador of a rich Jewish kingdom, he had arrived penniless in Venice.

When Reubeni left Egypt for Palestine, he did so in the company of Muslims and without the help of Jews. In Palestine, still disguised as a *sayyid*, he was embraced by Muslims who welcomed him into both the Cave of the Patriarchs in Hebron and the Dome of the Rock in Jerusalem. He also visited a church. The details that he provides of these places are highly accurate and lead one to believe that he did indeed visit them. Reubeni reports few interactions with Jews in Jerusalem, and none with any of the Jewish elites with which we are familiar. From his silence, one can perhaps deduce that he was unsuccessful in convincing them to support his project, perhaps reflecting the cautious attitude that Jerusalemite rabbis adopted towards messianic claimants during this period.[8] By contrast, in the smaller Jewish community of Gaza, populated by traveling Jewish merchants hailing from diverse places, Reubeni had somewhat greater success, obtaining funds for his trip to Venice.[9] On the way to Venice, Reubeni had another brief sojourn in Egypt, this time in Damietta and Alexandria. Although still disguised as a Muslim, he reported far more interactions with Jews and even managed to spend the Jewish New Year at an Alexandrian synagogue.[10] Reubeni's close interactions with Jews did not go unnoticed by some local Muslims, who were shocked that a man whom they believed to be a *sayyid* was not surrounding himself exclusively with coreligionists. Although they attempted to create difficulties for him, to his relief, nothing came of these attempts.

In Alexandria, Reubeni won his first follower, a Jewish drifter from Naples named Joseph, whom Reubeni describes as irascible, violent, and prone to thievery. Joseph volunteered to guide him to Rome, an offer that he accepted. While they were still in Egypt, Joseph was involved in a violent scuffle with Reubeni's Jewish hosts. Joseph threatened to denounce them to the governor of Egypt, but Reubeni was spared from this potentially dangerous involvement by the intervention of a local kabbalist, who talked Joseph out of doing so.[11] Undeterred by Joseph's risky behavior, or perhaps with little choice, Reubeni left Egypt for Venice with him as his guide. Joseph continued his misbehavior aboard ship and, indeed, all the way to Rome, sometimes bringing Reubeni unwanted outside attention.

Reubeni in Christendom

It was only once Reubeni reached the Christian world in 1524 that his activities began to have some modest success. His message was exquisitely well-tailored to the atmosphere of apocalyptic expectation that gripped the sixteenth-century Mediterranean. He arrived in an age that had experienced the Ottoman capture of Constantinople, the end of Muslim Spain, and the outlawing of all religions but Catholicism in Iberia. Europe was riven with conflicts. The religious crisis posed by the Reformation-era fragmentation of the Catholic Church had begun a radical reorientation of political loyalties. The political power of the papacy had never been weaker, and this had sparked a devastating war between the Holy Roman Emperor and the King of France over Italian territories, which culminated in the sack of Rome in 1527. Even as Christian kingdoms vied with one another, they looked with dread towards an ascendant Ottoman Empire. The armies of Suleyman the Magnificent were advancing westward, capturing vast swathes of the Balkans and Hungary, and reaching the gates of Vienna in 1529. Nevertheless, despite their fears of being conquered, Europeans stood at the dawn of a new era of global exploration, discovery, and vast imperial expansion. The Spanish encountered and soon conquered the great Aztec and Mayan civilizations of Central and South America. Never in their history had Europeans been so fascinated with the world beyond them. If these disruptions were not enough, the Mediterranean had been visited by a series of natural disasters, including earthquakes, severe flooding, and pandemics, news of which circulated more widely than in previous periods.[12] These tumultuous times led many Jews, Christians, and Muslims to interpret such events as harbingers of the Apocalypse. Imperial struggles for global rule were seen as preparing the ground for a millennial age in which all of humanity would be united in a common and purified faith under a single ruler.[13] It was widely believed that this final age of religious uniformity would be preceded by an intense battle between the forces of good and evil, represented by the Muslim and Christian worlds. Apocalyptic thinking was widespread across social classes, and there was an atmosphere of pervasive fear and anticipation of the coming of the End.[14]

Arriving penniless in Venice in early 1524, Reubeni was unlike most other ambassadors, who came in their own ships bearing expensive gifts.[15] Having no material resources with which to impress, he instead cultivated a reputation for piety and asceticism, manifested by frequent fasting and prayer. His first victory was in gaining the trust of Moses dal Castellazzo, a well-known artist as well a banker and entrepreneur with ties to elites across the region. With his help, Reubeni was able to win over some, but not all, of Venice's Jewish elites. He was also supported by the wealthy Jewish banker Simon ben Asher Meshullam, whose family was intermarried with the da Pisas, an influential family of Italian Jews who were to become Reubeni's key supporters.[16] In this way he was able to secure funds to travel to Rome and to obtain introductions to that city's Jewish leadership.

A Black Messiah in Rome

In Rome, Reubeni encountered a city rife with the practice of divinatory arts, prophecy, and eschatology. It was a city on edge, gripped by bouts of collective panic that seem to have affected most of its inhabitants, regardless of social class.[17] Reubeni was immediately able to attract a circle of Jews and Christians who were deeply engaged in apocalyptic speculation. Here, his appearance may have helped him. One of the first things that struck his interlocutors, whether Jewish or Christian, was the darkness of his skin. Daniel da Pisa, his closest supporter, described him as having "a black visage" (*shahor ha-mar'eh*), Abraham Farissol said he was "blackish" (*sheharhor*),[18] and Gedaliah ibn Yahya said he was "as black as a Nubian" (*shahor ke-kushi*). When Diogo Mendes, a leading converso businessman, was arrested by the Inquisition and questioned about Reubeni, he reported that he was "black" (*noir*).[19] Giovanni Battista Ramusio, an orientalist sent by the Venetians to investigate Reubeni, reported both that he was an Arabian and that he was "similar to the Indians of Prester John"—*Indians* being the term that Ramusio, among others in this period, confusingly used to refer to Abyssinians.[20] While such statements cannot shed definitive light on Reubeni's ethnic identity, which will likely never be known with certainty,[21] we do know that both Jewish and Christian dabblers in apocalyptic expectation would have found Reubeni's "black" skin evocative. Since the fifteenth century, rumors of the rediscovery of the ten lost Israelite tribes had increasingly circulated in Jewish communities. They described these tribesmen as powerful and courageous warriors, who fiercely defended an independent Jewish kingdom, located somewhere adjacent to the Muslim world. A parallel legend existed among European Christians concerning a mythical monarch, known as Prester John, who governed a powerful Christian kingdom that was surrounded by Muslims—according to some it was in Asia; according to others, in Africa. Many believed that Prester John would play a decisive role in an apocalyptic battle in which Islam would be vanquished and Mecca conquered. By the sixteenth century, European Christians came to identify Prester John with the real Christian emperor of Abyssinia and still hoped for his help against the Ottomans.[22] Jews, influenced by this Christian focus on Africa, increasingly envisaged apocalyptic battles as being fought by fierce Jewish warriors from the lost tribes, hidden in the African continent, and often at war with Prester John's kingdom.[23] Some Jewish scholars actively mined the works of Christian geographers to locate these tribes and discover other clues about the ways messianic battles might unfold.[24] Legends of the lost tribes and Prester John were reinforced by travelers' tales. For example, in an account published a decade before Reubeni reached Rome, Ludovico de Varthema, the first European Christian to visit Mecca, reported seeing a mountain in Arabia on which five thousand Jews dwelled. These Jews, he wrote, "go about naked, are five or six spans [about two and one-half feet] in height, have feminine voices, and are more black than any other color. They live entirely on sheep's flesh and eat nothing else. They are circumcised and confess that they are Jews. If they can get a Moor into their hands, they skin him alive."[25] Even in the work of a well-respected explorer like de Varthema, it was often difficult for a contemporary audience to distinguish fact from fantasy, and Reubeni surely benefited from this world of messianic speculation and geographical uncertainty. In an article provocatively titled "The Black Messiah," Ariel Toaff has argued that by the time Reubeni appeared in Europe, such legends and reports had led many Jews to place their hopes in lost Israelite tribes, located in Africa, and that this primed them to accept Reubeni as "a black messiah."[26] Many of Reubeni's supporters may thus have embraced him because of, rather than despite, his being a Jew of color.

Reubeni and the Jews of Rome

Reubeni's most important Jewish patron was the da Pisa banking family, described by one scholar as a Jewish "super elite."[27] Daniel da Pisa, with whom Reubeni had his closest interactions, was then regarded as the de facto head of the Jews of Rome, because of his close relationship with Pope Clement VII. Even as he was attending to Reubeni and serving as his intermediary with the pope, he was authoring an influential set of bylaws to govern Rome's Jews and ease tensions between the old Roman Jewish families and the newer Jewish families, which included many Iberian exiles.[28] The da Pisas felt a great responsibility to ameliorate the condition of Iberian Jewish refugees and spent a good deal of their money on ransoming those who had become captives.[29] Some family members were also known for their study of the Kabbalah and apocalyptic speculation. Indeed Yehiel da Pisa, Daniel's cousin who hosted Reubeni for some time, eventually chose to withdraw from his role in the family bank to pursue kabbalistic studies.[30] The da Pisa family was crucial in facilitating Reubeni's liaisons with key dignitaries, covering the expenses of his entourage, and facilitating his travel to Portugal.

Reubeni describes Rome as a city swirling with rumors and thick with intrigue and informers. According to his diary, he had many Jewish opponents and was often unsure about whom to trust. When Jews gathered to celebrate his receiving of letters of support from the pope, he found himself embarrassingly unable to distinguish between friend and foe. He misinterpreted the friendly gestures of Jewish community leaders, including the eminent Rabbi Obadiah Sforno, as attempts to undermine him, and publicly vented his anger against them. This chain of events somehow led to their arrest, although Reubeni was soon able to secure their release.[31] The Roman rumor mill also misled him about the intentions of his most important patron, Daniel da Pisa, with whom he briefly severed relations.[32] His mission was again endangered when his servant Joseph spread rumors that he intended to return Iberia's forced converts (conversos) to Judaism.

A community of such converts resided in Rome and, believing that these rumors jeopardized their precarious existence, they threatened to kill Joseph if he did not cease such talk.[33] Reubeni also faced some Jewish opponents who asked the pope to burn him at the stake, on the grounds that if he was indeed a divinely charged messenger as he claimed, God would protect him.[34] He was saved when the pope punished his accusers by dispatching them to a galley for hard labor. All these incidents recounted by Reubeni show him to be acutely aware of the dangers that his project posed both to himself and to the communities he visited.

Reubeni stresses that the help he received came from men and women alike. Help from women came in a variety of forms. Sometimes it was financial. While he was in Rome, the well-known businesswoman and philanthropist, Benvenida Abravanel, provided him with funds on three separate occasions.[35] She further gifted him the silk flag that he proudly unfurled everywhere he went, regarding it as an important martial symbol and witness to his status as a general.[36] Reubeni describes meeting many Italian women with high levels of literacy and education.[37] He also describes women occupying more traditional roles as devoted hosts and as caregivers, who tended to him when he was ill.[38] It is noteworthy that, in these pious homes, hospitality sometimes included women of the household dancing in front of and playing music for guests.[39]

Reubeni's relative popularity among Italian Jews led him to conclude that, whereas the Jews of Italy were "fit for war, valiant, and lionhearted," the Jews of Islamic lands were "timid, cowardly, fearful, and unfit for war."[40] The statement reflects Reubeni's disappointment that his mission to the Jews of Islamic lands had been a failure, despite his fluency in Arabic and cultural familiarity with the region. There were likely many reasons for this. Reubeni was certainly hampered by the fact that he had traveled through Egypt and Palestine disguised as a Muslim. The danger of harboring an individual weaving across religious boundaries would have been substantial, and Reubeni notes that he was told as much. But his failure to engage such Jews likely runs deeper. While Jews in Egypt and Palestine no doubt experienced tensions with the Muslim majority, their lives in these lands were stable, especially when compared to the ordeals suffered by Iberian Jews. Jews in smaller communities, like Gaza and Damietta, were content to host Reubeni and provide funds for his transportation, but they made no great sacrifices. Larger and more established communities, like those of Jerusalem and Cairo, were often reluctant to provide even minimal hospitality, given Reubeni's potential to disturb the stable and relatively safe status quo. By contrast, Italian Jews had not only witnessed the expulsions of their Iberian Jewish neighbors but, in parts of southern Italy, had faced such threats of expulsion themselves. They knew of the Inquisition and had seen Charles V allow its spread within his vast empire. They watched with trepidation as, throughout the 1520s, Charles attempted to expand his Italian territories, efforts which resulted in the 1527 sack of Rome. Concerned about this looming disruption of Jewish life, it is not surprising that some Italian Jews were inclined to take a risk by supporting Reubeni.[41]

Reubeni and the Christian Leadership of Rome

In Rome, Reubeni won the patronage of Cardinal Egidio di Viterbo, who paved the way for his audience with the pope. Egidio was one of the most accomplished humanists of the period—a poet, an orator, a philosopher, and an archaeologist. Crucially for Reubeni, he was a devoted Hebraist whose apocalyptic investigations led him to produce a highly influential synthesis of Christianity and the Kabbalah.[42] When Reubeni met Egidio, the latter had been studying kabbalistic texts for a decade and had developed a considerable mastery of Hebrew, perhaps even enough to understand Reubeni's speech. Although, with the exception of his Hebrew tutor Elijah Levita, Egidio was quite hostile to Jews, Judaism, and even to Jewish converts to Christianity, he considered the Kabbalah to be an important repository of truth and saw his role as that of liberating it from its impious Jewish guardians.[43] Egidio believed the world to be on the brink of a golden age in which all humanity would submit to a single religion. He saw the success of Portugal's eastern conquests in India and the Persian Gulf as evidence of this and plumbed the Kabbalah for further details as to how this age would come about. He was understandably excited by Reubeni, through whom he no doubt hoped to play a part in the apocalyptic events to which he had devoted so much of his life in study.[44] Also then residing with Egidio was Leo Africanus, the accomplished diplomat and geographer to whom Egidio had served as godfather when Leo had converted from Islam to Christianity.[45] Given their extensive involvement with Egidio, it would be reasonable to imagine that Elijah Levita and Leo Africanus assisted him in his conversations with Reubeni, who spoke only Hebrew and Arabic. One also wonders if they harbored suspicions about Reubeni and his story. But, to the enduring frustration of historians, they did not write about Reubeni and he did not write about them.[46]

Reubeni's diary shows him to be keenly aware of the political aspirations of the rulers with whom he interacted. This is first apparent in his opening gambit with Pope Clement VII—an offer to help make peace between Charles V, the Holy Roman Emperor, and King Francis I of France. Reubeni no doubt counted on this to appeal to the pope, because Clement's predecessor, Leo X, had sought to mobilize the combined forces of these two rulers to launch a crusade against the Ottomans. Leo's entreaties, however, had come to naught and it was not long before Charles and Francis went to war with each other in a conflict that ended only once Francis himself was finally captured in 1526.[47] Although, by 1524, relations between Francis and Charles had deteriorated too far to give any hope to an intervention by Reubeni, his offer to serve as a mediator established him as someone willing to make common cause with Christians against Muslims. Reubeni does not spell out what further requests he made of the pope. According to Daniel da Pisa, who conducted Reubeni's negotiations with the pope, Reubeni asked the pope for weapons that were to be delivered to the Arabian port of Jeddah for the purpose of fighting Muslim kingdoms in both Asia and Africa.[48] The pope delayed responding to Reubeni for a year and then told him to direct his requests to the King of Portugal, who, he said, was better able to help Reubeni achieve his goals.[49] In the letters of introduction he wrote for Reubeni to the King of Portugal and to the Emperor of Abyssinia, Dawit II, the pope said that although he could not verify Reubeni's story, he also did not want to dismiss it. In his view, Reubeni's proposal to make common cause with Christians, on the basis of his claim that his nation was embroiled in battle with Muslims, was not implausible, and it was also not unreasonable for Christians to take a similar position. Although Jews are the enemies of Christians, the pope concluded, "sometimes the Lord decrees vengeance upon His enemies by the hand of His enemies," and in any event, the commitment Reubeni sought was quite modest.[50] The pope was the first of several world leaders who were willing to grant Reubeni status as a diplomat; however, as we can see from his reasoning, this was not the result of a lack of sophistication. Rather, it was the product of a policy of caution in an environment in which everyone was profoundly aware of the inherent difficulties of attaining certainty.[51] Conventional geographical wisdom was being upended, peoples and lands hitherto unknown to Europeans were being discovered. In such an environment, many rulers thought it best to reserve judgment on matters pertaining to unknown lands. If Reubeni's tale were true, the rewards for Europe were potentially very great. So, they reasoned, why not take a small gamble on him?[52] Indeed, Reubeni was one of many false ambassadors who appeared in Europe in the sixteenth century, many of whom were beneficiaries of this policy of caution.[53]

Dawit II, Emperor of Abyssinia (r. 1508–1540).
Portrait by Cristofano dell'Altissimo.

Departure from Italy

Reubeni left Rome for Pisa. On the way he visited Ismael da Rieti, a wealthy Jewish banker who lived in Siena. Even though Ismael was an in-law of the da Pisas, he refused to help Reubeni. To Reubeni's shock, Ismael declared that he had no longing whatsoever for Jerusalem because he already had everything he wanted in Siena.[54] When Reubeni reached Pisa, he stayed at the luxurious home of Daniel's young cousin, Rabbi Yehiel, a banker and kabbalist.[55] Interestingly, Reubeni went with Yehiel to visit the bell tower of a cathedral, likely the Leaning Tower of Pisa. Climbing to the top, he reported seeing three icons, which he described as "three abominations with appearances too beautiful to be described."[56] Before Reubeni left, Yehiel's grandmother, Signora Sarah, upon whom he heaped much praise, gave him a Bible inscribed with her advice for him: "Be neither angry nor rash."[57] Reubeni, who recognized his irascible personality as his greatest flaw, was moved by her insight.

To obtain safe passage to Portugal, Reubeni applied to Dom Miguel da Silva, the bishop of Viseu and Portugal's ambassador to Rome. Dom Miguel was famous for his political machinations, and this is reflected in Reubeni's description of his creative delay tactics, which sent Reubeni and his entourage on a wild goose chase through Rome in search of him.[58] Fortunately for Reubeni, Dom Miguel was recalled to Portugal and Reubeni was welcomed by the new ambassador, who then arranged for his travel. Reubeni and a group of his new Italian Jewish supporters and servants promptly set sail for Portugal. Even with his letter from the pope, Reubeni discovered on his way to Portugal that he was unable to disembark in the Spanish town of Cádiz, where Judaism had been outlawed by royal decree since 1492.

The Conversos of Portugal

According to both Reubeni's diary and Inquisition documents, from the moment he arrived in Portugal on October 24, 1525, until he left a year and a half later, he was received by many of its conversos (forced converts) with the respect and reverence due to a king or even a messiah.[59] The practice of Judaism had been outlawed in Spain since 1492 and in Portugal since 1497, yet the effects of these decrees on conversos were very different. In Spain, the Catholic monarchs, Ferdinand and Isabella, had a fiery determination to create and enforce religious homogeneity. They expelled those Jews who were unwilling to submit to conversion and whose recalcitrance might compromise their project. They closely monitored those who converted and remained by vastly expanding the authority and resources of the Inquisition. Conversos in Spain who continued to observe Jewish rituals after 1492 did so in constant fear of the Inquisition and only with the utmost caution.[60] By contrast, Manuel I of Portugal did not pursue the goal of religious homogeneity with the fervor of the Spanish Crown. Unlike the Spanish, he did not offer the Jewish population the choice between conversion or expulsion, but instead simply converted all his Jewish subjects *en masse*. The resulting population of newly converted Christians thus included many who might otherwise have gone into exile for the sake of their faith and were therefore more likely to resist full assimilation to Christianity. Such resistance was further aided by Manuel's pragmatic decree that no inquiries into the beliefs of these new converts were to be made for a period of twenty years.[61] While, despite this, some official attempts were made to assimilate these conversos, they had little success and there is considerable evidence that many continued to observe Jewish rituals. These conversos were no doubt also emboldened by the presence of thousands of Spanish Jewish exiles, who had made the sacrifice to leave Spain in order to practice Judaism only to be forcibly converted to Christianity a few years later in their new home of Portugal. This atmosphere of widespread resistance to full assimilation to Christianity among Portuguese conversos was considerably curtailed in 1536, a decade after Reubeni's visit, when the Inquisition was introduced into Portugal.

Even in an age known for its intense messianism, conversos in both Spain and Portugal were regarded as extreme messianists. This characteristic was so well known that it became the topic of anti-converso polemics. In theatrical performances and in literature, as Yosef Yerushalmi has noted, "the verb *esperar* (to hope) became a catchword with which to identify the character who is of Jewish descent. *Experana* is the Jewish characteristic par excellence, and the satiric use of such terms is a leitmotif in the Spanish drama of the Golden Age."[62] Continual feelings of fear, marginalization, and resentment towards Christian authorities for their forced conversions and ongoing persecution drove many conversos to hope for justice, either through heavenly intervention and messianic deliverance or by more practical means. Indeed, as Matt Goldish has written, converso messianism was characterized by "a particular willingness to entertain a wide variety of messianic scenarios, and the reservation of a special place for the conversos in the messianic process."[63] Following the pogroms and forced conversions of 1391, messianic speculation began to increase.[64] For many, it was this hope that motivated them to continue their secret observance of Judaism. In the half century before Reubeni's arrival, there were a particularly large number of converso prophets, who foretold the impending arrival of the Messiah and the bringing of the conversos to the Holy Land.[65] One such figure was Inés Esteban, a preteen conversa, who prophesied the imminent advent of the messianic age. Once the Messiah arrived, she claimed, conversos would be pardoned for abandoning Judaism and would be taken to the Holy Land. In 1501, at the age of twelve, she and seventy-seven of her followers were burned at the stake.[66] Many conversos lived their lives in a state of mental preparedness for redemption. Women, for example, were known to always wear their jewelry, knowing that they could be transported to the Holy Land at any moment.[67] Converso messianic visions were also often characterized by a desire for their oppressors to receive retribution.[68] Many conversos were thus predisposed to respond favorably to Reubeni's martial image and promises of redemption, as is attested in a variety of documentary sources.[69]

Reubeni was greatly concerned about the welfare of the conversos. In recounting his travels through Italy, he names most of his Jewish hosts, but in Portugal, he does not usually identify his converso hosts by name, no doubt concerned that doing so might endanger them. Reubeni claimed that no harm came to the conversos as a result of their enthusiasm for his mission, but there is considerable evidence that this was not the case. According to his own admission, his presence resulted in bringing the conversos' often tenuous adherence to Christianity to the attention of the government. He also describes the great pains that the authorities took to ensure that he had no contact with conversos on his way out of Portugal.[70] The most damning evidence of his negative impact on conversos, however, comes from external sources. Many scholars now believe that it was in direct response to Reubeni's influence on conversos that the Inquisition was brought to Portugal. This process began in the late 1520s, when the Inquisitor of the Spanish town of Llerena, complaining about Reubeni's influence on the conversos, began to campaign for closer cooperation between the Inquisition and Portuguese authorities.[71] Then, in the early 1530s, King João III himself began negotiations with the pope to establish a tribunal for the Inquisition in Portugal, which was finally instituted in 1536.

Reubeni's Entourage in Portugal

In Portugal, Reubeni's entourage became increasingly difficult to manage. Often the most Reubeni could do was keep them well-dressed so that, at least at first glance, they resembled the attendants of a respected ambassador. A motley crew comprised of mainly dislocated and disaffected young men, their numbers included Jews from Italy and Morocco as well as conversos. Although some were loyal and upstanding, others were adventurers with few familial and communal ties. A case in point is the converso whom Reubeni refers to as "Aldequa the apostate." Aldequa had converted first to Islam and then to Christianity, but he confessed to Reubeni that he wished to revert to Judaism, his birth religion.[72] Although it was perhaps inevitable, given the extreme riskiness of his enterprise, that Reubeni would attract such rootless individuals, he further guaranteed their selection by magnanimously refusing to allow would-be attendants with young families to travel with him, on the grounds that they were more needed back home.[73] In an era when marriage was the social norm, even among those who traveled for a living, an entourage consisting of many unmarried men was bound to attract members who did not abide by social constraints. Reubeni reports constant fights among his entourage, sometimes with weapons, which nearly result in death. Often drunk, these young men publicly flirt with the women they meet and engage in frequent sexual antics, usually with enslaved women but sometimes with each other.[74] In his diary, Reubeni depicts them lying, cheating, and stealing, sometimes from him and sometimes from others, and at times endangering his mission by involving Christian authorities. To keep them in line, he unapologetically admits to threatening them, sometimes with his sword. When they are arrested, he occasionally lets them stew for a while in a local jail before coming to their rescue. While they are a disappointment to him, he is clearly aware that a person in his precarious position, a man with a desperate plan to save the Jews, cannot reasonably expect an entourage consisting exclusively of upstanding members of society. The many pages of the diary devoted to these trials and tribulations lead one to believe that Reubeni perhaps committed them to writing to impress upon future redeemers that the process of redemption is fundamentally more mundane than it is supernatural.

In Portugal, Reubeni reports many interactions with Moroccan Jews, some of whom he recruited to his entourage. Over the course of the six-teenth century, Portugal conquered much of the Moroccan coast and, be-cause Moroccan Jews were essential to the Portuguese imperial project, they were not subject to forced conversion. Those with official business in Portugal were even granted permission to journey there despite the 1497 decree that banned Jews from the country.[75] As a result of these contacts, Reubeni's message spread to the Maghreb, and he reports receiving communications from Jews who lived there. Indeed, his popularity was such that his activities became the subject of messianic poems in which Maghrebi Jews described the special role he had promised them in the recapturing of Jerusalem.[76]

Reubeni and the King of Portugal

In Portugal, Reubeni encountered another royal court saturated with apocalyptic expectation. Although King João III himself was relatively un-interested in millennial speculation, these ideas still had currency among his courtiers as a result of the beliefs of his recently deceased predecessor, Manuel I (r. 1495–1521). Millennial expectation had been a major factor driving Manuel's dizzying array of conquests in Africa and Asia that had the conquest of Jerusalem as their ultimate, if unrealized, goal.[77] He saw the Portuguese as God's chosen people, their enemies as the embodiments of demonic forces, and believed he was fulfilling the messianic role, normally accorded to Jesus, of realizing God's kingdom on earth. He and many in his regime understood his conquests as the beginnings of the ultimate apocalyptic battle.[78] King João III's court, still alive with the hopes of his predecessor, was thus a familiar environment for Reubeni. His meetings with the king were initially quite successful, with the king treating him as a respected foreign ambassador, providing for his lodging, and even giving him money. From the very first, Reubeni acted with the confident arrogance befitting the general and son of a monarch that he claimed to be. He portrayed himself as often furious and ready to fight those who opposed him with his sword, although his companions were usually able to dissuade him from such belligerence. On one occasion, however, he confessed to having thrown a monk out of a window after the latter denied that there was a king of Israel and said that Jews had no share in royal lineage.[79] Once Reubeni met the king, he continued this blustering approach. When he felt that the king's officials had not accorded him sufficient attention or respect, he made a scene at the palace, on occasion even reproaching the king himself. At other times, in high dudgeon, he simply refused to appear at court when he was summoned.[80]

Reubeni requested that the king provide him with weapons, weapon artisans, and ships to bear them to Jeddah.[81] His choice of Jeddah was no doubt calculated to appeal to the Portuguese interest in controlling this strategic port, which had indeed featured in several Christian apocalyptic visions.[82] In 1517, the Portuguese had laid siege to Jeddah, but were driven off by the combined efforts of the Ottomans and Mamluks.[83] When Reubeni arrived in Portugal, the Portuguese stood more in need than ever of an ally in the Red Sea region but, despite their need, they ultimately decided not to include Reubeni in this project. According to Reubeni, the king did initially promise to accede to his requests. Soon, however, Reubeni's diplomatic efforts were complicated by the appearance of the same Dom Miguel who had created difficulties for him in Rome. Dom Miguel warned the king that Reubeni would bring destruction to Portugal and would lead the conversos to revert to Judaism.[84] Matters came to a head when Diogo Pires, a converso who served as a high court judge, circumcised himself. Reubeni was summoned before the king and accused of directing the circumcision, returning the conversos to Judaism, and allowing them to kiss his hand and bow down to him, which was seen as an affront to the dignity of the king. Although Reubeni denied responsibility, the king ended negotiations with him.[85] The king then advised Reubeni to instead pursue his diplomatic project with either Charles V or Pope Clement VII, and Reubeni declared his intention to return to the pope.

The parting was initially amicable. The king gave him a letter granting him both safe passage and the sum of three hundred ducats. Reubeni, however, complained to the king that he had been dishonored because the letter had been written on paper rather than parchment. The king agreed to provide him with the letter on parchment but, unbeknownst to the king, it was Reubeni's old enemy, Dom Miguel, who rewrote it, and with much less favorable terms. In addition to denying Reubeni financial remuneration, the new letter stated in no uncertain terms that no conversos were to leave Portugal with him. This condition represented a break with previous royal policy towards conversos who, at that time, were still allowed to leave the country.[86] Reubeni's anger and arrogance, which had until then served him well in Portugal, had spectacularly backfired. Lamentingly, he recalled Signora Sarah's words of warning to him: "I see that you are always angry. If you can rid yourself of this anger, you will succeed in your enterprise."[87]

The End of Reubeni's Mission

Reubeni left Portugal for Livorno, but when a storm struck, his ship had to anchor at Almería, and he and his companions were arrested, because no Jew was allowed in Spain without the authorization of Charles V. The papal bull granting Reubeni safe passage was examined by the local authorities, but they would allow him to go no further without first consulting the emperor. Reubeni wrote letters to the emperor and to the queen, whom he had met in Portugal before her marriage, with the result that the emperor allowed him to travel in peace. When he reached the town of Cartagena, despite his letters from both the emperor and the pope, he was arrested on the orders of an inquisitor based in Murcia. Eventually, however, he was released, and that is where his diary ends.

In a section appended to the manuscript of the diary, Reubeni's companion, Solomon Cohen, continues the story. In 1527, Reubeni was arrested by an individual, referred to as the "Lord of Clermont," following a shipwreck off the coast of France.[88] Everything he possessed was seized on the grounds that he was "not the subject of anyone." This included the letter from his brother, King Joseph, that testified to his being the ambassador of a Jewish kingdom. According to one source, his two-year captivity ended when he was freed by order of the King of France; according to another, after a heavy ransom was paid by the Jews of Avignon and Carpentras.[89] Reubeni's imprisonment coincided with the devastation of his contacts in Rome as a result of the sack of the city in 1527 and the plague that followed. Reubeni's Christian patrons had more pressing concerns than negotiating for the release of foreign dignitaries from mysterious kingdoms. Pope Clement VII had managed to escape Rome with his life, but he had become severely ill and his wealth was much diminished. After a year in exile, he returned to Rome and, although he held onto power, he faced formidable challenges to his authority from both within the church and beyond it. Cardinal Egidio also escaped, although his famous library was ransacked and, like the pope, he too absented himself from Rome for a year. Rome's Jewish community was shattered by the death and looting that resulted from the invasion. Its once vibrant Jewish institutions were replaced with an environment where it was reportedly difficult to gather even the required quorum of ten men for prayer. Most disastrous for Reubeni was that his main patron, Daniel da Pisa, was among the dead.[90] The long period of Reubeni's imprisonment was likely the result of his remaining contacts in Rome being occupied by far more pressing concerns.

In 1530, Reubeni returned to Venice. There, Federigo, the Marquis of Mantua, invited Reubeni to visit him.[91] At this point, however, his luck ran out. He no longer had his brother's letter, which had been taken from him during his captivity. Considering it vital to his success, he decided to forge a new one. To get the letter right, Reubeni determined that he needed not just a scribe but seventy different Jews to individually forge the signatures of King Joseph's seventy elders. Reubeni's sway over Jews, however, was not what it had been previously. He was able to recruit only about twenty Jews, aged ten and older, to sign the letter, each of whom was sworn to secrecy. Determining that twenty signatures was not enough, he applied to the scribe to have the letter rewritten without the signatures. To lend authority in their place, he arranged for an official looking seal, bearing the insignia of King Joseph, to be made by a local craftsman, who had also been sworn to secrecy. Reubeni's clumsy involvement of so many people in such nefarious activities caused the tide to turn. The town's rabbis became aware of his embroilment of the Jewish community in his forgeries. Sensing danger, they absolved these Jews of the oaths they had sworn and reported the matter to the marquis. Reubeni was then handled with great cunning so as to better trap him in his lies. He was allowed to leave Mantua with his new letter, but the scribe had subtly marked it as a forgery. Not only were its signatures incompletely erased but the scribe had added his own signature to the document, craftily hiding it under King Joseph's supposed seal. The marquis then sent all this information to his representative in Rome with instructions to inform the pope, and it is possible that he also sent it elsewhere.

Perhaps in response to these events, Abraham ben Solomon Dienna, a rabbi from Mantua, circulated a fiery denunciation of Reubeni. Dienna described a world in which town after town flattered Reubeni, providing for his every whim and supplying him with huge sums of money. Dienna wished to add his voice to the small minority who opposed him. "Since the days of [the biblical villain] Haman the son of Hammedatha," he wrote, "no one has come to oppose us, rage against us, and cause us to perish, God forbid, like this enemy and adversary—this evil Haman." Dienna ruled that, since Reubeni had placed Jewish lives in danger, his life was legally forfeit. He lamented that, before Reubeni's arrival, the Jews were seen by Christians as tranquil but, thanks to him, they were now seen as bellicose, and that this put them in great danger.[92]

Despite the warnings sent by the marquis, it was some time before Reubeni was unmasked. In 1530, he received another letter of protection from the pope, and soon he was back in Venice.[93] At the end of that year, the Venetians assigned Giovanni Battista Ramusio, a learned orientalist and diplomat to examine and report on him.[94] Ramusio wrote that crowds of Venetian Jews, who treated Reubeni "like a messiah," came to hear him preaching.[95] Reubeni, he claimed, promised that his Jewish army would be victorious in Jerusalem because God would prevent the enemy's guns from firing. If Ramusio is to be relied upon, a miraculous dimension had entered Reubeni's promises, an aspect not evident in his diary.

The next we hear of Reubeni concerns his reunification with Diogo Pires, the converso whom he had refused to circumcise in Portugal. Born in 1501 near Lisbon to converso parents, Pires was a prodigy who, at the age of twenty, became a judge in the highest court of Portugal. According to Pires's account, his involvement with Reubeni began when he experienced a terrifying dream in which a heavenly power ordered him to be circumcised. Despite repeatedly asking Reubeni to interpret the dream, Pires says, the latter refused. Thinking that Reubeni's refusal was on account of his being uncircumcised, Pires circumcised himself. When he proudly shared this news with Reubeni, to his shock, the latter was angry with him, rebuking him for placing his mission in Portugal in danger. Reubeni's account of these events differs only in that he claims that Pires asked him to circumcise him.[96] Pires then took on the name Solomon Molkho, an allusion to the biblical King Solomon. He left Portugal and traveled through Italy and the Ottoman Empire. He soon developed a reputation for his deep knowledge of the Kabbalah and gained the admiration of such rabbinic luminaries as Joseph Karo and Shlomo Alkabets.[97] How he attained such knowledge, including an ability to write eloquently in Hebrew, is still not known. Molkho also began to attain a reputation for accurate prophecies and, at the same time, came to view himself as the Messiah son of Joseph, the messianic precursor to the final messiah, the Messiah son of David.[98] He correctly predicted massive flooding in Rome (1530), an earthquake in Portugal (1531), and the appearance of a great comet (Halley's comet in 1531). It was on account of these predictions that many came to embrace Molkho as an accomplished magician.[99] Crucially for Molkho, his accurate predictions won him Pope Clement VII's support. This paid off in 1531 when Molkho, condemned by the Inquisition to be burned at the stake for having converted to Judaism, was granted a reprieve by the pope, who substituted a condemned criminal for him at the last moment. This event further enhanced Molkho's stature, as reports multiplied about how he had emerged unscathed from the flames and was seen walking through the palaces of the Vatican.[100]

By the time Molkho reunited with Reubeni in Venice, he had a dedicated group of Jewish followers who accepted him as the Messiah, as well as several Christian supporters. Reubeni agreed to join forces with him, and together they journeyed to Regensburg to seek an audience with

Charles V. On the way, they met with the King of France. We know very little of this meeting. Some reports by Christian scholars claim both that they attempted to convert the king to Judaism and that the king offered Molkho the chair of Hebrew at the Collège de France.[101]

The extensive millennial expectation that centered on Charles V, the Holy Roman Emperor, must have led Reubeni to see him as suitable target for his proposals. Such expectations had been associated with Charles's family from the time of his grandparents, Ferdinand and Isabella of Spain, but were further accentuated as a result of the vast domains that he came to rule. His empire was the first to be described as one "on which the sun never sets" and many believed that, with such great power, he would succeed in conquering Jerusalem.[102] Reubeni no doubt saw the potential for exploiting such hopes.

When Josel of Rosheim, the great representative of Ashkenazi Jewry to the emperor, heard that Reubeni and Molkho were nearing Regensburg, he was so terrified by the prospect of their arrival that he left town to indicate that neither he nor the town's Jews had anything to do with them. The Jews of Habsburg lands under Charles V were in a precarious position. Judaism was already outlawed in his empire's Iberian territories, and Charles was known to be a strong supporter of the Inquisition, both strengthening its powers and allowing it to spread in his empire.[103] When, prior to Reubeni's arrival, Josel had successfully negotiated against the Jews' expulsion, he had to refute rumors that Jews were spying on the Habsburgs on behalf of the Ottomans. In Josel's mind, Reubeni and Molkho's plans to spark Christian-Muslim conflict were likely to reignite Charles's worst fears and suspicions about Jews.[104] For unknown reasons, Josel did not mention Reubeni in his writings, although we know from other sources that Reubeni had indeed been in Regensburg. Josel described Molkho's visit to the emperor thus: "At that time . . . the righteous convert, Rabbi Solomon Molkho, may his soul rest in Eden, came with his alien ideas to stir up the emperor by telling him that he had come to gather all the Jews to wage war against the Turks. When I heard about his plans, I wrote him a letter warning him not to provoke the emperor lest we be consumed by the great fire. I left Regensburg, so that the emperor should not say that I had a hand in his strange plans."[105]

Charles V, Holy Roman Emperor (r. 1519–1556). Portrait by Titian.

As it turned out, Josel's caution was well-warranted. Charles V rejected Reubeni and Molkho's proposal and had them both arrested. The two were dispatched to Mantua as prisoners, perhaps evidence that the emperor's displeasure was linked to his knowledge of the forged letters that Reubeni had produced there. Reubeni remained imprisoned for several years. He was transferred to a prison in Llerena where, in 1538, he was condemned by the Inquisition for converting Christians to Judaism and was "relaxed" to the secular authorities for burning at the stake. He was perhaps the only unconverted Jew apprehended by the Inquisition, and was charged with the only crime possible within its legal framework, that of proselytizing Judaism.[106]

Reubeni's Goals

What did Reubeni want? In his diary, he made clear to Jews and also to some Muslims that his goal was to return the Jews to the land of Israel. To Christians, Reubeni emphasized a different message. His Arabian kingdom, he claimed, was permanently engaged in war with the Muslims who surrounded it, and this made him a natural ally of Christians against their Muslim enemies.[107] Reubeni therefore asked Christian rulers for ships and weapons that were to be sent to the "East." From Reubeni's patron, Daniel da Pisa, we learn that he had specified to the pope that he wanted these weapons to be delivered to the Arabian port of Jeddah for the purpose of fighting Muslim kingdoms in Asia and Africa.[108] From this, some scholars have suggested that Reubeni's ultimate aim was that of sparking a world war between Muslims and Christians. Since both sides were already primed for such a war, many may have regarded this aim as easily attainable.[109] This hypothesis has recently been strengthened by Moti Benmelech, who has noted the close parallels between Reubeni's work and that of a contemporary mystic, Abraham ben Eliezer Halevi.[110] Halevi suggested that the final apocalyptic battle would occur once the Portuguese were lured into Arabia in the hopes of conquering Mecca, from which they would then be speedily routed by the Ottomans.[111] While it is impossible to know whether Reubeni himself had encountered Halevi's ideas, it is reasonable to imagine that some of Reubeni's supporters might have seen his activities in this light, since it is known that Halevi's works circulated in Italy and Venice. Moreover, many Christians openly anticipated and even welcomed such an apocalyptic battle between Ottoman Muslims and European Christians, and it is therefore conceivable that Reubeni's followers understood his mission as the Jewish narrative of such Christian prophecies.

What did Reubeni hope would happen after this conflict between Christians and Muslims? He may have thought that with both sides weakened by war, his ragtag group of Jews and conversos, newly supplied with weapons from Christian monarchs, would be able to seize the Holy Land for themselves. It is also likely, however, that Reubeni hoped for a decisive Muslim victory. As Cornell Fleischer has noted, "a betting man in 1500 would have put money on a universal Muslim victory."[112] And there are good grounds for supposing that Reubeni and his followers might have embraced such an outcome, as many Jews already had in their eschatologies. Asher Lemlein, a messianic claimant active in Italy a quarter century before Reubeni, predicted that an Ottoman victory against Rome was a necessary precursor to Jews regaining their land.[113] The famous Iberian rabbi and statesman, Isaac Abravanel (d. 1508), had a similar view: "It is quite possible that the Messiah will first appear in the land of the Ishmaelites [i.e., the Muslims]. . . . And who knows? Perhaps a king of Ishmael will accept the religion of Israel, bring about the salvation of Israel, and be an anointed one (mashiah)?"[114] There are also grounds for assuming that these views were held by some conversos. Historians of the Inquisition have shown how Mehmet II's conquest of Constantinople filled many conversos with messianic hope. For example, according to a 1464 Inquisition report, one converso told his neighbor: "You do not know who the Turk is. If God will favor us (the conversos), the Turk will be in Castile within a year and a half . . . for the Turk is called the Destroyer of Christianity and the Defender of the Jewish Faith. He is the Messiah whose coming is predicted by the Jewish Bible."[115] Reubeni seems to have largely shared these positive views of Muslims. He claimed to have spent time disguised as a Muslim in Africa, Egypt, and Palestine, and generally spoke positively of the morality of the Muslims whom he met. Later, when traveling in Iberia as a Jew, he describes how Muslims who had been forcibly converted to Christianity saw him as a natural ally and came to kiss his hand.[116] He did not see Muslims as an obstacle to his goal of returning the Jews to the land of Israel. After explaining to a Muslim dignitary from Morocco that his ultimate purpose was to send his army to conquer Jerusalem from the Muslims, Reubeni asked him, "Do you believe that the Kingdom of Ishmael will return the land to us?" And this dignitary, according to Reubeni, replied, "Yes, all the world believes that." Reubeni added that he envisioned Muslim rulers cooperating to help bring their Jewish populations to the land of Israel.[117] If this seems far-fetched to modern readers, it is worth keeping in mind that, following the Ottoman conquest of Constantinople, its new Muslim rulers actively encouraged Jewish migration to that city.[118]

How did Reubeni view his diary as contributing to his goal of returning the Jews to the land of Israel? Aside from the occasional remark about gathering the Jews in Israel and offering a sacrifice, the diary is devoid of the apocalyptic imagery that one might think would ignite the passions of a mass messianic movement. Indeed, its content is shockingly mundane. It details Reubeni's daily grind of mustering a following, recruiting and managing (often unruly) followers and servants, dealing with diplomatic victories and failures, as well as his struggles with his own emotions. It reports on the costs of clothing an entourage, entertaining guests, and buying lavish gifts to gain the favor of officials and dignitaries. It shows the extraordinary lengths to which Reubeni had to go to flatter those in power. The purpose of the diary may therefore be to emphasize to his readers that the business of returning the Jews to their land is mainly a naturalistic one. Many Jews nonetheless embraced Reubeni as the Messiah and, as Azriel Shohat has pointed out, Reubeni comfortably fits the naturalistic definition of the Messiah proposed by Moses Maimonides.[119] Yet Reubeni, true to the practical image that he wished to cultivate, reports in his diary that he had repeatedly and publicly denied being the Messiah and insisted that he was part diplomat, part military man.

Unlike other Jews who acquired audiences with Christian rulers, Reubeni displays no interest in using his tenuous access to power to petition on behalf of mistreated local Jewish communities. Insofar as he provides details on the lives of the Jews that he meets, it is mainly with a view to whether they have either potential for military service or an ability to make financial contributions. If he intervenes on behalf of a Jew in trouble, that Jew is usually one of his immediate supporters.[120] Reubeni seems to have seen one solution alone to the Jewish predicament, the relocation of Jews to their ancestral homeland. These practical concerns and single-minded focus on the necessity of a political solution to Jewish suffering have led some scholars to view Reubeni not so much as a messianic aspirant but as a proto-Zionist, a Theodor Herzl of the sixteenth century. Like Herzl, Reubeni desperately scoured the world both for political contacts and for Jews with political or military expertise in order to realize his dream of a Jewish polity.[121]

Reubeni's Legacy

For a decade, David Reubeni and Solomon Molkho filled the Jewish world with hope and occupied the attention of world leaders.[122] Unlike the seventeenth-century messianic claimant Shabbetai Tsvi, however, Reubeni's movement left few traces on subsequent Jewish history. Even Reubeni's companion Solomon Molkho had a more enduring remembrance. Molkho was revered as a martyr, most notably by Joseph Karo (d. 1575), the famous codifier of Jewish law, who wished that he could be martyred as Molkho had been.[123] Molkho's kabbalistic works were studied and his mantle, prayer shawl, and flag were taken to Prague, where they were treated for some time as relics.[124] In contrast, Reubeni was largely forgotten. Writing half a century after Reubeni's first appearance, Isaac Aqrish (d. after 1578), echoing general opinion, dismissively noted that Reubeni's tales were merely "inventions created in order *to steady tottering knees* (Isaiah 35:3) *and revive the hearts of the contrite* (Isaiah 57:15)."[125]

Reubeni's main legacy was his diary. While scholars are in no doubt that he played a role in its creation, they differ regarding whether he wrote it himself or was assisted by a collaborator.[126] The diary was largely unknown immediately after his death, although there is evidence that it was read by at least some conversos.[127] The first clear reference to the diary appears in an Inquisition document from 1639. According to this, a prospective chair of Hebrew at the University of Salamanca reported at his Inquisition trial that he had read a manuscript that he referred to as both, "The Embassy of Rabbi David" and "The Itinerary of Rabbi David."[128]

Scholars agree, based on his description of its contents, that the text was indeed the diary of David Reubeni.[129] The next we hear of the diary is its appearance in the collection of Heimann Joseph Michael (d. 1846), an avid bibliographer living in Frankfurt. Michael lent the manuscript to his friend Leopold Zunz, the founder of the academic study of Judaism, who, in 1841, summarized it in an article on Jewish geographers.[130] After Michael's death, his manuscript of Reubeni's diary was sold to the Bodleian library, from which, in 1867, it went missing. Fortunately, a facsimile made with pen and tracing paper had been completed before its loss, and it is upon that facsimile that we now rely.[131]

Nineteenth-century scholars of Reubeni's life and work did not look upon him with favor. They saw him as a sad manifestation of the irrationalities that had tragically gripped the vulnerable, premodern Jewish world. Heinrich Graetz, the first to reconstruct Reubeni's history, trenchantly concluded: "Molkho was a deluded enthusiast. . . . David was an adventurer who intentionally deceived others."[132] Some were even harsher. Adolf Poznański remarked that Reubeni's diary revealed him to be "a man, devoid of all wisdom and learning, capricious and ignorant, who was always squabbling with his servants and boasting about his humility."[133] The tide of sentiment against Reubeni, however, turned after the First World War. Reubeni ceased to be viewed as a swindler and instead began to be seen as "a unique patriot and fighter for the people who wished, in an altogether unusual but real way, with the aid of diplomacy and negotiations with kings and popes, to bring redemption to his miserable brethren."[134] The tangible earthliness of Reubeni's project, largely devoid of the magic rituals associated with other messianic claimants, was attractive to the early twentieth-century Jewish imagination. Reubeni was seen as a Herzl before Herzl. Without coopting the aid of cosmic powers, he had made a concrete attempt to redeem the Jewish people through diplomatic means and the building of a Jewish army. Those who read Reubeni in the original Hebrew were captivated by the fact that he wrote in the language of everyday speech, something unusual in an era that did not yet have realistic novels.[135] A flurry of historical fiction about Reubeni emerged, the greatest of which was surely Max Brod's brooding 1925 novel, *Reubeni: Prince of the Jews*.[136] Brod portrayed Reubeni as a Jew from Prague who determined that the only way of overcoming the cruel antisemitism that he himself had experienced was to fight it. He believed that the use of force and cunning was vital to his enterprise and even met with Niccolò Machiavelli to discuss these ideas with him. However, at his core, Brod's Reubeni hated all forms of violence and dishonesty. Ultimately his plan failed, owing not to the strength of his enemies but to the fanaticism of one of his disciples, which led both Reubeni and the disciple into the hands of the Inquisition. Perhaps taking their cue from Brod, other Zionist writers also began to see Reubeni's activities as representing the emergence of a military movement that prepared the ground for Jewish national liberation.[137] But it was not just Zionists who were inspired by Reubeni. After fleeing Nazi Berlin for the Soviet Union, David Bergelson, the indefatigable advocate of Joseph Stalin's Jewish Autonomous Oblast in Birobidzhan, wrote a Yiddish play about Reubeni. The last words of Bergelson's Reubeni were, "You fight, my people; that is, you live, my people." The director of the Moscow State Yiddish Theater who, in 1944, purchased the play for production said that, for him, Reubeni's figure meant "hope, resistance, and struggle."[138] For these Soviet Jews living in the shadow of the Holocaust, Reubeni's very failure was meaningful. It carried the message that Jewish struggles for survival and liberation, even in contexts in which these aims are likely unrealizable, are nonetheless of value and worthy of pursuit. Reubeni had failed because he had attempted a project all but doomed to failure, but by doing so, he had taken a vital stand on Jewish pride and dignity. He was thus an inspiration for Jews as they responded to persecution and developed their own national aspirations. Reubeni had taught that redemption did not involve waiting for a divinely sent messiah; it involved self-reliance, imagination, getting one's hands dirty, and taking big risks.

(CHAPTER 1)
AFRICA

I am David the son of King Solomon, of blessed memory. My older brother is King Joseph who, from his throne in the desert of Habor, rules over thirty myriads—over the tribes of Gad, Reuben, and half the tribe of Manasseh.[1] I left my brother the king and his advisors, the seventy elders, charged to go immediately to procure an audience with His Grace, the Pope. So I left them, setting out from the desert on a mountainous route. In ten days, I reached Jeddah and there I fell seriously ill and remained so for five weeks. To be cured, I was bled and blistered all over my body.[2] I then heard that a ship was traveling to the land of Kush. Still sick in bed, I made arrangements with the captain. I had an old slave, both deaf and mute, who used to cook and prepare all my food, and who was always ready and waiting to fulfil my needs. Together we boarded the ship, which was moored in the Sea of Reeds [Red Sea]. I remained sick. We sailed the Sea of Reeds for three days and three nights. On the fourth day, we reached Suakin in the land of Kush.[3] I took a house in that city and remained there for two months. I was bled in those lands as well, and between the cuppings at Jeddah and Suakin, I lost more than fifty liters of blood. I was also blistered with nails on my face and body more than one hundred times.

I then heard that a large company of merchants was traveling to the Kingdom of Soba [Sheba] via the Assua river in the land of Kush.[4] I summoned their chief, Umar Abu Kamil, who was a descendant of the Ishmaelite prophet, and purchased two camels in order to join them. Then my slave and I left Suakin with all our baggage, together with Abu Kamil, the merchants, and well over three thousand camels. Each day, my health improved. I made the two-month journey to the Kingdom of Kush, crossing great deserts, forests filled with abundant trees and vegetation, fine pastures, mountains, and rivers. There King Amara, who dwells by 8 the Nile, reigns over the Kingdom of Soba. He is a black king who rules over both Blacks and Whites. I stayed with him for ten months and Abu Kamil stayed with me, residing at the king's town of Lamul,[5] that is at the source of the Nile. This king was constantly on the move through his provinces and visited a different place each month. I always accompanied him on these journeys and at my service were more than sixty mounted descendants of the Prophet, who, together with their chief Abu Kamil, bestowed great honor upon me.

A Visit with the King of the Land of Kush

During my stay with the king in the land of Kush, I fasted every day and prayed day and night. I lived in fear and dread. I shunned merriment and frivolous company and would thus go from the king's house to my own only by a direct route. For that reason, on each and every journey, they would prepare a wooden hut for me near the king's hut. This king has innumerable servants. Among them are military commanders, provincial governors, and officers administering justice. Anyone who commits a transgression, whether great or small, is killed—and every day they render such judgments. This king has many horses with mounted riders. He has beautiful camels, innumerable cattle, and flocks of sheep. He also has gold dust. He has officials who go ahead of him to build wooden huts for him, his noblemen, and slaves. Whenever we arrived at a place at which such buildings had been erected, we saw how well-organized these journeys were. The rule is first in, last out. Then, when abandoning camp, they burn down all the huts.

In that land, there are trees and abundant vegetation, deserts, and mountains. The king whom I accompanied has male and female slaves, most of whom go about naked. The queen, the concubines, the noblewomen, and the female servants who serve her are adorned with gold bracelets: large ones on their hands and arms and two [smaller ones] on their legs. They cover their genitals with hand-crafted, golden chainwork, a cubit in width, that wraps around their loins and is fastened in the front and back. Their bodies are otherwise entirely naked apart from the gold rings that all the women wear in their noses. When they travel with the king, they do not dwell in huts.[6] Even when it rains, they stay outside naked,
9 together with their animals, and sleep on the ground. Each one, whether

male or female, builds a fire in front of and behind them to keep warm. They eat elephants, wolves, leopards, dogs, camels, scorpions, frogs, and snakes. They also eat human flesh.

The king used to summon me every day and ask: "What do you seek from me, oh my master, oh descendant of the Prophet? Whether you want slaves, camels, or horses, you may take them."

"I do not want anything from you," I responded; "I simply heard of the glory of your kingdom and, with love and good will, I brought you gifts—a silk garment and seven hundred ducats (gold florins). I do not want anything in return from you." Then I added: "I love you and will give you my blessing, my ancestors' blessing, and the Prophet Muhammad's blessing. I will grant you pardon and forgiveness and the right to a place in the Garden of Eden for you, your sons, your daughters, and all the people of your house. And may you visit us next year in the town of Mecca, the place for the atonement of sins."

After that, the king sent four virgin slave girls and four slaves to my house, all of them completely naked. "Our master the king sends you a thousand greetings. Accept these slaves and slave girls as a gift," the messenger declared, before leaving the slaves with me and going on his way.

I stood there in my house with the eight of them standing completely nude in front of me, until I gave them each a garment to cover their nakedness. That night, the evil inclination stood at my right to seduce me with one of those slave girls, a beautiful young girl, and I drew her onto my bed. But then my good inclination prevailed and I said to myself: "Consider where you came from, where you are going to, and what this deed is that you wish to commit. God, may He be exalted, takes no delight in such wicked deeds. Remember your Creator and He will remember you. If you sin tonight, God will send your enemies against you. They will lay you low and you will not be able to continue your mission." May the Creator 10 who saved me from this sin be exalted. All night long I did not sleep but prayed, cried, and begged God for mercy. At the light of day, I took all the slaves and led them to the king's wife. "The king gave me these slaves as a gift and I now give them to you with love and good will," I said. "I want nothing from you in return but give you heavenly pardon and forgiveness and a good abode in the Garden of Eden."

When the king heard about this, he summoned me to ask why I had not accepted his gift. "I did accept it from you, but I gave it with love and good will to the queen," I responded. On account of this act of affection, the king bestowed great honor upon me, upon the descendants of the Prophet in the land of Kush, upon their chief, Abu Kamil, and likewise upon their attendants. The king and all his officials loved and respected me. They thought that I was like an angel of God and were in awe of me. I fasted every day and prayed day and night. I did not speak much in front of them and, if they spoke to me, I would reply to them only briefly.[7] When I would ride my horse and go ahead of the king, he would order his finest slaves to accompany me on whatever road I took.

An Encounter with an Enemy from Mecca

After these events, a certain Ishmaelite, who had come from Mecca, went to Abu Kamil's house. Abu Kamil came to me and said: "Do you know that one of the Meccan descendants of the Prophet has just joined us? The three of us will form a single fellowship, united like brothers. We will swear not to deny your words. Whatever you command we will do, inclining neither to the right nor to the left, and we will be like sons to you."

This Ishmaelite scoundrel then came to me with Abu Kamil and together they swore by their holy book that they would honor me by agreeing to say nothing to the king without my permission. I asked this scoundrel, "Why did you come to this land and what do you seek from the king?"

"I come from Mecca bringing a book from the house of the Prophet which I want to give as a gift to the king," he replied. "I will promise him a place in paradise and forgiveness for his sins and will ask him for gold, slaves, and camels."

"Do not ask the king for this because to do so is shameful for us," I said to this mischief-making scoundrel. But the evildoer replied: "I beseech you and Abu Kamil to visit the king with me. I will read the book to him and you will speak well of me. I will tell him that, since this book is from the Prophet's house, it is worth more than one thousand florins, and that it will give him a place in paradise, make his kingdom prosper, and grant him pardon for all his sins. I ask that you do me the kindness of advocating for me to the king about these things."

Abu Kamil and I accompanied him to the king and this scoundrel took out his book of lies and, in front of the king and his officials, read from it. The king said to me and Abu Kamil: "Do you know this man?"

"He is our relative, a descendant of the Prophet, and this book is from the house of the Prophet, from those who guard his grave," we replied. "This is a great religious opportunity. Keep the book in your house and your kingdom will prosper and all your sins will be pardoned. This is surely worth more than one thousand gold dinars."

So the king said to his slaves: "Give the owner of this book thirty camels and a horse." And they gave these to him.

After these events, this cursed one went secretly to the king and denounced me. "This man in whom you believe is not a descendant of the Prophet," he said, "he is merely a Jew from the desert of Habor."

When the king heard this, he sent for Abu Kamil and told him this informer's story. "What do you have to say about this allegation that your new kinsman, whom you introduced to me, has made?" he demanded. "What do you know about these two men?"

"I know about neither the one nor the other," Abu Kamil responded, "but I see that the first is honorable and humble. He fasts all day and fears God. He does not pursue women and frivolous things and has no love of money. But the second does indeed love gold and silver. He does many evil things and talks a lot."

"You speak with honesty," the king declared. Abu Kamil left the king and told me about this conversation.

Later, the king's wife, to whom I had given the slaves, heard the informer's allegations and sent for me. "Do not stay in this land any longer," she told me, "because your new Meccan kinsman has grievously slandered you to the king and has incited many people to urge him to kill you."

"But how will I be able to leave without the king's permission?" I asked.

"The king will be at my house tonight," the queen answered. "I will send for you and you will come before us and ask him for permission. I will be there to help you. The king will grant you permission and tomorrow you will go on your way in peace. May you remember me well all the days of your life."

At the third hour of the night,[8] the queen sent for me and I appeared before the king. There was no one with him but his wife. "What is my crime and how have I offended you?" I asked him:

> I came to you, with love and good will, bearing gifts. I wanted neither silver nor gold from you, neither male nor female servants. You are a king who is wiser and more discerning than all others. Know that the scoundrel who has slandered me loves gold and silver and gave you nothing but a single book, and we do not know whether it is one of truth or falsehood. Abu Kamil and I were at my house when this scoundrel first approached me and I demanded of him: "Why have you come to the king and what do you seek from him?" He replied: "I heard that you were the most important person to the king and that he hearkens to your words and accords you great honor. I heard that he gave you slaves, horses, and camels, and that you did not accept them. I ask you to accept everything that the king gives you and to give it to me for I am your kinsman." I did not want to obey him and commit this act. You, oh king, like the great sea, are deficient in nothing, yet if you condemn an innocent man, will not your kingdom and your riches be deficient? If, however, you encounter an evildoer and punish him justly, God will make your kingdom great, for justice is the prerogative of God and kings. I have now stayed with you for ten months. Consult all your servants and officials. They will tell you if they have noticed any misconduct on my part, whether great or small, or anything shameful. Therefore, in your kindness, for the sake of the Almighty God, give me permission to go on my way. I will pray for you and bless you.

The queen then spoke to him: "Give permission to this man to go on his way for he is honorable and loyal. He has stayed with us for ten months. We found no fault with him and there were only good reports about him."

"Whatever you desire, whether slaves, camels, or horses, take them and go in peace," the king said to me.

"I want nothing from you except permission to leave tomorrow at dawn, because I know that I have evil enemies who stand against me," I replied. "Therefore, may it please you to send one of your honorable servants to accompany me to the minister of your treasury." The king then summoned a servant and ordered him to go with me. He gave us two horses and the king ordered a messenger to tell Obadiah, the ruler of that area, to guide me to Abu Kamil.

[A passage is likely missing from the manuscript near the end of this section.⁹]

Leaving the Land of Kush

That morning, I left the king's residence in Lamul at the source of the Nile with my old companion and the king's servant. We crossed many rivers and passed through grazing grounds for elephants—and there were lots of elephants in that land. There was also one very muddy river into which horses can sink up to their bellies in mire. Although many men and horses have sunk and died there, we rode our horses right through it—blessed be God who saved us, Amen. We traveled for eight days until we reached Sennar, the residence of Obadiah, the ruler of that area. The king's messenger who accompanied me called on him and instructed him as he had been instructed by the king: "Guide this man, our master, to Abu Kamil, who is at the town of Soba on the Nile."

Then Obadiah summoned me. "Oh our master, what do you desire? All that you demand of me I will willingly and devotedly do," he said.

"I desire nothing from you except that you acquire for me at my own expense three good camels and some leather waterskins for them to carry," I replied. Nonetheless, he provided me with a slave to accompany me to Abu Kamil.

In the morning, I left Sennar with my slave and the messenger. We journeyed along the Nile for five days until we reached the town of Soba, which was a desolate ruin, yet they do have some homes there made of wood.

Abu Kamil then came to me. "How is it that you have come from the king and yet he has not presented you with any slaves?" he asked. "I know that the king loves and honors you, yet you have arrived here having taken nothing from him. Therefore, stay at my house and I will go to the king and entreat his favor."

"I will agree to this," I replied.

That night, as I slept in Abu Kamil's house, my father, of blessed memory, appeared to me in a dream. I recognized him and said: "Your form is like the form of my father."

"Yes, I am your father," he replied.

"Why have you come to this far-off land?" I asked him.

"I came because I love you and want to be of help to you. Why are you still staying in this place?"

"My master, my father," I said, "Abu Kamil told me that he wished to visit the king and return to me. I am going to wait for him here until he returns."

Still in the dream, my father answered: "If you go tomorrow, you will go in peace. No evil will befall you and you will go with God's blessing, but if you delay until Abu Kamil returns, know that you will die. Therefore, go without fail tomorrow and do not delay."

After midnight I woke up, went to Abu Kamil, and woke him up. "Send me on my way tomorrow without fail," I told him, "I do not want you to go to the king." And Abu Kamil promised to send me on my way in the morning.

At daybreak, I left Soba, Abu Kamil's abode. He gave me his brother as an escort and, in ten days, I reached the Kingdom of Al Ga'l,[10] which is part of the Kingdom of Soba under the dominion of Amram [Amara].[11] Abu Aqrab was the king of Al Ga'l. We came before him and Abu Kamil's brother said to him: "The king commands you to guide our master, this descendant of the Prophet, and give him everything he needs for his journey." I stayed with that king for three days. I then traveled with my old slave until I reached Mount Ataqqi[12] and met a great chief named Abd al-Wahhab. He advised me to travel by way of a short desert route to the land of Dongola.

I stayed in his house for six days. On the sixth day, messengers arrived from King Amram. While we were standing on one bank of the Nile, one of them called to Abd al-Wahhab from the opposite bank: "Tell our master that he must not leave because the king regrets the evil that he caused him, seeks his forgiveness, and is sending him slaves and camels. Tell him to wait until the king's messengers arrive with these gifts."

Abd al-Wahhab then called to me. "I have good news for you," he cried. "The king is sending you a big gift!"

When I heard these words, I said to him: "Do me the great kindness of accompanying me on my way this very night so that it may be a memento between us." I gave him twenty ducats and some garments and within the hour he had filled six waterskins for us and loaded them onto three camels. I then set out with my slaves and Abd al-Wahhab on a ten-day journey through the desert. I had two slaves with me . . .

[A passage is missing from the manuscript.]

. . . until we reached the town of Dongola, a half-day's journey. We saw many men on horseback. I said to Abd al-Wahhab: "Go and call on the owner of these horses and he will tell you what this land is like." So Abd al-Wahhab mounted his camel and sped off, catching up with them at the edge of the desert, at the border of Amram's Kingdom.

"We are searching for some runaway slaves," the horsemen said to Abd al-Wahhab.

"We have not seen them," he answered. He then asked them whether 15 this land was good or bad.

"This land is good," they replied, "but last night some of King Amram's sons came with two hundred men and we heard that one of the king's sons was gravely ill and that they were searching for a doctor to treat him."

When Abd al-Wahhab reported this to me, I said to him: "If you deal kindly with me, your reward from God and from me will be great. It is not good for me to stay in this land while King Amram's sons are here. I have no desire to see them. Therefore, if I have found favor in your eyes, show me the way to Massawa. It is located on the Nile River at the border of the Kingdom of Soba, a five-day journey from here, and its people are enemies of this king."

"I will do as you say," he replied, "and if you so desire, I will go even as far as Egypt."

When I heard his words, I bowed down to the God of heaven and earth. We went together to the edge of the desert. There were huge sand dunes that we had to traverse as one would mountains. I fasted for three consecutive days until I reached the town of the king's enemies.

After that, I went to the river and there before me was an Egyptian Ishmaelite sheikh. This sheikh lived with his wife and sons in a town called al-Habir. He came, kissed my hand, and declared: "Come oh blessed one of God, you who are our master and the descendant of our master. Do me the kindness of visiting my house so that I may receive your blessing. I have straw, fodder, and a place for you to stay the night." I went with that sheikh, whose name was Usman, and he cleared his home for me and my slaves.

"Could you show me the way to Egypt?" I asked him. "The route that proceeds from Lamul is a good one," he replied, "but the route by which you plan to go to Egypt is not. If you travel by river, you will be killed. Even if the Prophet himself were with you, they would kill him. Therefore, stay in safety at my house while we determine which route is best and then you may go." After hearing the sheikh's words, I gave Abd al-Wahhab ten ducats and he returned to his land.

While I was in that land, five young men from the two [lost Israelite] tribes presented themselves to me and gave me a gift of two lion cubs. I accepted them, intending to bring them with me to Egypt, and the young men returned to their land.

I had been staying with my slaves in the honorable sheikh's house for a month when he said: "Your camels are extremely weak. They will not be able to traverse this desert unless you first feed them for two or three months until they are fat enough to make the journey. There are parts of the desert where one can journey for three days without finding vegetation, grazing grounds, or anything for camels to eat. They will have to make do without food and with what little water they can find until you reach Girga on the Nile, which is near Cairo."

"What should I do?" I asked the sheikh. "Advise me. How should I make this journey? If you know of people who are traveling to Egypt, please introduce them to me, and procure good camels for me that are capable of conveying me through this desert."

"I will do as you request," the sheikh answered.

I bought a beautiful she-camel from him for twenty ducats and the sheikh bought two strong camels for me in exchange for seventy ducats. I also put the camels I had towards the exchange. The people of the town and surrounding area then came to the sheikh's home to offer me their tithe, filling his house with wheat, barley, buckwheat, young goats, and cattle. I took only what the camels needed to eat and gifted the rest to the sheikh and to the poor.

After that, the sheikh said: "Know that there are Ishmaelite merchants who want to set out through the desert tomorrow, the 17th of Heshvan [November 17, 1522], and there are others who will set out on the first of Kislev [December 13, 1522]."

"Summon the leaders of these travelers for me," I replied. He summoned them and I said to them: "I wish to go with you to Egypt by way of the great desert."

"We are your servants," they responded. "We would be honored if you would accompany us. Set your affairs in order tonight and be ready tomorrow."

They agreed to fill the waterskins and load them onto the camels for the journey. I slept through the night and, in the morning, I called to the sheikh, "Prepare what I need for me."

"I have everything prepared," he answered, "but I'm waiting for your slave, who left the house but has not yet returned."

"Go after the slave," I instructed him.

They searched for the slave but could not find him, so I said to the merchants, "Wait for me until midday so that I can find my slave."

We waited until midday but the slave did not appear, so I let them go on their way. I stayed with the sheikh for many days and did not leave his home. Even when chiefs and notables visited, I did not stir from my place. After the merchants had left al-Habir, I said to the sheikh: "Come with me to King Muhammad."

So the sheikh and I went there together, while my old slave remained at the house with all my baggage. We appeared before the king, who had many servants, and found him drinking date wine and eating mutton without bread. The king rejoiced and greeted me: "This day is blessed because 17 our master, the descendant of our master the Prophet, has come to us. I desire you to stay in my home. If you agree, you will be greatly honored."

"May you be blessed by Him whose name is blessed," I replied. "I will pray for you and grant you forgiveness and absolution for all your sins. I am here to request that you dispatch your servants to find the slave who fled from me today, for I know that he is in your kingdom. May God reward you for this kindness that you do for me."

"I myself will go out to search for him with my servants," said the king. And so the king himself went with all his officers to search for the slave. Indeed, he sent his servants searching throughout his land and beyond, riding on camels and running on foot. I returned to the sheikh's house and stood there in prayer until evening, when the king arrived with my slave.

"For my sake," he said, "please do not beat the slave this time."

After the king returned to his home, I put iron shackles on the slave's neck and feet. After spending another seven days in the sheikh's house, the merchants who had departed on the 17th of Heshvan returned, stripped naked and beaten from head to foot.

"After we left, we journeyed for three days," they told me. "On the fourth, a large band of bloodthirsty men attacked us, slaughtering many and taking the camels, slaves, and other spoils. We do not know who among our party is still alive and who was killed."

The next day another two of them arrived and, in the evening, another three. Each day more came, all stripped naked. So I gave them clothes to cover their nakedness and alms worth fifty ducats and these ravaged people served me and ate at my table until, on the 14th of Kislev [December 13, 1522], I left the sheikh's house, accompanied by many people, to journey through the great desert.

CHAPTER 2

EGYPT AND THE HOLY LAND

I fasted and prayed to God continually, when I lay down and when I got up, wherever I went and wherever I traveled. I vowed to eat and drink only at intervals of three days and nights and not to eat while traveling between oases. In this desert, the intervals between oases are journeys of three days and nights, and sometimes even four or five days and nights. We drank solely from the water that was loaded on the camels until, after forty-five days, we reached the town of Girga in the Rif. We had a knowledgeable guide who led us through the desert like a ship's captain navigates the sea. At night, he navigated by the stars and during the day by his wisdom, for the desert is like the ocean.

"Come with me to my home until I find a way to get you to Cairo," this wise man said to me. His name was Shalom in Hebrew and Salam in Arabic. I went to his house, which was a mile away at the edge of the town, and he gave me lodging, a bed, and a servant to attend to all my needs and those of my slaves. His place was on the bank of the Nile. I stayed with this man for twenty days, then I sold my camels for one hundred gold florins and embarked on a small boat down the Nile until I reached the gates of Cairo. At the gate, the Ishmaelite Turks detained me and searched through all my baggage and boxes to assess the customs tax. They wanted twenty florins for my slaves, for no one can enter at the city gates with Kushite slaves without paying twenty florins per slave. When the Turks saw my two lions, they asked for them as a gift in exchange for which they would exempt me from customs, the slaves' tax, and other expenses. So I gave them the two lions to avoid the other expenses. As a result, they honored me greatly and there was great rejoicing, because they told me that they wanted to send the lions to the King of the Turks.

18

An Incalculable Swindle in Cairo

I entered Cairo in the early evening on the first of Adar, 5283 [February 26, 1523], accompanied by a man who had friends in Cairo. "Spend the night at my house," he offered. "In the morning, with God's help, I will find you a better place to stay."

Taking my slaves and baggage with me, I went with him. His spacious house included a garden with large trees. He gave me a room and provided me with bread and cheese to eat. But I said to the people of the house: "I don't eat cheese, please only give me eggs."[1] So they gave me eggs and I ate, then fell asleep until morning. In the morning, I took out some gold pieces and said to this man: "Come with me to sell this gold to the Jews, for they are more knowledgeable in this business than the locals." So this man accompanied me to the street of the Jews. I stood at the entrance to a store in which there were some Jewish silversmiths.

"Who is your leader?" I asked them in Hebrew, so the Ishmaelite would not understand.

"I will take you to him," one replied. While the Ishmaelite waited at the store, we left together and arrived at the house of R. Abraham [de Castro], who was the Chief of the Mint and the most powerful Jew in Cairo.

"I am a Jew," I told him. "I want to stay with you for three or four days and reveal a secret to you. Also, if you know of a way to get me to Jerusalem, please direct me. I want neither silver, gold, nor food from you, only lodging."

"I cannot let you enter my house," R. Abraham responded, "for you have come disguised as an Ishmaelite. If you were to stay in my home, you would bring trouble upon me."

Although R. Abraham did not want to let me lodge at his home under any circumstances, I pressed him, saying, "For the love of God and our ancestors, do me a kindness, because 'the reward for performing a commandment is the opportunity to perform another one.'"[2]

"It is a weighty commandment for me, as well as for all the Jews of Cairo, that you not be permitted to enter my house," R. Abraham replied. So I left him and returned to the Ishmaelite.[3]

"If you know of a righteous and distinguished man who observes the commandments, do tell me," I said to him. He responded that there was indeed a good, honorable, and worthy man in the city and his name was Sharaf al-Din. "Come with me," I said, "and let's go meet him."

So I went to Sharaf al-Din and said to him, "I have heard that you are the most honorable and pious person in Cairo. Could you in your kindness lodge me in your house until I leave for Jerusalem and would you show me how to get there?" He gave me an apartment there and the apartment that Sharaf al-Din prepared for me . . . [A passage is missing from the manuscript.]

My old slave fell ill and was bedridden for five days, dying at midnight on the fifth. This slave had been a loyal guardian of all that I owned and had been my cook. I had brought him out from the desert [of Habor], even though he was deaf and mute, and had a wife and children. The second slave that I had bought, however, was a thief and so, after the old slave died, I had to remain in the apartment alone, guarding my belongings while others went to bury him. I was in great distress. My thoughts were troubled and I did not know what to do. In the end, I decided to return to R. Abraham, the Chief of the Mint, but I first went to Sharaf al-Din and said: "I am going out to attend to some business and am entrusting you with the safekeeping of this slave. Guard my apartment!"

I opened a chest in front of him and brought out four fine pearls, but I did not show him what else was in it. I then closed the chest—putting the pearls back inside before his very eyes—and locked it with the keys. I had also shown him a thousand gold florins that were kept there. I then said to him, "This apartment, this chest, and this slave are now entrusted to you until I return."

That same day after the death of my servant, I went to see the Jews. When I returned to the apartment, I fell asleep until morning. I saw myself in a dream walking naked among people, covering my genitals with my hands. The dream greatly distressed me and troubled my thoughts. I was in anguish. After that, I locked the chests and took the keys with me. I left the room key and the slave with Sharaf al-Din and went to the market. When I returned to the room in which the slave and money had been, I found that the chest containing the money was missing.

The moment I realized it was not there, I was like a body without soul or spirit. I went to find Sharaf al-Din, but came upon his son. "Why did you move the chest?" I reprimanded him. "Call your father!"

The son left and, when he returned, he informed me that his father was in the market. I was in anguish and could not think clearly until Sharaf al-Din returned and I approached him. "Why did you move the chest from its place?" I demanded.

"Because I wanted to keep all the chests safe for you in my room. Do not fear."

"Retrieve the chests because I need to get something from them," I told him.

"I went to eat at another house and forgot the keys there," he replied. I then realized that he was playing tricks on me. I wanted to get angry with him, but I was a guest in his house.

"Send for the keys!" I demanded.

"No messenger will know where they are and so I myself will have to go," Sharaf al-Din replied. He left and did not return until midnight, at which point I asked him, "Give me the chest because I need to retrieve one of the pearls as well as another item."

"I will not give you anything unless you take my daughter as a wife," he replied. "Let me give her to you and I will return everything and will deal kindly with you."

It is impossible to calculate the worth of the treasures that Sharaf al-Din stole from me, so precious were they, and I will not write down in this book what he took until the time for judgment and justice comes.

I left Sharaf al-Din's house with my Kushite slave and what remained of my belongings and went to the house of a certain Turkish Ishmaelite, whose name is Zachariah (in Hebrew) and Yahya ibn Abdallah (in Arabic). When I told him everything that Sharaf al-Din had done to me, he said, "I already know about this man and his dealings. He is a swindler. Although he presents himself as righteous and God-fearing, he is a great evildoer. Stay in my house until morning and I will go and speak with him and reprove him for what he has done."

So the Turk met with Sharaf al-Din. "Why have you wronged this descendant of the Prophet who has come to my house?" he asked him. "He told me that he deposited a chest filled with many things in your house and that you will not return it to him? Why did you do this to our master who is a descendant of the Prophet?'"

"No," Sharaf al-Din replied, "he gave me nothing at all. He came to my house with nothing but two slaves: the old one, who died on him, and the Kushite slave, whom he took with him. After making these claims, he took his slave and left. I am most aggrieved that he should say such things. I want to summon him and a judge to my house so that justice can be rendered between us—let men of law determine the worth of his claims against me. Let them levy a penalty of one thousand gold florins on me if he has indeed entrusted me with anything in front of witnesses. However, if he can bring no proof against me, he must pay me the thousand florins."

The Turk returned and reported all this to me. "Advise me what to do because I am afraid of him," I said. "Tell me what I should do and what my strategy should be."

"I know that if you ask him for what you have entrusted him with," he replied, "you will bring serious trouble upon yourself. I can see that he is filled with malice and seeks to kill you. Neither his slaves, servants, nor students will testify against him. If you heed my advice, go on your way and do not ask Sharaf al-Din for anything."

So I sold my Kushite slave to that Turk for two hundred gold florins and left Cairo with a large party of Turks. Among these Ishmaelites was a righteous merchant from Gaza, whose name was also Sharaf al-Din. I was riding on a bad camel when this righteous man said to me: "Ride on my camel, it is better than yours." His camel had a pretty caparison painted like the window of a house.

Assistance from Jews in Gaza

I arrived in Gaza at a house so large it was like an inn. Since I had come 22 on my own, they gave me one of the upper rooms, which I shared with a Jewish merchant from Beirut named Abraham Dunas. After staying in the same room with him for two days without saying a word, praying all day and speaking to no one, I asked him his name. "Abraham," he answered.

"What do you people pray for at this time, for the falling of rain or for the falling of dew?"[4] I asked.

"We are now praying for the falling of rain," he replied, adding that although he had met many Ishmaelites and many descendants of the Prophet, he had never met one as wise as me.

"I know by my own calculation that today is a joyful one for you because it is the holiday of Purim," I observed.

"You speak truly," he exclaimed. "Who taught you all of this?"

"There are many wise and eminent Jews in my land and their homes are close to mine. Some are my friends and they dine at my table, eating fruit but no meat. They love me and I love them."

"How is it that we Jews in this land cannot even speak to an Ishmaelite, let alone a descendant of the Prophet, for they hate us so?" he asked. "They like dogs better than they like Israelites."

"Do not fear," I replied, "for the End is nigh and the Holy One Blessed Be He will humble the wicked and elevate the humble. The time is at hand when you will see great things, terrible disorder, and conflict between kings. And as for you, Abraham, do me a great kindness and find some merchants who can lead me to the Temple, but first to Hebron."

"I will do so," he said, and left to contact some merchants and muleteers. When he returned, he presented me with a mule, and we made the necessary business arrangements. I decided not to immediately reveal my secret to him, but to give him some inkling of it when we were on the road. Later he came to me with a silversmith named Joseph, who was a shop owner. Joseph had a brother, whose name was Jacob, and their old father was still alive.[5] He and Joseph stayed with me for about two hours, and I continued to conceal my secret from them, giving them only hints. I stayed in Gaza for five days, during which time the local Jews secretly arranged for Abraham the Jew to provide me with bread and meat.

A Sign at the Cave of the Patriarchs in Hebron

23 On 19 Adar 5283 [March 16, 1523], I set off from Gaza on the road to Hebron. I traveled, day and night, until I reached the Cave of the Patriarchs in Hebron at noon on 23 Adar [March 20]. The guardians of the cave approached me and kissed my hands and feet, declaring, "Come oh blessed one of God, our master and descendant of our master." Two sheikhs, the guardians of the Mosque of Abraham, then arrived. Both were very wise and had been appointed over all the other mosque guard-

ians as well as over the judges of Hebron. Taking me by the hand, they brought me to a certain tomb and said: "This is the tomb of Abraham our father." I prayed there until completing the prayer.

Afterwards, they showed me a small chapel to the left which contained the tomb of Sarah our mother. In between the tombs of Abraham and Sarah was a chapel in which the Ishmaelites prayed. In the main mosque, above Abraham's tomb, was that of Isaac, and next to it, above Sarah's tomb, was Rebecca's tomb. Below Abraham's tomb is another chapel in which there is an inscription for Jacob's tomb and, near that, an inscription for Leah's tomb, which is opposite that of Sarah.

I gave them ten florins as alms to buy lamp oil and said to the guardians: "These grave markers are incorrect. The truth is that Abraham, Isaac, and Jacob are buried together in a single underground cave. They are not buried on the surface."

"Your words are true," they answered.

"Show me the cave," I told them.

So I went with them and they showed me the entrance to the cave at the mouth of the well. There was a single lamp lit in that well, day and night. They lowered it into the well on a rope, and I saw an opening in its wall that was about the size of a man. I believed that this was truly the cave and I rejoiced. I sent the Ishmaelites away and prayed at the mouth of the well until I completed my prayer.

I then called the oldest of the guardians and said to them: "This is not the entrance to the cave, there is another entrance."

"You are correct," they responded. "In ancient times, there was an opening to the cave in the middle of the main mosque that contains the marker for Isaac's tomb."

"Show me the location of that entrance," I replied.

I followed them and they removed the rugs from the floor of the mosque and showed me the location of the door, which had been blocked with large stones and lead that no one would be able to remove. After that, 24 I told them to cover the floor with the rugs and asked, "Do you have any idea who built this entryway to the cave?"

They retrieved a book and read to me that a certain king, who had been one of Muhammad's caliphs, had built the cave's entryway after the

Ishmaelites had conquered the Temple from the Christians. That king had sent four men, each with a lamp, into the cave, where they stayed for about an hour. Upon leaving, three of them immediately died. The fourth was struck dumb for three days. The king then asked him, "What did you see in the cave?"

"I saw the following things," he replied. "Our father Abraham was in his coffin at the place above where they marked his tomb. His coffin was covered with beautiful fabric and around it were lamps and many books. Near Abraham our father was Sarah our mother. Isaac and Rebecca were above them and Jacob and Leah were below. There were lamps surrounding the coffins. On each of the coffins there was an image of a man or a woman. The lamps in our hands were then extinguished and the cave was lit with light as bright as the sun. After we saw this, there was a pleasant scent in the air like incense. As the four of us left, we passed by Rebecca's tomb and, as we did so, the image of the man on Isaac's coffin cried out to us in a loud voice and we exited the cave breathless." This was the description of the tombs by the fourth man, who had been struck dumb. The entryway to the cave was closed by the king and remains closed until this very day.

I stood in prayer at the mouth of the well. I focused my gaze on the entryway to the cave from Sabbath eve until dawn. In the morning, I remained standing in prayer until evening. Then, on Saturday night, I prayed at the mouth of the cave, staying awake until morning. The seventy elders had told me that on Tuesday I would discover a certain sign, and I stood there silently wondering what it would be.

On Sunday morning, before the sun rose, the guardians joyously shared this news with me. "Our master and descendant of our master the Prophet," they said, "arise and rejoice for great happiness has come to us. Water has risen from this mosque's cistern, and no water has risen from it in four years." I went with them to see the water and it was beautiful and
25 pure, flowing to the cistern from a far-off land.

A Sign at the Temple in Jerusalem

I left Hebron for Jerusalem on 24 Adar [March 21, 1523]. When bandits were sighted on the way, my companions cried out, "Our master, descendant of the Prophet, there are enemies ahead of us!"

"Fear not," I reassured them, "for it is they who are in danger and you who are safe." I had not even finished speaking when the Ottoman judge from Hebron appeared with many servants. The bandits saw him and they all fled. I went with him to Jerusalem, arriving on 25 Adar 1523 [March 22, 1523], and that very day I entered the abode of the Holy of Holies. When I arrived at the Temple, all the Ishmaelite guardians came to kiss my feet. "Come oh blessed one of God," they called out, "our master and descendant of our Prophet."

The two most eminent of them ushered me into the cave under the Foundation Stone (even ha-shetiyah) and told me: "This is the place of Elijah the Prophet, this is the place of King David, this is the place of King Solomon, this is the place of Abraham and Isaac, this is the place of Muhammad." They showed me the places of the prophets both under and above the stone. "Since I now know all these places," I told the guardians, "you can go on your way for I wish to pray. In the morning I will give you alms."

They went on their way. I already knew their words to be empty and false. I prayed until the Ishmaelites left the courtyard after completing their prayers at the second hour of the night. Then, while they returned to their homes, I went under the Foundation Stone. The guards then extinguished all but four of the lamps in the courtyard. Before they closed the doors, they searched around to see if anyone was sleeping in the cave so that they could drive them out and there they found me.

"Leave this place," they demanded, "for we are its guards. We have sworn to the king not to let anyone sleep here. If you do not leave, we will go to the governor and he will remove you against your will."

When I heard their harsh words, I left the courtyard and they closed its gates. It was Tuesday evening; I prayed all night long and fasted. In the morning when the Ishmaelites came to pray in the courtyard, I entered with them. Once they had completed their prayers, I called out to them loudly: "Where are the guardians?" When all of them had gathered around me, I said: "I am your master and the descendant of your master the Prophet. I have come from a far-off land to this sacred house. I wanted to remain inside it to pray, not to sleep, but four guards came and drove me out. I am your master, the descendant of your Prophet. If you want peace with me, well and good, I will bless you. If not, I will take vengeance upon you and will write to the Turk of your evil deeds."

"Forgive us this time," they pleaded, "we want to serve you. We will be like slaves to you and will do your will so long as you are in the Temple." I gave them ten ducats as alms and stayed in the Temple. I fasted in the Holy of Holies for five weeks. I ate no bread or water except on the Sabbath. I prayed both below and above the Foundation Stone.

Ten emissaries from my brother, King Joseph, and the elders came to me but comported themselves as if they were strangers.

[A passage is likely missing from the manuscript.]

At the top of the courtyard's dome, the Ishmaelites had erected an image of a crescent moon facing west.[6] However, on the first day of Shavuot 5283 [May 30, 1523], it turned east. When they noticed this, there was a great outcry.

"Why are you crying out?" I inquired.

"Because of our sins, the crescent moon has turned eastward and that is a bad omen for the Ishmaelites," they answered.

That same day some Ishmaelite craftsmen restored the crescent moon to its original orientation, but the next day it again reoriented itself to the east. As I prayed, the Ishmaelites cried out and wept, seeking but being unable to restore the crescent moon to its original state. The elders had already told me, "When you see the sign, go to Rome." I saw the gates of mercy and the gates of repentance, and I went below to the sanctuary, which was a large building like the one above. Under the sanctuary, I did what the elders had commanded me in a place where no one could interfere with me. The image of the crescent moon was restored only after I had done what the elders had commanded me under the Temple.

After that, I ascended the Mount of Olives where I visited two caves. I then returned to Jerusalem and ascended Mount Zion. There are two houses of worship there in a single building: the upper part is controlled by Christians, the lower part by Ishmaelites.[7] The Ishmaelites opened their part for me and showed me a tomb, telling me that it was that of King David, peace be upon him. I prayed there, then left for the upper house of worship. The Christians opened it for me and I entered their church and prayed there. I then descended from Mount Zion to Jerusalem and visited the house of a Jew named Abraham the Proselyte, who was a metalsmith. He lived above a synagogue and I saw old women there shining the synagogue lamps.

"What is your name?" I asked. "Abraham," he responded. I dismissed the Ishmaelites, saying that I needed to do some work with the metalsmith, and they went on their way.

"What are you praying for now, the falling of rain or the falling of dew?" I asked.

"We are praying for the falling of dew," he answered, utterly astonished.

I spoke with him a great deal, but I did not tell him that I was Jewish until my third visit to his home, just before I was to leave Jerusalem. "I want to go to Rome. Would you draw me a map of Venice, Rome, and Portugal?" I inquired.

"Why are you going?" he asked.

"I am going for a worthy cause, but its nature is a secret that I cannot reveal. I want you to advise me how I should go on my way." I then gave Abraham a letter that I had written at the Temple and asked him to deliver it to the Nagid, R. Isaac.[8]

On 24 Sivan 5283 [June 17, 1523], I left Jerusalem with a party of Ishmaelites on horseback, who accompanied me for five miles. In the month of Tammuz [June or July], I reached the place where I had first stayed in Gaza. An old Jewish spice merchant visited me. "Summon Joseph the metalsmith and tell him to bring his gold and silver measures and his seal dies to show them off to me in front of the Ishmaelites," I instructed him.

The old man did so and the two of them returned to me. I asked after the welfare of Joseph's brother Jacob and his elderly father, and he told me that they were well. After that, four [Jewish] elders visited me and I identified myself to them: "I am a Jew and so too are my father, King Solomon, and my older brother, King Joseph, who rules over thirty myriads in the desert of Habor."

That night, we ate and drank wine. I had not drunk wine since I had 28 embarked on my journey from the desert of Habor. They asked me if I had been in Egypt and I told them all that had happened to me in the house of R. Abraham, the Chief of the Mint, and how this had led me to lose the fortune that Sharaf al-Din stole from me.

They told me that a certain Ishmaelite had found a stone with engraved Hebrew inscriptions and had sold it to a Jew for four ducats. I asked where the stone was and they told me that they had hidden it in the cemetery. Two of them left to retrieve it and brought it to me. Once I had examined it, they returned it to its place.

That night old Ephraim and I went to the house of R. Daniel, the richest Jew in Gaza. He told me about all the governors who had come to Gaza from Anatolia. He was honorable and pious but he had a son, a strong and handsome man named Solomon, whom the Jews hated because he was wild. I called Solomon aside and reproved him, saying: "Repent of your evil deeds before Jerusalem is ensnared. If you do not repent, your blood is on your head." He swore to me that he would repent.

That Sabbath eve, R. Ishmael sent old Ephraim to me with a thousand greetings, begging me to dine with him that night and I did so. I stayed there until midnight, at which point I asked them to show me the synagogue. I went there and prayed for about two hours before returning to R. Ishmael's house.

"For the sake of God's love, love of the elders, and love of the rest of the House of Israel, do me the favor of finding a ship that will take me speedily to Alexandria," I implored him.

"There is a ship that sails to Damietta this week and some Jerusalemite Jews are traveling on it. This old man, R. Ephraim, will go with you and I will pay his wage," he responded.

"Be blessed by God. Remove baseless hate from among you and return to God so that He may hasten our redemption and the redemption of the House of Israel, for thus have the elders declared," I said.

I returned to my dwelling on the Sabbath morning and remained there. Later I sent an Ishmaelite to summon the shipowner, who came to me.

"I hear that you are sailing to Damietta," I said to him.

"Yes," he replied, "but I want to set out at dawn tomorrow. If you still
29 have business to do, finish it today."

Alexandria and the Voyage to Venice

I left Gaza on 15 Tammuz 5283 [July 8, 1523], arrived in Damietta two days later, and took accommodation. A few days later, I went to the home of a Jew named R. Mordecai—whose brother, R. Samuel, lived in Cairo—and spent the Sabbath with him. On Sunday, he led me overland along the coast, on a single camel, for a distance of twenty miles. I then boarded a ship and, on 24 Tammuz [July 17], reached Alexandria and lodged at the travelers' inn. The kabbalist R. Mordecai visited me.

"I am Jewish. My brother is the king of the desert of Habor. Could you tell me how to go by sea to Rome?" I asked him.

"Go to the consul," R. Mordecai replied, "he will advise you what to do because he is an honorable man and do let me know what he tells you." So I went to the consul.

"I am the brother of the King of the desert of Habor," I told him, "I come at the urging of my brother, King Joseph, and the seventy elders. It is my desire to meet the pope and, after that, the King of Portugal. Could you advise me what I should do and find me a ship to travel there?"

"There is a ship traveling to Apulia," the consul mused, "but your presence on it might cause trouble for me. I therefore advise you to wait until a galley sails to Venice with Ishmaelites aboard who can direct you."

I returned to my residence and then went to R. Mordecai's house. A young man named Joseph visited. His father and mother were from Naples and he had a wife in the land of the Turks.[9]

"I will go with this man to Rome," Joseph told R. Mordecai.

"This is good news!" exclaimed R. Mordecai, "this young man will be an interpreter for you on your way there."

That night I stayed in R. Mordecai's house. The next day, I saw a beautiful house within the complex of a mosque and I asked the caretaker, whose name was Birr al-Din, whether he would let me stay there for a few days.

"Both the mosque and the house belong to a woman, who inherited them from her father. Her husband, however, is an evildoer and she can do nothing without his permission," he answered.

I went to Phillipo the consul and told him all this. He sent for the woman's husband and persuaded him to let me use the house. But then

some Ishmaelite evildoers, who lived nearby, became aggrieved because Joseph the interpreter worked for me and Jews were not permitted to enter their mosque. When I became aware of this, I visited my Ishmaelite neigh-
30 bor, who was an utterly wicked Jew-hater. The moment he saw me he exclaimed: "Oh our master and descendant of our master, welcome! This night is blessed on account of your visiting our house."

"I have come here only out of love for you. How can you heed these slanderers who speak falsely against my Jewish servant, though he is loyal and devotedly serves me?" I challenged him.

"There are many Ishmaelites who can serve you," this evildoer responded. "The Jews are our enemies and enemies of the Prophet. It is not appropriate for one to serve you."

"I have found faith lacking among Ishmaelites," I answered him. "I, your master and descendant of the Prophet, have traveled through many lands. I have encountered Ishmaelites, and even descendants of the Prophet who are my relatives, who have cheated me and stolen my money. Now you wish to anger me, may evil befall you."

"If you want a good servant, I will give you one," the scoundrel offered. "If you wish, I myself will serve you." And so, in anger, I left him.

In the morning, I went to R. Mordecai's house and told him what that Ishmaelite had said about Joseph. And I warned Joseph, "Make sure that you do not come to my house because there are Ishmaelites who are conspiring to kill you."

I returned to my house and stayed there until the eve of Rosh Hashanah 5284 [September 19, 1523]. I then summoned R. Mordecai and said: "Tell the Jew who is staying in the big synagogue that I will be staying in the small synagogue." And that is what I did. I prayed in that synagogue on Rosh Hashanah eve together with my landlord, Isaac Bukapzi, and a Jew named R. Benjamin, after which we left to dine with the landlord. I then returned to the synagogue to pray until morning.

That morning, R. Isaac and R. Benjamin came to pray with me after which we left to eat. When I returned to the synagogue, I said to the landlord: "Do not open the door to anyone because I am afraid. I want to stay at the synagogue until after the holiday." He did so, but then Joseph came and knocked at the door.

"Open up," Joseph demanded, "I want to speak with R. David so that we can arrange our trip to Rome."

"No," R. Isaac responded, "He commanded me not to open the door."

But Joseph would not listen and set at the door to break it down. So they opened it and struck him, with the result that Joseph left and went to the big synagogue, where he told all the Jews: "I went to the synagogue in which the emissary of the desert of Habor is staying and R. Isaac and his wife struck me. Now I want to bring a case against them to the governor." R. Mordecai the kabbalist then arrived and reprimanded him. It was the Jews who told me about all these events. I stayed at the synagogue for the remainder of Rosh Hashanah before returning to my house. On Sukkot, I went to R. Mordecai's house, where I stayed for the first two days [October 4–5] of the holiday. Joseph visited me there. "I sinned against you because my anger dispelled my judgment," he wept, and I forgave him. R. Mordecai then advised me that Joseph would still be useful as an interpreter 31 between me and the Christians.

Later, I was walking in the market and happened upon the stall of a Jew who said to me: "Know that your servant Joseph is sick and bedridden."

"Take him to your house, feed him, and sustain him," I said, and gave him some coins.

I stayed in Alexandria until I heard that the galley was departing for Venice. I went to the Turkish governor, who was surrounded by high-ranking officials.

"My desire is to go to Venice," I declared, and received permission from him in front of them all. "Do me a favor out of love for me and for the Prophet, and I will pray for the Prophet to grant you a place in the Garden of Eden," I added. "Speak to the captain of the galleys and order him to put me on a ship to Venice." They did this, sending their servants who boarded the galley with me. They gave instructions to the captain, who replied, "I will do so."

❨ CHAPTER 3 ❩
ITALY

My servant Joseph and I left Alexandria in the middle of Kislev 1523 [2 December 1523]. I fasted all day and prayed day and night. I brought all kinds of food from Alexandria for Joseph, but it was of no use to me because it was mixed up with that of the Christians. Joseph used to eat using the Christians' utensils. Although I scolded him for this, he did not listen. When we reached Candia [Crete], I bought many kinds of food. The Christians, including the captain, would berate me about Joseph. The captain complained that he had stolen bread and wine from the ship's crew. Although I was very ashamed of him, I could do nothing about it because Joseph would not listen to me. When I reached Venice, I went to the captain's house and he gave me a place to stay. I fasted in his house for six days and six nights, neither drinking water nor eating bread, and praying day and night. After I had completed my prayers, I noticed that there was a man standing behind me.

"Who are you?" I asked him in the Holy Tongue.

"I am a Jew," he answered.

"Who told you that I would be here?"

"Joseph your servant said that you are a divinely charged emissary."

"What is your name?"

"Elhanan."

I asked about his father and mother. "My father is deceased and my mother is alive, but she does not live in this town," he replied.

On another occasion, Elhanan returned with a Jew, whose name was R. Moses dal Castellazzo, the painter.[1] I said to R. Moses, "I am in great
32 need of seven ducats because my servant Joseph is poor and sick. I have already spent a lot of money on him in Alexandria and on our way here."

"Come to my house and I will call the wardens (*parnasim*)," R. Moses responded.

I went with him to the ghetto (the Jewish quarter). There, a distinguished Jew, R. Matsliah, presented himself to me. When I discussed the issue of expenses, he said that we needed to visit R. Hiyya [Meir], and off we went.[2]

I introduced myself to R. Hiyya: "I am a Jew from the desert of Habor, charged with a mission by the seventy elders." But to R. Hiyya, I seemed like a joker.

"I need seven ducats," I persisted, "Would you ask the wardens if they are willing to provide them?"

"If the rest of the Jews give, I will give my share," he responded.

"This is the sixth day of my fast and I cannot eat until nightfall. Would you send me a little wine?" I asked, before returning to my lodging at the captain's house. But R. Hiyya did not send me anything, so I ate only eggs, bread, and water.

The honorable R. Matsliah tried his utmost for me, with the result that R. Simon ben Asher Meshullam visited me.[3] "I have heard that you are an emissary charged by the seventy elders to go to Rome," he said. "Tell me your mission and I will send two Jews with you and will pay all your expenses."

"I am going to meet the pope," I said, "but, for the good of all Israel, I am not able to tell anyone but him about my mission. If you would do me the kindness of sending two men to accompany me to Rome—for the love of God, the elders, and all Israel—you will be credited with this good deed and they will return bearing good news."

After that, I went with R. Moses the painter to the captain's house. I bade him farewell and took all my belongings to R. Moses's house in the ghetto. When R. Matsliah visited, I said, "Would you find me a ship bound for Rome?" and he did.

I remained at R. Moses's house until nightfall and then boarded a gondola, which conveyed me to a ship. I fasted and stayed aboard until morning when the customs officers came to make inspections. I was greatly afraid because I did not know where Joseph had gone. But Joseph did re- 33 appear and on Friday, 1 Adar 5284 [February 15, 1524], we departed. I spent the Sabbath on the ship. When it reached Pesaro, I went to R. Moses Foligno's home.[4]

"Do me a favor," I requested, "show me the way to Rome, for I do not want to spend the night here."

He left and got me horses and Joseph and I traveled to another city in which Jews dwelled. In this way, evening by evening, journey by journey, and meeting many Jews along the way, we reached Castelnuovo [di Porto], a town near Rome, on the eve of Purim. There I went to the house of a Jew named R. Samuel and stayed with him over Purim. That day, I bought the well-known bull and did with it as the elders had commanded me.[5] The next day I left and arrived in Rome, praise be to God.

A Meeting with the Pope in Rome

I am David the son of King Solomon, of blessed memory, from the desert of Habor. I arrived at the gates of Rome on the 15th of Adar I, 5284 [February 29, 1524]. A gentile Venetian approached me and spoke to me in Arabic, and I became angry with him.

I arrived at the pope's courtyard, riding an old white horse, my servant preceding me, and the Jews accompanying me.[6] I entered the pope's palace, still on horseback, and presented myself to Cardinal Egidio [di Viterbo].[7] All the other cardinals and officials came to see me. Attending the cardinal
34 was our honored master and teacher R. Joseph Ashkenazi,[8] who was the cardinal's tutor. Our honored master and teacher R. Joseph Tsarfati[9] also presented himself to us. With my journey companion as my interpreter, I spoke to the cardinal—and these Jews heard everything I said to him.

"I speak to you now in brief," I assured him, "but I will elaborate on my words in front of the pope."

I stayed with the cardinal until nightfall on the Sabbath eve. The Jews then asked the cardinal if I could stay with them until after the Sabbath.

"If you wish to go with them you may go," the cardinal said. "If you would like a room in my house, I will give one to you. Tomorrow I will appear before the pope and will send word to you of what he tells me."

I left with R. Joseph Ashkenazi and old R. Raphael, who lived together in a house. We ate the Sabbath evening meal and slept until morning. I went to synagogue with them to recite the blessing of the redeemer upon the Torah and remained in prayer until the end of the service.[10] As we walked back to old R. Raphael's house, men, women, and children came to see

Pope Clement VII (r. 1523–1534). Portrait by Sebastiano del Piombo.

me. I fasted right through the Sabbath. All that day until nightfall, men and women, Jews and Christians, came to visit me. Cardinal Egidio sent for R. Joseph Ashkenazi, who returned with the message that the pope had commanded the cardinal to bring me to him without fail on Sunday at the 11th hour. He said that the pope had greatly rejoiced and longed to see me.

In the morning before prayers, they gave me a horse and I went along the Borghetto Santo Egidio to the house of R. Moses Tsarfati's elderly brother-in-law and I prayed there. Many Jews visited me, may the Holy One Blessed Be He protect them and multiply them one thousandfold.

At the eighth hour, I went to the pope's palace and entered Cardinal Egidio's chamber together with twelve old and distinguished Jews—none of them young. As soon as he saw me, the cardinal rose from his seat and the two of us went together to the pope's apartment. I spoke with the pope, who received me graciously, saying: "This matter is from God."

"King Joseph and the elders," I declared, "commanded me to urge you to make peace between the emperor and the French king in any manner possible. This peace will be good both for you and for them. Would you write a letter for me to these two kings so that they can aid us and we can aid them? Also, would you write a letter for me to King Prester John?"[11]

"I cannot make peace between these two kings," the pope responded. "However, if you insist on helping, the King of Portugal can assist you. I will write to him and he will do the rest. His land is 'closer' to your land because his subjects are more accustomed to sailing the ocean throughout the year than those of the two kings whom you mentioned."

"I desire everything that you desire and will not depart to the left or to the right from what you command me," I said. "I have come here to serve God and not for any other purpose. I am ready to serve you at your pleasure and for your benefit all the days of your life."

The pope then sent for Cardinal Egidio. "Where is this ambassador staying?" he asked.

"The Jews asked him to stay with them on the Sabbath," he replied.

The distinguished Jews who were present said to the pope: "Leave the ambassador with us. We will honor him in your honor."

"If you do me this honor, I will defray all the expenses that you incur," the pope declared.

"I want to visit you once every two days," I said to the pope, "because to see your face is like seeing the face of God."

The pope said that he would instruct Cardinal Egidio to bring me each time he visited him and to take care of all my needs. With that, I took my leave and departed with the Jews, happy and glad-hearted. I walked back along Borgo Sant'Angelo to the old man's house but Aaron the alderman, may God protect and preserve him, was annoyed that I had gone there. He approached Cardinal Egidio, saying: "The community leaders and the   36 entire Jewish community have arranged a house for the ambassador where he will be able to stay by himself. It is furnished with everything he needs and they will provide him with servants."

The cardinal wrote to me saying that I should go with them and they gave me the letter. So I went with them and they arranged a beautiful house for me with three pleasant and spacious rooms. The name of the homeowner was Joseph and he had three sons. The eldest was Moses, the second Benjamin, and the third Judah, and they all looked after me. I stayed in their house for three weeks. For five days, I continued to frequent the cardinal's house, because other cardinals came to consult me there from morning until evening. While I was in Joseph's house, I fasted for six consecutive days and nights, neither eating bread nor drinking water.

Illness and Joseph Tsarfati and His Family

On Sabbath eve, they boiled water with herbs for me. Everything they did was done out of love for me and they did this because they said that it was a medicine used after fasting. When I felt fatigued and wanted water, they gave me some boiled water and I drank a bellyful. That water made me fall seriously ill with a severe chest ailment, because I was not accustomed to drinking this kind of water after fasting. In Jerusalem I had fasted six times for seven days and seven nights and in Venice for six days and six nights. After all these fasts, I had drunk nothing but water sweetened with fine sugar, which did me no harm. But since they had prepared this water especially for my benefit and were not familiar with my constitution, blessed be my hosts and the community leaders.

When this serious illness came upon me, I said to them: "Go and find me a bathhouse!" A man named Yomtov made arrangements and I went to the bathhouse with five or six servants. I stayed there until midnight, together with the servants, whereupon they arranged a room with a good bed in that very bathhouse and I slept there. Right through the night until the following day I was bled and, the next day, all my limbs were cupped. When my host arrived, he said: "If you wish, you may come home with me."

"May you be blessed by God, but I detest your house on account of my sickness there and I cannot enter it. Could you arrange another house for me?"

So Yomtov Halevi arranged another house and I went there with him and lodged in the room that he had prepared. It was a house filled with residents and my room was a thoroughfare for all of them. So I sent for R. Joseph Tsarfati the sage, who came to me.

"See the conditions in which I am living," I said. "If you want to acquire a good name for yourself, arrange a room for me in your house and I will stay with you until my sickness has passed."

He left and, after receiving permission from his mother and sisters, returned to me with the news that he had arranged a room in his house for me with a good bed. I went with him and entered the room that he had prepared. The room, which belonged to his sister Dinah, was beautiful and had a good bed. I stayed there for three months and, gladly and willingly, he saw to all my needs and expenses, while his sisters took care of me and his old mother attended to my every need. May God bless them! They fed me and prepared a variety of different medicines for me. They warmed herbs and, on many nights, placed them on my feet. They frequently served me warmed wine. They washed my feet and anointed me. They filled a large tub with hot olive oil in which I immersed myself and then ensconced myself in my fine bed. I did this four times and each time they changed the sheets!

I was like a dead man. When they examined the appearance of my urine, they saw gravel at the edges. But I did not believe them.

"Look at its appearance," I demanded, "If this sign is really present, it is indeed grave."

I then examined it and found that their words were true, but I told them that I would not die from this sickness until I gathered [Israel] in

Jerusalem, built the altar, and offered a sacrifice. And they all rejoiced in God. Despite my good constitution . . . [There is a break in the text here.] sleep would not come to me. My servants carried me back and forth on their shoulders all night long. Then, at dawn, they put me in bed. I was distressed and in great pain, hovering between life and death. They saw my pain and believed that I was about to die. I urinated a little and Dinah and her brother, R. Joseph Tsarfati, showed it to me.

"Do not fear for me," I reassured them, "for I know with certainty that I will not die from this sickness."

"If you wish, you may recite the deathbed confession, for that will neither hasten nor delay death," they suggested.   38

But I became angry with them and said, "Go in peace. I have no wish to recite the confession. I trust that God will be with me and that He will save me on account of the service I have performed—indeed He will be with me always." They were astonished and rejoiced at my words. That day the Holy One Blessed Be He caused me to have a great sweat and I recovered from the terrible sickness.

My servants stayed with me: Hayyim, the cantor, Mathias, Shemtov, David Pirani, Simha, Solomon the Gibeonite, and Joshua and his two brothers, Moses and Shabbetai, who were from the Maghreb. Like Joseph Tsarfati, all these people stayed in the house, day and night, taking care of me and sleeping with me. A terrible sickness then came upon my servant, the cantor. He returned to his home and was confined there for forty days, because they were afraid that he was sick with the plague. But the Holy One Blessed Be He saved him and came to his aid. After that, I called Dinah and her mother and told them that I disliked their house on account of my sickness there and that I wanted another house. "I do not want to stay here under any circumstances," I said to them.

They were greatly distressed and even cried, for they did not want me to go to another house. "I will stay elsewhere until I convalesce," I insisted. I summoned R. Joseph Tsarfati. "Find me a warm bathhouse," I said. So he arranged a bath for me in the Sephardic synagogue, which had a beautiful bath. After I had bathed, Judah Gattegno prepared a great feast which lasted about an hour.[12]

A Guest of the Abudarham Family

After that, I returned to R. Joseph Tsarfati's house. I called the doctor, R. Moses Abudarham,[13] who came to me. "Find me a house," I urged him. He told me that he had a beautiful house with "a good room prepared to meet all your needs." So I went there with him and he showed me into a beautiful room with a good bed. "I have three sons, Joseph, Samuel, and Isaac," he said. "They and I will take care of you and so will my two nephews."

39   I stayed with him from Wednesday until the end of the Sabbath. He had a young daughter who had read all twenty-four books of the Bible and used to pray every day, morning and evening.[14] On the Sabbath she had greatly rejoiced and danced but, on Sunday, she was struck by the plague. I had just completed the morning prayer when a wise woman named Ravit visited me. Although she was wealthy, she used to teach children, including this young girl.

"Pray for R. Moses Abudarham's daughter," she urged me, "for tonight she has been struck with fever."

The moment I heard this woman's words, I summoned R. Moses. "I need to leave for an orchard, could you find me one?" I asked him. Once he had, I sent for the servants who had attended me at R. Joseph Tsarfati's house. Together we went to the orchard, where we were joined by R. Moses's three sons. At nightfall, after spending the entire day there, I sent Joseph [R. Moses's son] to tell his father that I would not return to their house until eight days had passed and we knew the outcome of his daughter's illness. When Joseph returned, he told me that he had arranged a room that would have all I needed in the house of Isaac Abudarham, who was his uncle. I walked there with him and discovered that it was a bad house with a bad smell. But Isaac had a wise and worthy wife, named Perna, who spoke Arabic, and they arranged a room for me with a good bed and I stayed with them. The three sons of his brother, R. Moses, also stayed in this house until their sister's illness had passed. Isaac, his wife, their son Moses, and Abraham Abudarham, all took care of me with their persons and with their money. I stayed there for three months. All my expenses were paid by R. Moses Abudarham and his brother Abraham sent me gifts each week, but it was Isaac and his wife, *most blessed of women* (Judges 5:24),[15] who served me with all their strength. R. Moses Abudarham's daughter died within a week and her brothers, R. Moses's sons, stayed with me until forty days had passed. I stayed in that house only on account of my love for them because the house was a very, very bad one.

A New Residence Is Provided by the Jewish Aldermen of Rome

Since Christian noblemen were now visiting me at a house that was not respectable, I sent a letter to the cardinal. I explained that I had left Joseph Tsarfati's house because I had been struck ill there and that I was now staying in a house that was neither fitting nor respectable. The moment the cardinal saw my letter, he sent for the Jewish aldermen: "Find him a nice house that is fitting and respectable. Honor him and provide everything that he and his four servants need," he urged them. The Jewish aldermen then came to the house and said to me: "We searched for a house and found two. Send your servants to see which is better and we will get it for you."

"I will come on foot," I replied and went with them, even though Isaac and his wife were saddened.

We visited a large house in which they showed me a beautiful room, but it was a house filled with residents. "This house is not good for me," I said to the Jewish aldermen. I went with them to another large and nice house. When I entered, I found that there were four rooms, all already prepared for me. The house had no residents other than those on the floor below—an old woman, and her sons and daughters who looked after her. "I wish to stay in this house and will not leave it," I told the Jewish aldermen. So they rented the house for six months from the old woman and paid all the rent. David ibn Forno,[16] Moses and Judah Gattegno, of blessed memory, together with my servants, organized the house for me. They set up the rooms nicely, preparing a good bed for me and turning the large room into a synagogue, that had a Torah scroll and thirty lighted lamps.

The servants who attended me did so on account of their love of God and did not ask for any payment. They had sworn to go with me wherever I went, but I did not want them to on account of the children they would leave behind. I had a secretary, R. Elijah the teacher, the son of Joab. His two brothers, the cantor and Benjamin, also used to attend me throughout

my stay in Rome. My own servants also attended me the entire time I was
41 there. I sent Joseph the scoundrel (the servant who had accompanied me
from Alexandria)[17] back to his father in Naples, because he would create
strife and discord among my other servants every day and wanted to rule
over them. He also slandered me to the King of Portugal's ambassador,
Dom Miguel, saying that I had come here for the sole purpose of returning
the conversos to Judaism. When the conversos of Rome heard this slander,
they came to me, saying: "We want to kill your servant."[18] I begged them
to do him no evil and then summoned Joseph. I gave him clothes and
money and sent him away to his father in Naples.

I stayed in that house until Rosh Hashanah [September 8, 1524]. My
servants, Hayyim, Mathias, and the cantor, then informed me that the cardinal had decided to go to Viterbo and would not return for two months.

"Everything is from God," I reassured them. "If He has closed one
door, He will open another better one."

Once the cardinal sent word to me about this matter, I dispatched
all the aforementioned servants to him. In front of them, the cardinal instructed the pope's secretary: "If the Jewish ambassador needs anything
from the pope, be there to help him." The cardinal then introduced him to
my servant Hayyim [who would serve as a go-between]. When the notary
heard this conversation, he said to Hayyim, "If the ambassador needs anything from the pope, I will take care of everything." Hayyim returned to
me and told me all these things.

Enlisting the Aid of Daniel da Pisa

When Cardinal Egidio left for Viterbo, I wondered to myself: "Who will
now help me and serve as an interpreter during my meetings with the
pope?" I met a man named R. Daniel da Pisa,[19] who had met with the pope
and was staying in a house close to his. He was rich and well-respected, a
sage and a kabbalist, and I decided that I should appeal to him. So I sent
42 for him and he came to my house.

"I see that you are respected by the pope and by all the cardinals and
that you are a great and important man," I began. "I want you to be my
interpreter and advisor in my dealings with the pope. Show me the right
way for the love of God, King Joseph my brother, the elders in the desert

of Habor, and God's people, Israel. May God bestow on you great glory, more than you already have, on account of this service to Him. I have come from the East to the West for the sake of His service and for the love of Israel, who are under the rule of Edom and Ishmael."

I told him all the secrets of my heart as well as the secrets that King Joseph my brother, may God protect and preserve him, had confided to me. I revealed everything to him, nothing remained which I had not told him—all the hints and secrets—and this I did because I saw that he was good and righteous in the eyes of God and humankind. Having done this, I said to him: *God's secret is with those who fear him* (Psalms 25:14).

A Second Meeting with the Pope

R. Daniel swore to me that he would not leave Rome until I had received all the letters I needed from the pope and that he would be my interpreter. He also swore to provide forthright guidance and to accompany me to the ship I was to board.

"Be glad hearted," he said, "because I will take care of everything. I will lead you on a good and straight path because of my love for God and for King Joseph your brother."

That day he wrote a letter on my behalf to the pope, which I sent with my servant Hayyim to the notary.[20] The notary was with many officials and other people when Hayyim arrived, but he immediately addressed Hayyim: "Has the ambassador sent you with something?"

"The ambassador sends you a thousand greetings and this letter," my servant responded. "Would you convey it to the pope and give me his answer? And please let me know at what hour I should return for his response."

He took the letter and said to Hayyim, "Go in peace. You may return for a response at the eighteenth hour." When Hayyim came back to me, I summoned R. Daniel and told him everything.

On Monday, I sent Hayyim again to the notary. The moment he was admitted, the notary said, "Go quickly and call your master, the ambassador, to come before the pope, because he has been summoned."

On that very day, R. Daniel da Pisa, of blessed memory, had a horse delivered to me. Accompanied by all my servants, I rode to the pope's 43 palace. They ushered me through many rooms until I entered the one adjoining that of the pope.

"I do not want to appear before the pope until R. Daniel da Pisa arrives, because he is my interpreter," I told the officials, who were guarding the pope's room. I sent for him and, while I was still speaking with them, R. Daniel arrived.

"Go in first to meet the pope," I instructed him. He entered, returned, and then together we came before the pope and I addressed him: "I have stayed here for almost a year and have desired, for the sake of the Holy One Blessed Be He and for the sake of Your Eminence, that you write for me the letters that I had requested from your Eminence—the letters to Prester John and to the Christians, great and small, through whose lands I will pass."

And His Excellency, R. Daniel, spoke to the pope and the pope responded in the affirmative: "I will do everything that the ambassador wishes." R. Daniel da Pisa and I then took our leave, happy and in good spirits, and returned to my house in peace.

Reubeni's Jewish Adversaries

There were at that time forty-five informers in Rome—may God inspire repentance in their hearts so that they desist from their evil machinations. There were also courageous Jews in Rome and in the Kingdom of Italy, fit for war, valiant, and lionhearted. By contrast, the Jews in Jerusalem, Egypt, and throughout the Kingdom of Ishmael are timid, cowardly, and fearful, and are not fit for war like those in Italy. May the Holy One Blessed Be He strengthen them, multiply them one thousandfold, and bless them.

There was then in Rome a true bastard[21] named Reuben, who was regarded as a rabbinic sage. He was a great and mighty informer, who felt no mercy whatsoever for any Jew. He was a doctor and, on account of his abundant wickedness, he would go about the market with his hat in his hand bowing to all the Christians. Never in all my days, from the time I was in my own land until I reached Rome, had I seen someone as wicked as he. He said some villainous things about me in front of the cardinals and the pope's secretaries, but they did not heed him, for all the Christians knew him to be a bastard and frequent informer on all the Jews. When this informer came to my house, people advised me, "For God's sake, do not get angry with him." Despite this advice, I wanted to seize him and give him such a lashing that it would reach the ears of the pope. But when he came before me, he kissed my hand. I forgave him for his past slanders and he promised that he would not repeat them. He left me in peace, swearing to do no further evil, but afterwards he did the opposite. Every day he slandered me and all of Israel.

Two other informers from among the wicked of Israel in Rome went to the pope and said, "Since this Jewish ambassador claims to be a divinely-charged messenger, light a fire and burn him, and see if God will save him from the fire." The pope was furious with the first informer. He had him arrested and sent to a galley on which he was sentenced to serve for the rest of his life. I had no knowledge of these events until the informer's wife came and accused me of having told the pope to send him to the galley. I told her that I knew nothing about this matter and she left.

There was a man named Moses Alatino[22] who always opposed me. He used to speak every day to Dom Miguel, the King of Portugal's ambassador, about things that are not decent—he spoke against God and against all Israel. One day this Moses Alatino was sent by the Cardinal of Venice to summon me to him. While at my house, he saw Dinah, R. Joseph Tsarfati's sister, who was visiting me. He wanted to marry her, but she refused and so he appealed to all the cardinals to help him to take her as his wife. But R. Joseph and Dinah greatly hated him. Each week he would call upon R. Joseph to negotiate the matter and he squandered a lot of money doing so. Moses Alatino was convinced that I wanted to take Dinah for a wife and was envious. All the Jews used to laugh at him and so too did the Christians.

Riding on a horse, I went with him to meet the Cardinal of Venice, and many Jews accompanied me. On the way, I saw Reuben the bastard riding by on a mule and bowing to all the Jews and Christians as he passed. When he saw me, however, he put his hat on his head and insolently cut ahead of me. I entered the Cardinal of Venice's residence and the latter asked me some questions.

"When but three people are left to attend you," I said to him, "I will tell Your Excellency everything and one of my servants will be the interpreter." So the cardinal dismissed all the Jews and Christians. Remaining before him were two Christians, Moses Alatino, and me and my two servants. "Send Moses Alatino out!" I demanded, and the cardinal dismissed him. Moses Alatino was greatly offended at being sent away but I did so because, while I was on my way there, Dinah had warned me: "Be sure that, no matter what, Moses Alatino is not present when you speak to the Cardinal." It was for that reason that I did all of this.

After Moses left, he went to Dom Miguel's house and accused me of things too indecent to repeat. I did not resent this because he did have a certain right to do so, given that he was a man of respected lineage and I had expelled him from the Cardinal's house. May God inspire him and all the informers of Israel to repent—except for Reuben the bastard, may the Holy One Blessed Be He never forgive him.

That day I spoke with the cardinal concerning a variety of things for about an hour and then returned home. R. Mordecai Bonfils, a student of R. Joseph Ashkenazi, came to visit me. He told me that, because of the plague, his half-brother had been detained in a certain city and that the authorities were demanding a fee of two hundred ducats because they had lodged him in a prison.[23] I wrote a letter to the pope saying that the detained man was my servant. "Hand this letter to the notary who will give it to the pope," I instructed Mordecai. "Send him my regards and tell him when you will return for a reply." Mordecai left with the letter and delivered it to the notary. "Come back tomorrow for the reply," the latter advised him. Mordecai returned and told me what had happened. The next day he went to the notary, who gave him a letter with the pope's seal, ordering the city leadership to release the detainee without any payment. And so he went to that city and, without making any payment, procured his release.

A Dispute with Daniel da Pisa

I stayed in the house that the Jewish aldermen had arranged for me. Each month they would give me five ducats and R. Daniel da Pisa would see to all my needs. But I had no need of what the Jewish aldermen were giving me, since R. Daniel would fulfil my every needs each day. Indeed, he would come once or twice a day to inquire as to what I needed and would see to everything. He himself would even provide the candles for the synagogue that was in my house. When he was honored as the *hatan Torah*, he arranged a sumptuous meal at my house.[24] When all the Jews came to rejoice and feast, they saw that R. Daniel da Pisa, driven by his love of God, was serving me with his person and with his wealth.

A well-respected Roman Jew from a good family contacted me and slandered R. Daniel. As a result, I became very angry with R. Daniel and he too became very angry. He left and avoided me for two days. He was greatly upset because I had commanded all my servants to neither visit his house nor speak with him. But then my servant Hayyim asked for my permission to contact him. "Don't be angry with me," he said, "but I want to go to R. Daniel's house. I assure you I won't have a prolonged discussion with him." And off he went.

The moment R. Daniel saw his former servant Hayyim, he dismissed everyone who was with him, because the slanderers had been in his house. He then spoke to Hayyim and inquired after my welfare. "Go speak to your master," he told him. "I know that his anger against me is on account of what that slanderer said—it does not come from his heart. I want to meet with him."

Hayyim returned and recounted what R. Daniel had said. Then R. Daniel came and spoke with me:

"The slanderers now believe that I will abandon you and join them against you, perish the thought that I should do such a thing against God. I know that your anger does not emanate from your heart. You are angry only because you believe what the slanderers say about me. God forbid that I did what they said. They say this only because, driven by my love of God, I have served you with all my strength and because I speak against them to the pope, the cardinals, the ambassador, and all the officials. When they questioned me about your reputation, I responded by honoring you and scolding the slanderers in front of all the people of influence."

This made me feel regretful. "I came here driven by my love of God and my love of serving Him," I said to R. Daniel. "I came on account of my love of Israel and for the sake of Jerusalem, the holy city. I traveled from the East to the West only for this. I came to Rome and found none of its Jews to be as good, righteous, and God-fearing as you are. You well

deserve to be a part of this worthy undertaking. May you gain a good
name for yourself and for your children before all Israel."

47   "Never listen to a word that the slanderers say because they come only
for the purpose of testing you by denying your words." R. Daniel replied. "I
will do my utmost and will not return to my town until I have received all
the letters that you seek from the pope. I will guide you on the right path."

Reubeni Receives His Letters from the Pope

R. Daniel then went home and, within a few days, had obtained letters
from the pope. I sent my servants Hayyim and Mathias with him to the
pope, and the secretaries collected the letters and gave them to them.
That night, many Jews came to my house to celebrate my receiving the
letters. Among them, however, there were slanderers and spies, although
I did not then know it. Four respected leaders of the Jewish community
of Rome were also in attendance: R. Obadiah Sforno,[25] R. Judah Ascoli
the physician,[26] and two others. They wanted to copy the pope's letters
in order to memorialize them for further rejoicing, but I became very
angry with them. I was angry because the slanderers had told me that
these leaders were informers, who would give reports to the secretaries
and corrupt my words. This made my mind race with distressing thoughts.
The four leaders left me, deeply saddened, and I too was saddened that
I had let them leave empty-handed. I then became very angry with the
slanderer who had libeled them. "It was you who caused all of this," I
reproached him.

The next day, the pope's secretaries arrested the four men who had
visited me. The moment I heard that they had been arrested, I sent for the
secretary who had ordered the arrest. "If you do not release them this very
night," I warned him, "I will appeal to the pope and will procure their
release against your will. If you wish to be in my good favor, go now and
release them." And so this secretary released them from prison and these
former prisoners became more devoted to me than all the holy congrega-
tion of Rome.

48   After that, the pope summoned R. Daniel da Pisa and spoke to him
about me. He told him that if I wanted to travel, he would grant me leave,
and ordered me to appear before him at the eighteenth hour on the 24th

of Adar I [February 27, 1525]. R. Daniel and I then met with him together and stayed for about two hours.

"I have already written a letter to Prester John for you," he said, "and I also wrote to the King of Portugal and to all the Christians whom you will encounter, telling them to honor and assist you for the sake of their love for God and their love for me."

"Be strong and resolute and do not fear because God is with you," the pope said to me.[27]

"I yield to no one but to God and to you," I answered. "I will be at your command all the days of my life, as will King Joseph my brother, and all the people of our nation."

The pope ordered that I be given a sign and shield to show to King Joseph and, while I was still standing before him, he handed it to R. Daniel, who passed it to me.

"Show this shield of mine to King Joseph your brother," the pope instructed me.

He also gave me one hundred gold ducats. I did not want to accept the money, but he forced it on me, saying, "Take it for your servants." I left him and went home in peace, joyful and in good spirits.

Dom Miguel, The King of Portugal's Ambassador

I then went with R. Daniel to obtain a letter of safe passage at the house of Dom Miguel, the King of Portugal's ambassador. "Would you write me a letter of safe passage?" I asked him. "If you go to Pisa," he replied, "I will write it for you and entrust it with two servants, who will accompany you to the King of Portugal." But this was just an evasion, because he did not want to write the letter at all. I told R. Daniel that Dom Miguel was a villain, who wished to do me great harm. Indeed I had already requested this letter from him during my very first week in Rome and he had evaded me by summoning me to meet him at his house. I went there, only to have his servants tell me that he was at the pope's palace. Since R. Daniel and my servants were with me, I sent them to the pope's palace, but they returned saying that he was not there. Dom Miguel's servants then told me that he was at the notary. Again, I sent servants to check if he was there, but they did not see him.

Because of the delay, R. Daniel had to return home to attend to his business affairs. "Stay here and wait for him until he comes and then send for me and I will come immediately," he said. So I waited at Dom Miguel's house from midday until nightfall. When he finally returned, I sent for R. Daniel. I was so angry with Dom Miguel that I wanted to strike him with his own sword, but R. Daniel grabbed my arms, preventing me from doing so. After that, I left him in a fury and returned to my house for the night.

When the pope heard about all of this, he spoke to Dom Miguel: "I know that the Jewish ambassador is angry with you on account of the letter of safe passage that you have not written for him. Come what may, write the letter for him because I have already written about this to the King of Portugal."

But Dom Miguel did not listen to the pope. He left Rome to go hunting and a week passed before he returned. On the night of the 15th of Adar II [March 20, 1525], I went with R. Daniel da Pisa and all my servants to again ask him for the letter of safe passage. He told me that he would certainly send it after I left for Pisa. I believed him and returned with R. Daniel to my house. I told R. Daniel that no matter what happened I wanted to leave Rome the next day, in the middle of the month, just as our forefathers had left Egypt. Under no circumstances would I stay in Rome any longer. I had made up my mind to go on the morrow, come what may.

Servants for the Journey

I summoned the servants who had sworn to come with me: Hayyim, Mathias, Simha, and the cantor. The cantor had requested leave and pardon from me a week earlier and I gave him leave and pardon. There was no love between Hayyim, Mathias, and Simha, who would secretly inform on each other to me, but they asked for neither leave nor pardon, daily declaring that, come what may, they would accompany me. Then the time for departure arrived and each said to me: "I am unable to come."

I stayed in Rome until noon of the 15th of Adar to arrange my affairs and, together with R. Daniel, to find a companion for the journey. I found two servants. The first, R. Raphael Cohen, had been a prayer leader and musician[28] in my house from the day I had arrived in Rome. He was a

strong and belligerent man whom my servants had hated and denounced 50
as a scoundrel. Because of these slanderers, I had not wanted him to stay in
my house but then, just when I was about to leave, he said: "Did I not tell
you that I alone would accompany you on your entire journey?" And with
that he swore to accompany me. The second servant was Joseph Halevi,
who was as strong or even stronger than Raphael Cohen. He had served
me since I had arrived in Rome but, because the slanderers had described
him as a scoundrel, I had also not wanted him to stay in my house until
the very day I was to leave when he too swore to accompany me. I gave
them each five ducats so that they could clear their debts. A third servant,
Nissim, came to me. He spoke Arabic and had served me since I had left
R. Joseph Tsarfati's house. He was a respectable man and had a wife and
small children.

"It is not appropriate for you to accompany me. You have small children and your first duty is to serve and provide for them," I told him. R.
Daniel then promised to procure further servants for me. In Rome, he
gave me a third servant—Tobias the evildoer.

I left Rome at midday on the fifteenth of Adar just as I had entered
Rome at midday on the fifteenth of Adar. I had thus stayed a full year in
Rome, from midday to midday of the fifteenth of Adar. Some Roman Jews
came to accompany me for a distance of five miles and with them was an
escort of thirty men on horseback.

The Journey from Rome

At Ronciglione, I met a brigade of the King of France's army, which had
about five hundred horses. They accorded us great honor, thank God! I arrived at R. Joseph Cohen's house in Viterbo. My servants Raphael Cohen,
Joseph Halevi, and Tobias were with me. Because he had been delayed
in Rome, R. Daniel had also sent Joab to accompany me, telling him to
take me to R. Yehiel da Pisa and promising that he would follow later. In
Viterbo, we stayed at the house of R. Joseph Cohen, a well-respected Jew.
His young sons and his mother, of blessed memory, got me everything I
needed. The Jews of Viterbo came to see me. They were riven by quarrels,
disputes, and senseless hatred until, through my effective persuasion, I succeeded in uniting them in peace. 51

The Grand Master of Rhodes summoned me.[29] I visited him with R. Yehiel and R. Moses and spoke with him for a very long time.[30] He was an old and distinguished gentleman. I then left Viterbo with an escort of some ten horses. We stopped in Bolsena, where we spent the Sabbath in the house of the aforementioned R. Joseph, of blessed memory, who was a rich man.[31] His first wife had died and left him a son, who was now an important and respected man. R. Joseph had then married a widow, who had borne him another son. We stayed with him until Sunday and he treated us with great honor, more than was customary.

On Sunday we set off for Siena. We arrived at the house of a distinguished man named Ismael da Rieti, may God protect and preserve him, but he had not yet returned from town.[32] When he arrived, he showed us into a large room while he arranged a room and bed for me. His house was large and he was very rich.

"Which do you prefer?" I asked him. "To go to Jerusalem or to stay here forever?"

"I have no desire for Jerusalem," he replied, "I desire nothing but to stay here in Siena."

I was greatly astounded by this. Although God had bestowed great wealth on him, he was unwilling to use it to serve God by performing meritorious deeds. He was a man who would never be satisfied with his own riches. To quote Ecclesiastes, *He that loveth silver shall not be satisfied with silver* (Ecclesiastes 5:9). He swore to generously provide for my servants, but then changed his mind and, choosing not to earn a good name for himself in Israel, did not do anything that he had vowed.

Delayed in Pisa by Dom Miguel

52 On Monday I left Siena and arrived at R. Yehiel's house in Pisa.[33] May the memory of R. Yehiel, his mother, and his grandmother be blessed a thousandfold. R. Yehiel was like an angel of God. He was well-versed in the Bible and Talmud, humble, pious, and generous. His soul clung to Jerusalem, the holy city. His house was open to the poor of Israel and all who came there dined at his table. He distributed charity to the poor every day. He gave with his own hand and his mother and grandmother gave with theirs. I witnessed all their good deeds with my own eyes. I saw that

they were pious and loyal and that their good deeds exceeded anything I had witnessed in Italy. I stayed at their house for seven months.

My servants, Raphael Cohen and Joseph Halevi, stayed only for the first month and a half. I then had to send them back to Rome because of the gossip caused by Tobias's quarrels with them. They had wanted to kill him in R. Yehiel's house but I became angry with them and, since they were loyal to me, they accepted my rebuke. In the end, however, although they wanted to accompany me on my journey, I had to give in to the wishes of others and send them back to Rome. I kept on Tobias out of respect for R. Daniel da Pisa, who had given him to me as a housekeeper, saying, "Tobias will serve you until you reach Portugal."

Meanwhile, the evildoer, Dom Miguel, had not sent me the letter of safe passage that he had promised. When R. Daniel arrived in Pisa, he advised me to send Aaron, an old man, back to Rome to ask Dom Miguel for it. So I sent Aaron, who had been traveling with me to Portugal in order to visit his brothers and relatives in Tavira, back to Rome. He returned within a month but without the letter of safe passage. Instead, he brought letters from Dom Miguel which said: "The king does not wish you to go to Portugal this year." This was all lies and deception because the king had not written a word about this to him.

I was in great anguish and stayed, grief-stricken, at R. Yehiel's house. They arranged a room for me with a nice bed on the top floor. There were many rooms on the top floor and, by God, it was a large house. Many officials came to visit me there. I fasted six times for six days and 53 six nights, neither eating bread nor drinking water and, every forty days I fasted for three days and three nights. My hosts brought me all sorts of dishes, spices, and rose and violet water.[34] They served me all kinds of delicacies, so numerous they cannot be described. In addition, R. Yehiel's mother, Signora Leora, *most blessed of women*, served me in all things, as did her mother, the magnificent Signora Sarah, who treated me with kindness and loyalty and, like her daughter, gave me very generous gifts. R. Yehiel also gave me gifts, including silk clothes and money for my servants.

During my great fasts, people came to visit me at the house of R. Yehiel and his wife, Diamante, who was the daughter of R. Asher Meshullam of Venice. Signora Sarah, her daughter, Signora Leora, and other young women would come and dance in my room.

"We come to honor you during your fasts, to dispel your grief and give you cheer," they declared, and then asked: "Do you enjoy our dancing and cittern music?"

"You mean to do me well," I told them, "but only the Holy One Blessed Be He knows the emotions of my heart, for my heart clings to Him day and night. I have no desire to hear the music of the cittern and flute, nor the sounds of rejoicing."

Many gentiles came to see me. They gathered in R. Yehiel da Pisa's house and played trumpets and sang to busk for money. When I stayed in Rome, the papal trumpeters also used to visit to busk for money. The same was true in Viterbo and Bolsena. Trumpeters trailed me all the way from Rome to Pisa—and even Tobias played the trumpet.

I stayed on the beautiful upper floor room of R. Yehiel da Pisa's house. David Romano was one of the four servants who had traveled with me from Rome. Unlike Raphael, Joseph Halevi, and Tobias, who rode on horses, he went on foot and asked me for neither money nor clothes. I entrusted him with the supervision of my clothes and money and he proved to be faithful and God-fearing. I greatly loved him, much more than my other servants, and he stayed with me in Pisa until my ship sailed to Portugal.

54

I composed a letter to the King of Portugal and R. Yehiel wrote it down. I gave it to a converso priest, who was a friend of mine, with instructions to deliver it to the king. He promised to do his best and sailed away while I remained in Pisa, delayed by Dom Miguel the ambassador. When David Romano saw that because of this delay I would not be able to travel that year, he said to me: "Give me leave to visit my mother in Rome, then I will return." He swore to return immediately if he heard news of a ship on which I could travel and so I granted him leave. He then went to R. Daniel da Pisa, who was then in Florence, and he provided him with four ducats for his travel expenses. R. Daniel also gave twelve gold ducats to Joseph and Raphael, who had accompanied me from Rome.

After David Romano departed, I was left in R. Yehiel's house with no servants except Tobias. But R. Yehiel, who had many servants, said to me:

"Fear not, all my servants as well as I and my family are at your service."
Every day he came up to my room to see me, three to four times per day,
and I went with them for morning, afternoon, and evening prayers at the
synagogue. The rest of the Jews of Pisa were poor people, may God be
gracious to them and have mercy on them!

Troubles with Servants

A short time later, Signora Sarah's brother, R. Shabbetai, may God protect and preserve him, arrived from Turkey to visit his sister and obtain
money from her. He was a wise and respected doctor and stayed with us
in R. Yehiel's house. He had a servant, named Jacob, who had traveled
with him from Turkey and who could speak Arabic as well as the local
language.

"If you want," Signora Sarah offered, "my brother's servant can enter
your service. I am sure that he will serve you better than your servants do."
Although R. Yehiel said the same to me, I told them: "I know their nature
and they all deceive me. They get clothes and money from me and then off
they go on their way."

But then R. Shabbetai himself came to me. "He is a good and honorable servant," he assured me. "If you want him, I will let him serve you;
if not, I want him to travel with me on my journey for I am without ser- 55
vants." So I summoned the servant and asked him: "Do you want to serve
me and accompany me on my way?"

"Yes," he replied. So I bought him new clothes and he entered my
service. Despite knowing both Arabic and the Holy Tongue, he was both
a good-for-nothing and stubborn and rebellious. Everyone hated him on
account of the true accusations that Tobias had made against him. As for
Tobias himself, he started a serious argument with me in Pisa because he
did not want anyone else to accompany me.

R. Yehiel, his wife, his mother, and I went for a walk in his orchard.
The orchard, which was filled with olive trees, contained a large pavilion
with many rooms, each of which had tables and upholstered furniture.
It was bordered by a great mountain that rose above it. From its peak, a
large river cascaded that flowed from Pisa to the Mediterranean Sea. A
boat could thus sail close to R. Yehiel's pavilion and collect wood from the

orchard to deliver to his house. We would usually come by boat from Pisa to the orchard. (Once we rode there on horses and, by the time we reached the orchard, Tobias was on the verge of killing my servant Jacob then and there.[35]) [A passage is likely missing from the manuscript.] R. Yehiel's wife would play the cittern and many officials would come to visit. We spent two days in the pavilion before returning to Pisa.

R. Shabbetai returned to Turkey, but his companion Jacob stayed with me and had daily arguments and quarrels with Tobias. I had not heard a bad word about him from Tobias until he and R. Yehiel's mother showed me the Passover matzah they had found in Jacob's bed.

"Isn't there enough matzah at the table for him to eat?" they asked me. "Why does he need to stash it away?"

Everyone in the house resented Jacob because of this. "Send this servant away because he is not fit to serve you," R. Yehiel and his grandmother Sarah advised me. "It is shameful to have him stay in your home." So I listened to them and sent him away. I gave him clothes worth eight ducats and a prayer book. I also bought him a sword. I then sent him to R. Daniel in Florence and he stayed at his home. Later, the servants who laid the table there informed me that Jacob was still staying with R. Daniel and eating at his table. R. Daniel, who had good and well-mannered ser-

56 vants, had noticed that Jacob was both discourteous and villainous. He had let Jacob stay for eight days, however, because of my request that he be permitted to stay there on account of his quarrel with Tobias. I therefore wrote to R. Daniel saying that, if he provided me with another of his servants, I would send Jacob away.

Jacob had asked R. Daniel for money to go to the tavern. Each day he ate at R. Daniel's table and then went to eat at the tavern. In the end, R. Daniel gave him two ducats and said: "Go on your way because I do not want you to serve R. David." So Jacob stole a garment worth eight ducats from R. Daniel and left.

I was distressed because I had no one to serve me other than Tobias. R. Yehiel da Pisa, however, had a young man named Emmanuel who worked with him in his store. He was respectable, loyal, and God-fearing. He came to serve me and proved to be *pure-hearted and upright* (Job 1:8).

I went with R. Yehiel to visit a church, which had a great tower.[36] We climbed to the top and saw three abominations with appearances too beautiful to be described. We returned to the house and stayed there for a few days before riding to the orchard. R. Daniel then arrived from Florence and met us at the orchard pavilion. R. Daniel and R. Yehiel soon returned to Pisa to attend to their business affairs, but we stayed at the orchard until the following day before returning. R. Daniel then left for Florence, but R. Yehiel stayed a few more days before announcing that he would follow R. Daniel to obtain the four thousand ducats that he owed him. He went in peace and stayed there two months before returning to Pisa. R. Yehiel had written a Torah scroll. When I was in Pisa, I made the blessing on this Torah scroll on many Sabbaths and it was very beautifully written.

Female Patrons

The Signora of Naples,[37] *most blessed of women*, sent a beautiful, antique silk flag to me in Pisa, inscribed with the Decalogue in two columns and decorated with gold. She also sent a golden shawl for me to wear in her honor. Prior to this, she had sent me money three times while I had been in Rome. I heard that she fasted every day. Stories of her renown had reached me when I was in Alexandria and Jerusalem. It was there that I heard how she had redeemed more than one thousand captives and gave charity to everyone who asked her. May she be blessed before God.

As for the esteemed Signora Sarah da Pisa, of blessed memory, I saw with my own eyes that she had accomplished more good deeds than can be counted. She gave me a gold signet ring, saying, "Let it be a witness to the friendship between us." She also gave me a large book, written on parchment, containing the books of Psalms, Job, Proverbs, and the Five Scrolls. On the first page, she inscribed some advice in her own hand so that I would act accordingly and memorialize her deeds. This is what she wrote: "Be neither angry nor rash."[38] She also gave me a prayer book, saying: "Pray from it out of affection for me."

Signora Sarah was responsible for her young niece, Deborah—the daughter of her brother, who lived in Jerusalem. The girl was intelligent,

virtuous, and well-versed in scripture and she prayed frequently. She had a
teacher named Solomon Cohen, who was a little deaf but was nevertheless
a very learned, young man. It was Signora Sarah herself, however, who
educated her in the art of refinement, wisdom, and culture.

While I was staying at R. Yehiel's house, R. Eliezer, the young teacher
of R. Daniel's nephew, declared his desire to marry Deborah, *most blessed of*
women, but Signora Sarah did not want to give her to him. "Why don't you
marry her off to this young man who is learned and honorable?" I asked
her. "She does not wish to be given to anyone in the world until she goes to
Jerusalem and there she will marry whom she pleases." May God provide
58 what her good soul yearns for and fulfill her heart's desires. Amen!

Permission to Travel to Portugal

A few days later, the King of Portugal recalled Dom Miguel and sent Dom
Martin as his new ambassador.[39] When Dom Martin arrived in Rome, he
immediately wrote to me in Pisa: "The King of Portugal has heard of your
desire to serve him and is very pleased, so get ready to sail!"

There was a large ship bound for Portugal that was docked in Livorno.
Its captain had been delayed in Rome on account of business with the
pope. While waiting for the captain's return, I sent for R. Daniel, who was
in Florence. When he returned to Pisa, I consulted him.

"I don't want you to travel with the letters Dom Martin sent," he advised me. "Let us instead send a messenger to Rome to obtain other letters
from Dom Martin as well as from the Pope."

R. Daniel then sent a delegation to Rome. All the expenses for the
horses and messengers came from his own pocket, and this was in addition
to what he already given to me and my servants. He then left for Florence.

R. Joseph Tsarfati of Rome came to Florence, but he did not want
to travel to visit me in Pisa. That greatly astounded me because he had
once been an interpreter between me and the Pope. In fact, however, he
had ignored what I had wanted him to convey to the pope and spoke instead about his own affairs. Even when we had visited the cardinal, he had
spoken about his own affairs and said little about mine. Nevertheless, he
used to assure me that he liked me and I, in my naiveté, liked him back.
So I had remained in his house, and all the while he talked and talked.

On the same day that Joseph Tsarfati arrived in Florence, a letter arrived from Rome informing me that my secretary, R. Elijah, may God protect and preserve him, was confined to his home because the plague had struck his family, and his wife and children had died. I felt great sorrow for him.

My servant David Romano returned from Rome, joined me at R. Yehiel's house, and briefed me on everything that had happened. I was overjoyed to see him and entrusted him with the keeping of my money and my clothes. Joseph Halevi of Rome, accompanied by his servant Francesco, also visited. They all stayed with me at R. Yehiel's house.   59

The ship's captain arrived and was in a hurry to set sail, so I sent Tobias racing to R. Daniel[40] in Florence, asking him to come quickly to me as soon as he received my letter. But three days passed and neither R. Daniel nor Tobias came.

I had stayed with my servants in R. Yehiel's house for almost seven months and, during that time, R. Yehiel had seen to all our needs and paid all our expenses. It is impossible to enumerate his many acts of kindness to us. On our last day, shortly before my departure, he gave me ten ducats. Then the ship's master arrived. "If you want to travel with me, make sure that, come what may, we depart tomorrow," he said. "We have arranged a nice room on the ship for you and will gladly provide you with everything you need until you reach the king in Portugal." He then went on his way.

The next day, I packed all my baggage, loaded it onto mules, and sent it to Livorno. Then, together with R. Yehiel and R. Reuben and his sons, I set out. R. Yehiel's mother, however, was sick in bed, may God heal her. Joseph Halevi and David Romano also accompanied me, but Francesco, the servant who had arrived with Joseph Halevi, had fallen ill. I did not know if it was with the plague or with some other illness.

Sailing from Livorno

We arrived in Livorno with all our belongings and went to an inn. I was fasting for the second night of what would be a three-day fast. By contrast, during the major fasts I had undertaken in Pisa, I had fasted six times for six days and six nights and every forty days for three days and three nights. At the inn in Livorno, I became very worried, my heart filled with great anguish, because neither R. Daniel nor my servant Tobias, whom I had sent to find him, had returned. That night, the ship's captain visited to tell me that they would depart early the next morning and then he left. They arranged a bed for me at the inn. I slept while R. Yehiel dined together with both his servants and mine. These included Benzion, a young man from Correggio whom R. Daniel had sent to me and who had accompanied me to Livorno. After eating, they all retired to their beds and slept until midnight when R. Daniel finally arrived. He had departed from

60　Florence that morning and had reached Pisa. When he had not found us there, he followed us to Livorno. I was still sleeping when he arrived. He spoke with me and I greatly rejoiced at seeing him. He then left in the middle of the night to contact the ship's captain before returning to the inn. I slept until morning.

In the morning, R. Daniel gave me some gifts from the pope: a new red Damascene brocade robe and a black velvet cap. R. Daniel himself, may his memory be a blessing, also gave me a black and green, double-length, robe. He then appointed Solomon Cohen of Prato to accompany me and paid him twelve ducats. He also paid six ducats to Benzion, ten ducats each to David Romano and Tobias, and two ducats to Joseph Halevi for a return trip to Rome. I gave a further two ducats to the latter because Tobias had declared: "If you want Joseph Halevi to come with you, I will stay behind." Since Tobias was indispensable as a cook, I had to send Joseph back to Rome.

The ship's captain then arrived. "If you need 300 or 500 ducats, I will give them to you and when you reach the king, you can reimburse me," he offered. "I also bought everything you need—bread, eggs, and poultry."

R. Daniel then gave me 120 ducats.[41] "Take them as a token of my friendship," he urged me.

So I took all my belongings and brought them to the big ship. Tobias played the trumpet as R. Daniel and R. Yehiel stood on the bank. We had a beautiful cabin. The captain who had made us all those promises was delayed in Livorno but said he would follow us by land. Then R. Daniel and R. Yehiel boarded the big ship, came to my cabin to see me, and stayed a while to chat. We exchanged goodbyes and they went on their way. Then R. Solomon Cohen, Tobias, David Romano, Benzion, and I sailed from Livorno with a good wind, thank God. May God keep us safe, Selah!

CHAPTER 4

PORTUGAL

We set sail with a good wind on the Mediterranean Sea heading west to the King of Portugal. We docked near Cádiz, a town in the territory of the [Holy Roman] Empire.[1] I sent Tobias ahead to the magistrate with the pope's letter. Tobias found him and asked whether we could disembark 61 to spend a day in town before returning, but the magistrate would not permit it. When Tobias returned, he informed me that the townspeople had spoken to him with malice in front of the magistrate. Their leader permitted our captain to visit the town. When he returned, he informed me that the magistrate had summoned him to appear before all the important town officials.

"Their opinion of you is unanimous," he said. "They say that the Jewish king is allying himself with the King of Portugal, who is weak, and they think that together we will fight against the emperor. They have ordered your arrest and are requisitioning horses with which to send you to the emperor."

I was happy with all that the Holy One Blessed Be He had done and thought to myself that if men did come to forcibly arrest me, God would compel them to act in my interests and in the interests of all Israel. I remained confident in my mission to serve God and observe His commandments. Though my servants were trembling with fear, I was joyful. "Be not alarmed and afraid," I reassured them.

The captain came a second time. "It is best that you leave this ship and board another that belongs to the King of Portugal," he said. We left the ship in the middle of night, leaving all our baggage in our cabin and locking the door. We took a small boat to the King of Portugal's ship, which we boarded. The captain of that ship was asleep in bed. When he was alerted to our arrival, he got up and we were ushered into his cabin, where we showed him the letter from the King of Portugal. Our captain spoke to the King of Portugal's captain at length about what the magistrates and officials of Cádiz had said. We stayed with them until dawn. Then, while we went to the town of Almería, I sent Tobias with the two captains, who presented themselves before the magistrates and officials.[2] When they returned, they reported that the magistrates and officials had argued with them over whether to arrest us.

Arriving at Tavira

The captain of our ship then advised us to go to Tavira, which was under the authority of the Kingdom of Portugal. They gave us our baggage and transferred us from the big ship to the King of Portugal's ship. I gave seventy-five ducats to the captain of our first ship as payment for his trouble and he went on his way. We stayed with our new captain until midnight and then found a place for ourselves on his ship, which was filled with wheat bound for Tavira.

62

When we arrived at the coast near Tavira, I sent Tobias with the pope's and the King of Portugal's letters to the magistrate of Tavira, who was an appointee of the king. He immediately returned with two of the magistrate's servants and a good mule. They boarded the ship and I disembarked. When the townspeople heard that I had arrived on the coast, Christian officials and conversos, women and children, immediately came to greet me. As I rode the mule along the coast towards town, the road filled with men and women too numerous to count. I reached Tavira and went to the house of a converso, where they had arranged beds and a table for us. This converso and his wife were very well-respected people. The town magistrate visited and greatly rejoiced at our arrival. "I am at your service, ready and willing for you to command," he declared. Indeed, he would call on me twice a day.

The magistrate wrote to the king saying that we had arrived and were with him in Tavira. I also wrote a letter to the king and sent David Romano to him. I stayed at the converso's house waiting for the king's reply. That converso and his wife were very kind to us. They did not want us to spend a single coin from our purses but wanted to bear each and every one of our expenses, whether for eating or for drinking. We stayed in their house for forty days until the King of Portugal's messenger arrived in Tavira.

At that time, it happened that a Spanish monk was speaking with R. Solomon and the latter became angry with him. "What is your problem with this monk?" I asked R. Solomon. But it was the wicked monk himself who responded, telling me that there was no King of Israel and that we had no claim to royal lineage. He was standing in front of a big window and I, filled with God's zeal, threw him out the window in front of all the gentiles, who laughed at him and were afraid to speak against me. When the chief magistrate heard about this, he greatly rejoiced.

The messenger I had sent to the king returned with two letters. The first said that I should appear before the king and that he would do my will. The second was written to the magistrates of his kingdom, ordering them to respect me, escort me from town to town, and arrange a house with a table, chair, and lamp wherever I stayed.[3] After giving me these letters, the messenger said: "Go tomorrow to the king for I have made all the arrangements that he has commanded. As the king has commanded, I am assigning four strong and intelligent captains to you and am providing you with five hundred ducats. One of the king's scribes will be responsible for your expenses and I will arrange for everything you need on the road including the horses. Just be ready to leave tomorrow. If you have business in town, do it today so that you will be ready to go tomorrow without delay." And with that, he left. The next morning, they gave me horses and I rode away with all my servants.

When I left Tavira, the magistrate, all the important town officials, and the king's secretaries, poured out of the town to bid me farewell. More people than can be enumerated, great and small, accompanied me for two parasangs before returning. I traveled with the four distinguished captains and the king's secretary, who was responsible for expenses. In total, thirty people from Tavira came with me on my way to the king. Throughout the journey, the king's secretary went ahead to contact the magistrates of each town and arrange a house with a table, chair, and lamp, as had been commanded by the king.

Greeted by Crowds at Beja and Évora

We were three parasangs from the town of Beja when people began to come out to greet me. The magistrates and important town officials, both Christians and conversos, arrived on horseback and, as we drew closer, more and more people appeared—men, women, and children, too many to count. When we reached Beja, we lodged at a pleasant house belonging to a converso. All the magistrates and people, both Christians and conversos, visited me there until midnight. We stayed for the night, then left the next day with magistrates, officials, and many people accompanying me on my way for two parasangs.

64   On Sabbath eve, we reached the large town of Évora. When I was two parasangs away, some magistrates came to meet me, accompanied by many people. Once in the town, which was a large one that had a residence for the king and many communities of respected conversos, we went to a converso's house. Wherever I went in town, conversos, great and small, men and women, came to kiss my hand in front of the Christians. The Christians became angry at the conversos for kissing my hand and reproached them: "Treat him with great honor but do not kiss his hand because that privilege is reserved for the King of Portugal alone." But among the conversos there were those who felt encouraged, believing in me with complete faith just as Israel had believed in Moses, our teacher, of blessed memory. Everywhere we went, I would tell them: "I am the son of King Solomon. I have not come to you with a sign or miracle or by way of the Kabbalah but as someone who has been a man of war from his youth until now. I have come to give aid to the king and to you. We will see by what way God will guide me to the Land of Israel."

I stayed at that converso's house on the Sabbath and on Sunday. On Monday I left Évora. The magistrates, many respected officials, and people too numerous to count accompanied me for two parasangs before returning to town.

Before I left Évora, my servant Tobias, who was my cook, got into a brawl in the market with some Christians. He had drawn his sword and they wanted to kill him. These Christians approached me but, out of respect for me, they pardoned him and made peace. In Tavira, Tobias had also picked many fights with the gentiles and I had been furious with him because it had caused me great expense. Each of my servants had received thirty ducats from Solomon Cohen, not counting what they had received from R. Daniel da Pisa and what the conversos had given to me for them. Tobias would pick fights with all my servants and would steal everything 65 that I had given them.

First Meeting with the King of Portugal

Throughout my journey, conversos would come from all corners to accompany me and give me gifts and some righteous Christians did the same. The King of Portugal had fled the plague in Lisbon and was staying in Almeirim.[4] When I was two parasangs away, I wrote to tell him where I had reached. I told him that I would stay there until he instructed me regarding how to present myself to him. I sent the letter with an old and respected Christian, who left with the king's secretary (the one in charge of my expenses who had accompanied me from Tavira). When they returned, they told me that the king had summoned his counselors, who had advised him on the matter. Some had advised him one way and others had advised him another. Some had said: "Accord him honor and send respected officials to accompany him because he has journeyed from a faraway land to seek your favor and serve you." Dom Miguel, my enemy from Rome whom I had wanted to kill with a sword, had become the king's deputy and confident. He spoke against me to the king and to the messengers I had sent him. This led some courtiers to question the secretary as to whether conversos accorded me greater honor than Christians did.

The secretary answered that they did indeed accord me great honor and that, wherever I went, they, their wives, their sons, and their daughters would come to kiss my hand. At this, Dom Miguel turned to the king and his advisors and exclaimed: "Did I not tell you that he came to destroy your kingdom and to make the conversos Jews again?! If you send your officials to accompany him, all the conversos will go out to accompany him—they, their wives, their sons, and their daughters—and they will plot against the Christians and will become Jews again."

The wicked Dom Miguel said all these things in front of the king, his advisors, the old man I had sent, and the secretary, who had accompanied me. And it was the old man who told me all of this.

João III, King of Portugal (r. 1521–1557). Portrait by Cristóvão Lopes.

66   The king sent for his advisors. "How should I respond to the Jewish king?" he asked them.

"Tell him that your grandmother died," they said. "Say that you are now in mourning for a year and our custom makes you unable to accord him the honor that you would otherwise accord him. Let him know that you remain at his command and will treat him with honor when he comes before you but that, at this time, you ask for his forgiveness and pardon. Let the ambassador come before you thus with his servants, your servants, and the men who came with him from Tavira."

When I heard what the king, his advisors, and officials had said, I mounted my horse and rode to him with all my servants and with all the people who had accompanied me. In total, there were about fifty people and fifteen horses with me, not to mention all the mules that were carrying my baggage. I reached the King's courtyard in Almeirim on Wednesday. I had been fasting since Sunday, neither eating bread nor drinking water. I stood before the king with my servants, each with *his sword upon his thigh* (Song of Songs 3:8). I spoke thus to the king and his wife, the queen, who was with him: "I am tired and weary from the journey. I have been fasting and am unable to speak to you today. Would you be so kind as to let us go to the house where I have arranged to spend the night and later you and I can speak together." But I did not want to kiss his hand, neither when I arrived nor when I left, because of the vexation that the wicked Dom Miguel had caused us both.

Santarém

Having received the king's permission, I went to the house that they had arranged for me in Santarém. The house belonged to a converso and was spacious. Its owner was an absolute villain, but his wife was very honorable. The house had a second door that opened from the room in which we were staying and from which everything could be seen, but the owner had locked it. My servants Tobias and Benzion told me that this wicked converso had boarded up the door so that we would not be able to throw water or anything else outside. Having examined the door and seen that it was well-blocked, I found an axe, smashed the obstruction, and opened it for them. The wicked converso then came to me, acknowledged he was 67 in the wrong, and begged for forgiveness, so I forgave him for the sake of his righteous wife.

An Arabic-speaking converso, who had arrived on one of the king's ships, visited me. The king sent him every two years to the land of the Blacks. This converso told me that he had often traveled to a certain Mediterranean island, a half-day's journey away—but by "day" they mean one hour in those places. On the island, there was a great mountain from which fire erupted day and night, such that the entire mountain was aflame with smoke billowing up to the sky. The previous King [João] of Portugal had sent the young sons of conversos there and had left them near that mountain, where they remain until this very day. They live near an island tribe who eat human flesh.[5] This converso was also knowledgeable in astrology, as are all the people of Portugal.

A captain of one of the king's ships visited me. He told me that he had once set out from Hormuz and journeyed to the capital of my kingdom.[6] He even told the king all about how, some twenty years earlier, hearing [in Hormuz] that there was a king of the Jews named King Solomon, peace be upon him, he had gone and spent a year there during the time of my father, of blessed memory. The captain was an honorable man. He reported these great things to the King of Portugal and the king was fond of him. He was also my friend in Portugal and I too was fond of him. He asked me for a sign—my autograph—that would serve us as a memento until the arrival of the Hour. So I signed and gave it to him and it became a secret between us. He was a sincere Christian and he loved all Jews.

I fasted for six days and six nights. All the Christians and conversos, great and small, came to see me at my house. Day and night, the king's servants visited me with trumpets, citterns, and all kinds of wind instruments.

My servant, the wicked Tobias, then picked a fight with a converso who had joined us in Tavira and whom I loved as much as my servants and perhaps more. They were standing at the table in front of me when Tobias drew his sword, intending to kill him. The converso fled to the room in which I was standing. He closed the door behind him and stood in front of me. Tobias then broke down the door and entered my room with his sword drawn, determined to kill the converso. The wicked Tobias ignored my shouts and protests until I stood up to him and seized the sword from his hand. I wanted to kill him, but instead sent the converso to summon the town magistrates. After that, Tobias left for the market with a big stick in his hand, searching for the converso in all the lanes and stalls, while all the people, young and old, ridiculed him. It was then that Tobias realized that the magistrates were heading to my house and so he contacted my servant David Romano, and the two of them fled Santarém and crossed the river. By the time the magistrates arrived, all the Christians and conversos were discussing the evil deeds of Tobias, David Romano, and the converso, and were saying that they had broken the law. I told the chief magistrate to send his servants to apprehend Tobias and David and return them to me, and they did so. I instructed the magistrates to put them in irons and imprison them, and this too was done. Before that fight, Tobias had stabbed one of the king's Christian servants and the king knew all about it.

A Meeting with the King and Dom Miguel in Almeirim

It was Wednesday and now, eight days after my arrival, the king sent for me. I appeared before him with my servants, the old man Solomon Cohen, and Benzion. The king had summoned an old converso physician to serve us as an interpreter of the Holy Tongue. The old man was a little deaf and when he spoke to the king and me, he was terrified. It was the same with the elderly Solomon Cohen of Prato, who was also deaf and whose words the king could not hear because his speech was slurred. Benzion, who was a young man, spoke to the king well, but he was less distinguished. It was for this reason that the king said to me:

"I have heard that you speak Arabic well. I have an official who also speaks Arabic well. He will be able to listen to your words from beginning to end and relay them to me. As it is, I can understand neither the translations of your servants nor those of the converso, who convey only a tenth of what you say. My only option is to use this official who knows Arabic."

Dom Miguel, who was with the king, spoke against me. Although I saw him doing so, I did not then recognize this man as Dom Miguel and my servants did not tell me that it was him. Each time I said something 69 to the king in the Holy Tongue, he would turn to consult Dom Miguel and the latter would respond: "Pay no attention to what he says in the Holy Tongue, pay attention only to what he says in Arabic." So the king summoned the official who knew Arabic. "Speak with this ambassador in Arabic," he ordered.

But when he began to speak to me in Arabic, I told the king in the Holy Tongue: "I do not want to speak with this Ishmaelite because Ishmaelites are my enemies. I can tell from the way this official speaks that he, his mother, and his father are Ishmaelites."

"But my father, my mother, and I are Christians, not Ishmaelites," the Arabic interpreter replied to me. He was greatly afraid and trembled before the king on account of what I had said.

Dom Miguel again spoke against me with the result that the king turned to me and said: "If you speak in Arabic to this official, I will do

all that you request. I will listen, understand, and do all that King Joseph
your brother and the Pope of Rome have commanded. This official is my
servant and he will not twist your words. He is loyal to my house and he
will be our interpreter." All of this had been the plan of Dom Miguel, who
was with the king.

After that, I spoke in Arabic with this interpreter and he relayed everything I said to the king. I gave the king all my letters of introduction,
which he read and passed to Dom Miguel. I told the king about my
mission to him and about the journey I had taken from the time I left the
desert until I reached him. I said this all in Arabic and the interpreter
successfully communicated it to the king. I also conveyed King Joseph's
request of his kingdom: "He asks you for artisans skilled in manufacturing weapons."

Dom Miguel again spoke against me but the king did not accept anything he said. Instead, he greatly rejoiced at what I had said and was
pleased with me. "This is from God," he declared, "I am persuaded and
desire it." The matter also pleased all his officials. After that, the king said
to me, "I propose that you leave Santarém for Almeirim, which is nearby
to me." He commanded an old official to arrange a house for me close to
his and this the old man did, setting up a large house.

While I had been speaking to the king that day, he had asked me: "Do
you know Dom Miguel?" I told him that I had got to know him as I had
70 been in Rome for an entire year and we had met in the presence of the
pope. The king then said to me, "Look and see if the man before me is
Dom Miguel."

I scrutinized the man, discovered that I did indeed recognize him, and
addressed some harsh words to him in front of the king. "I did not realize
that he was Dom Miguel until now because he has played the stranger," I
explained to the king. "If you wish to do what is good in the eyes of God,
King Joseph my brother, and the pope, do not let Dom Miguel remain
before us. He is God's enemy and he is also your enemy. Driven by my
love for you, I came all the way from the East to the West, yet this Dom
Miguel was intent on delaying me in Rome and thus preventing me from
meeting you. Although he was your servant, he wished to impede me from

traveling to you. It was this that so angered me in Rome that I wanted to kill him with his own sword."

Dom Miguel was greatly humiliated in front of the king and all his officials. "Do not be angry in your heart on account of this for I want to do all that you want," the king assured me. "So go now until I call for you and we will speak then about your affairs."

Troubles with Reubeni's Entourage

I left the king and sent everything from my house in Santarém—the beds, the linens, and all the furnishings—to the house that they had arranged for me near the king's residence in Almeirim. I also sent word to the prison warden to release my servants, Tobias and David Romano. They were released and met me at the house. I discovered that they had sold their clothes in Almeirim, the place where the king dwelled.

"Repent of your evil ways and return to serve me," I told them. "If you obey me, you will be honored. You traveled with me from your land to a faraway place. I never wanted to cause you distress but only to honor you. All the people of our nation have witnessed the honor that I have bestowed on you. When the king questioned me about your evil deeds, I told him that you were young men who meant well and that I loved you. So what is your desire, to stay with me or to go?"

"Give us your authorization[7] and we will return to our land and will not remain with you," they answered.

"Give you my authorization?!" I exclaimed. "Under no circumstances." But after that, I gave them money and garments and they stayed with me for ten days, during which time their evil deeds and quarrels continued.

We stayed in the house that the king had arranged for us. From morn- 71 ing to evening each day, it was filled with people, both Christians and conversos. A table was laid for them in the morning, at noon, and in the evening. In the evening, it was set at great expense for anyone who came to visit me from afar.

Day after day, Tobias would say to me: "Buy a maidservant for us who can help me with the cooking and clothes washing and who can take care of household matters." He calculated that old Solomon Cohen paid half a florin per week for clothes washing, another half florin for drinking water, and one florin for the water that the horses drank.

It was then that an old converso came to visit me. "I have an Ishmaelite maidservant whom I want to sell," he offered.

"Bring her to me tomorrow so that I can take a look at her," I replied.

So the converso returned the next day with the maidservant and I saw that she was a young woman, *beautiful in form and nice to look upon* (Genesis 29:17),[8] and she knew Arabic. I spoke to her in front of the converso.

"Do you want me to buy you and to become a Jew?" I asked her.[9]

"Yes," she agreed.

I paid forty ducats to the converso, who returned to his home in Santarém. The maidservant stayed in my house until nightfall. I then called in a respected female converso, who knew Arabic, and told her to cut the maidservant's hair and fingernails.[10] After that, I summoned my servants, Tobias and David Romano, and instructed them in the presence of the female converso:

"I have acquired this maidservant to take care of household matters. You are warned not to touch her with lascivious intent. In thirty days' time, I intend to give her as a wife to whomever of you is most obedient to me. I have converted her and there will be no fornication in my house."

I likewise commanded the maidservant: "Be on your guard so that no man touches you. If I see you doing anything evil in my house, I will kill you. Behave respectably in my house and I will give you one of my servants as a husband and you will be free."

I gave her the inner room—my room was in the middle and my servants' room was outside. She stayed for eight days, helping Tobias with the cooking, doing all the housework, washing clothes, and drawing water. After dinner, I usually retired to my room to sleep, fleeing the many visitors, but my servants would draw out their meals until the sixth hour of
72 the night. After one such dinner, Tobias got up to slaughter and pluck the chickens with the maidservant, all the while flirting with her, until midnight. And, as he was every night, Tobias was very drunk.

From my bed I could hear them talking, though I could not discern what they said. I summoned Tobias and told him to go to sleep in his bed. I also summoned the maidservant, cursed her, and ordered her to go to sleep. Tobias passed by me in my room, making as if to go to sleep, and I also pretended to them that I was asleep. But later, he returned to the maidservant's bed and had sex with her. I could hear it. I crept out of my bed and stood over the night-stool in the center of the house. I then called for Tobias, who was riding the maidservant, and I called for the maidservant, who said, "Tobias won't let me get up, he's on top of me." This time I called for Tobias in a loud voice: "Come here right now. If you don't, I'm going to kill you." So Tobias came to me wearing nothing but a shift. And the maidservant too wore only a shift.

"What have you been doing in my house?" I asked Tobias. "I warned you both against committing evil and fornication here."

"I have sinned, transgressed, and done wrong.[11] I am drunk and have erred under the influence of the wine," Tobias answered.

"By way of penalty, you will make a contract with me," I said. "You will stay with me for a full year. I will give you this maidservant to be your wife. I will give you both a complete trousseau and you two will be the caretakers of my household."

But Tobias rejoined, "I cannot do such a thing unless you give me at least fifty ducats to send to my son in Italy."

At that I became angry with him. "Go sleep in your own bed!" I said, and he went. I could say no more, neither good nor bad, because in the house that I shared with my servants, there were about ten sleeping people, some on beds and some on the ground, and I could not speak for shame of them hearing. Later, however, I did speak to the maidservant.

"I converted you and made you a Jew," I said, "and you have done evil in God's eyes and in my eyes. You have transgressed God's commandments and mine."

The maidservant explained that this was the third night that Tobias had come to her in her bed with his sword at her neck. "He came to me against my will and without my consent," she said.

"Why didn't you call out to me?" I retorted. "Return to your bed and go to sleep," and there she went.   73

I stayed in my bed until dawn, then got up, and called Benzion and the maidservant. "Go with Benzion and return to your former master in Santarém," I ordered her. Though she wept, I did not listen to her. "Go!"

I said. She went with Benzion to the house of her former master, who then visited me.

"Why did you abandon the maidservant after she had become a Jew and wanted to stay with you?"[12] the old converso asked.

"Because she disobeyed my orders and brought disgrace to my house. She did things that should not be done. It is for that reason that I do not want her and I ask that you return the money I paid for her," I replied.

Hearing that the king had granted me permission to return to Rome, the old converso left for the town of Évora, intending to thereby avoid repaying me. He stayed in Évora for more than a month and I received nothing from him but the belt that I had given to the Arabic interpreter and a little money—not all of it, because the man was a scoundrel. All of this had been brought upon me by Tobias the wicked cook.

Before I returned that maidservant to her master, the Arabic interpreter visited me and saw her in my house. "Why is this maidservant in your house?" he asked.

"Because she is a maidservant and I bought her," I answered.

After that, he questioned her, saying many things to her in Arabic as well as in the local language, and she replied: "The ambassador bought me and made me a Jew."

The Arabic interpreter then asked me: "Is it true that you made her a Jew?"

"Yes, it's true," I said. He left and relayed this to the King of Portugal, who summoned me. When I appeared before him, he spoke at length before asking about the maidservant.

"I have heard that you bought a maidservant and made her a Jew," he remarked.

"What you have said is true," I replied. "I bought her and, since she was an Ishmaelite, I made her a Jew."

"What do you mean you made her a Jew?" the king inquired.

"I sent Solomon Cohen the elder and two of my servants with her to the river, and Solomon washed and immersed her in the water three times. After they returned to the house, I ordered her to cut her fingernails and some of her hair. I made her swear to do no evil behind my back to ensure

that she would conduct herself appropriately in my house. I also told her
that if she wanted a husband, I would give her one and set her free, providing that her husband was obedient to me."

Having heard me out, the king said: "You did well."

In the Kingdom of Portugal, there are many Ishmaelites. This was because there had been a great famine and plague in the Maghreb, in which
many had died, and some had sold their sons and daughters to the Kingdom of Portugal to keep them alive.[13] The famine had lasted eight years
and had afflicted Ishmaelites in both the East and the West. Everywhere
I had gone, from my home in the desert to the West, I saw Ishmaelites
suffering from this famine. With my own eyes, I had seen them and their
children die from extreme want. And the maidservant whom I had bought
was one of them.

When I returned to my house, the wicked Tobias went out to deliver
some clothes to a Kushite maidservant for washing. He took my new shirt,
which was worth more than four ducats, and gave it to the black maidservant to wash. After collecting the linens and my clothes from her, Tobias
informed me that she had lost the shirt. To convince me, he brought the
black maidservant to me. She begged for forgiveness, so I told her, "Go in
peace." Later some people told me that Tobias had given the black maidservant my shirt so that he could carry on with her.

Emissaries from Muslim Lands Contact Reubeni

Al-Mughira,[14] an important Ishmaelite official and one of the King of
Fez's magistrates, had been sent by his king as an emissary to the King
of Portugal. He was a distinguished man, who was favorably disposed
to Jews. He visited me at my house—and with him were ten servants—
because the King of Fez had heard about me and had commanded him
to first meet with the King of Portugal and after that to call on me. He
delivered letters from the Jews of Fez and from R. Abraham Benzamerro
of Safi[15]—because the Jews love me.[16] He also gave me a third letter from
the Captaincy General in Tangiers.

After handing me the letters, he asked me about my land and if there
were many Jews there. I told him that my land is the desert of Habor,

75 where three hundred thousand Jews flourish under the rule of my brother, King Joseph. King Joseph has seventy elders as advisors, and many officials, and I am the commander of the army.

"What is it that you seek from this kingdom that led you to journey from the East to the West?" the judge asked me.

"From our youth we are trained in war and fight with the sword, spear, and bow," I replied. "With God's help, we want to journey to Jerusalem and conquer the land of Israel from the Ishmaelites, for the End and salvation has arrived. As for me, I have come in search of artisans—skilled in manufacturing weapons and firearms—to travel to my land to manufacture them and teach our soldiers."

The judge was greatly amazed. "We believe that the kingdom will return to you in our time. If it does, will you deal kindly with us?" he asked.

"Yes, we will deal kindly with you and with all who deal kindly with Israel, who are in exile in the Kingdom of Ishmael and the Kingdom of Edom," I replied. Then I asked him, "Do you believe that the Kingdom of Ishmael will return the land to us?"

"Yes, all the world believes it," he answered.

I told him: "We are royalty and our fathers have been royalty in the desert of Habor since the Temple was destroyed. We rule over the tribes of Reuben, Gad, and the half-tribe of Manasseh in the desert of Habor. In the land of Kush, there are nine and a half tribes, who are also ruled by kings. The two tribes that dwell closest to us are those of Simon and Benjamin. They live on the Nile above the Kingdom of Soba between the two rivers, the white river and the black one (that is, the Nile). Their land is good and vast, and they have a king whose name is Baruch, the son of King Japheth. He has four sons, the eldest is Saadya, the second Abraham, the third Hoter,[17] and the fourth Moses. They, like us, number three hundred thousand souls, and together we form a single alliance."

After that, the judge said, "Do you wish to write a letter for me to deliver to the King of Fez?"

76 "There is no need for a letter," I said, "just tell him all of this in your own language and give him a thousand greetings from me. Tell him that the Jews who live under his rule are under his protection and that he should

respect them. This will be the starting point of the peace between us and him, and between our seed and his seed."

"What will become of the Jews living in the kingdoms of the West?" the judge asked me. "Is it your desire to come to the West for them or how is it that your words will reach them?" I told him that, to begin with, we will take the Land of Israel and the surrounding area. After that, the army commanders will go to the East and to the West to gather *the dispersed people of Israel* (Psalms 147:2). Whichever Ishmaelite king is wise will bring the Jews who live under his rule to Jerusalem and he will be greatly honored above all other Ishmaelite kings. Then God will deliver all the kingdoms into the hands of the King of Jerusalem.

The judge said, "The Jews of Fez and its environs, and even the Ishmaelites, say that you are either a prophet or the Messiah."

"God forbid!" I exclaimed. "I am a greater sinner before God than any one of them. I have killed many people. In a single day, I once killed forty enemies. I am not a sage or a kabbalist, neither am I *a prophet nor the son of a prophet* (Amos 7:14). I am merely an army commander. I am the son of King Solomon of the line of David son of Jesse and my brother is King Joseph, who rules over three hundred thousand people in the desert of Habor."

The conversos of the Kingdom of Portugal and the Jews of Italy and of all the places that I passed through thought that I was a sage, a kabbalist, a prophet or the son of a prophet, but I always said to them: "God forbid, because I am a sinner. I have been a man of war from my youth until now."

The judge begged me to write a letter to the Jews of Fez and to R. Abraham Benzamerro of Safi. So I wrote to them and gave him the letters, and he went on his way in peace.

A captain of the King of Portugal's fleet in India, who had served there since the reign of Manuel [I] the Elder of Portugal [r. 1495–1521], had recently arrived in Portugal. The king had arrested him following a financial audit of the ships and detained him in one of the royal residences. 77 When I went on my way from my house to the king, he would peer out of a window at me. When he questioned the king's servants about me, they told him about my business with the king. I had a fine horse that they had bought for me for one hundred ducats, not counting the saddlery, and that imprisoned captain wanted it. He sent word to me, asking if I wanted to sell it for one hundred ducats, but I responded that I would not sell it even if he gave me two hundred ducats.

After that, a high-ranking official visited the king. He was related to the kings of Hormuz, which is in the Indian Ocean near the Habor desert.[18] He did so because the captain, who had been arrested, had killed his brother and robbed him of all his money. The king respected this official, who was an Ishmaelite, and asked him about me: "Have you any knowledge of the desert of Habor?"

"Yes," he replied. "In the desert of Habor there are many prosperous, cattle-owning, Jews. They are now ruled by a king and his name is King Joseph. He is advised by seventy elders. The Jews of our land tell us many great things about the desert of Habor." And he spoke to the king at great length about them in front of all his officials. There were conversos in the audience and they reported all of this to me.

Each day, the king's servants visited my house and played trumpets and all kinds of wind instruments to busk for money. Indeed, musicians from everywhere would visit, many of whom had followed me all the way from Tavira. They accompanied me when I visited the king and stayed at my house and ate at my table. They made music day and night, arriving behind the house before dawn, and playing and singing loudly to receive money.

One day, Joseph Cordelha[19] visited and delivered a letter, written to
78 me in Arabic, from a king who ruled a land west of Fez at the edge of the world. There are no kingdoms beyond his, nothing but desert, but they do have Arab-Ishmaelite neighbors who dwell in this desert in tents. That Ishmaelite king, whose name is Sharif, is a descendant of their prophet.[20] His kingdom is much bigger than others because he killed the kings who preceded him and replaced them. He is a strong and wise king. There are Jews who dwell in his kingdom on a great mountain called al-Sus, which is at the edge of the world.[21] The Jews who live there are farmers. Most of them are poor, but they are strong. One of them paid me a visit. He was a *kohen*[22] and had the heart of a lion—unlike the other Jews who live under Ishmaelite rule.

The letter said: "I heard that you have traveled from the tribes to the King of Portugal. Have you heard tidings about the nation that has emerged from the desert between me and the Blacks? They have captured all the Arabs who dwell in the desert—they, their women, children, cattle, and everything they had—and no one whom they have taken has returned. We do not know if they have killed them or what they have done with them. One refugee fled to me and told me all of this. I have sent Jews to investigate but none have returned. We are astounded by this nation. I have written this to you so that you, in your kindness, can tell me all you know for certain about these lands. Conceal nothing from me about your region and about the tribes, tell me everything."

When this letter reached me, I summoned the Arabic interpreter, who interpreted for the king and me. He read it to me and, in that way, I understood all that was in it. In reply, I dictated a letter, which he wrote down. I told that Ishmaelite king that I am from the desert of Habor in which there are three hundred thousand Jews, may God increase their number one thousandfold, and that these Jews are from the tribes of Reuben, Gad, and the half-tribe of Manasseh. King Joseph my brother rules over them and I am the commander of the army in charge of war. The nine and a half other tribes live in the land of the Blacks in four regions of Kush. The tribe 79 of Moses lives in a different area, beyond the Sambatyon River. The two tribes, that is Simon and Benjamin, live at the source of the Nile and the white river lies beyond them. They are located between two rivers, above the Kingdom of Soba. These two tribes send messengers to us and we to them. Because they live in the land of the Blacks while we live far away in the East, they tell us what they know and hear about the other tribes that dwell near them.

I wrote all these things and sent the letter to King Sharif. The messenger left and so too did R. Abraham Benzamerro, because King Sharif had sent for him. This R. Abraham was a great man who was well-respected both by the Christians and their kings and by the Ishmaelites and their kings. King Sharif had told R. Abraham about all these matters. R. Abraham returned to his land before last Rosh Hashanah 5287 [September 18, 1526]. From Safi, he wrote to me about everything that the king told him concerning the people emerging from the desert. They say that it is an immense desert, the size of the Mediterranean, so large that they cannot tell where it ends.

Jews living throughout the Kingdom of Ishmael had heard of me. They sent messengers and many letters to me in Portugal from Tlemcen, Meknes, Oran, Fez and environs, and many other places.

The King of Portugal had some Ishmaelite slaves. Their supervisor was a magistrate, who resided at his palace and administered all his affairs. The king ordered this magistrate and his slaves to be at my service for all matters. These slaves, who were about five in number, would eat and drink at my house—but they were thieves. At night they would steal, although by day they behaved like angels.

Some distinguished conversos came to tell me that they had seen four flags appear in the sky. After that, many people reported this to me and to Solomon Cohen, including Christians, monks, and conversos. So too did a group of the conversos' little children—they were four years old and piously fasted on Mondays and Thursdays, awaiting God's deliverance.[23] "Trust in God and do good because *the great and dreadful day of the Lord* (Malachi 4:5) is approaching," I said to them.

I made peace among the conversos wherever I went and they obeyed me. Among them there are strong warriors, men trained in the use of firearms, and artisans. I saw that these conversos were stronger and more capable than any of the Jews I had previously met.

The King's Feast

The Arabic interpreter visited my house and said: "The king is having a big feast and it will be a day of great joy for him. They are setting up a table for him outside. If you please, come with me today to the king. If he sees you, he will rejoice." So I went to the king's palace, where they were preparing the table with things too wonderful to describe. All the dishes, big and small, were made of silver, and the large water vessel was made of gold. After concluding their prayers, the king and his brothers stood at his table. The palace was filled with officials—four rooms full of them—and outside there were crowds of people who had come to see how the king eats. Each official attending the king had his hat in his hand and their sons, ages ten and older, stood around the king's table, each bowing down on one knee. There were four magistrates before the king. Each had a cane with which they struck and drove people away from him. The King of Portugal gives a cane to each of his magistrates—a sign from this good king that he must be feared throughout his kingdom. At the start of the meal, I was sitting among the people, but then the king signaled to me to come to him and so there I went. Since I had two servants and the Arabic interpreter with me, the king called to one of the magistrates, "Drive out the people who are in front of the window"—and they were high-ranking officials—"and let the Jewish ambassador be stationed before me by the window with his servants." This they did and I seated myself in the place 81 the king had arranged for me. There were people playing trumpets and all kinds of wind instruments. The king was at the table with his three brothers behind him. He was offered a large silver bowl and golden ewer for washing his hands. Two of his brothers stood up, bowed to him, and kissed the silver bowl before he washed his hands and the man who washed his hands first drank some of the water before washing them. Then, after the king's hands had been washed, the cardinal, who was the king's brother, bowed down to him and kissed the bowl.

They stood at the banquet. On the table, there was a sheep that had been slaughtered without severing its neck.[24] They had removed its stomach, but it was otherwise whole from its head to its legs. They had set golden horns on it and laid it on the table in front of the king. Also on the table were four pigs, whole from head to tail, that had also been slaughtered without severing their necks, and there was much poultry. They served these to the king in that order, removing each after he had finished. The king ate and so too did his brothers behind him. They gave him water to drink and he drank. They then gave water to his brothers. They drank and then returned to eating. They gave the king cuts of all the different kinds of meat and he ate a little of each. They also did this for his brothers. Each of them had servants at the table. These again gave the king water to drink and then did the same for his brothers. All in all, water was consumed three times at the meal. They then served whole fruit, first to the king and then to his brothers. After that, they served many kinds of sweet dishes before removing the tablecloths. The king then stood at the table and the monks blessed him, while all the people bowed. After that, the king went to his wife, the queen, and I followed him with my servants and the Arabic interpreter. Some high-ranking officials also went in after me to the queen.

That day they brought in the captain, who had returned from India and been arrested, and so both he and I stood before the king. The king asked him in front of me: "Are there Jews in the land of India and Calicut?"

82   "Yes," he answered, "there are Jews too numerous to count in Shingoli, which is a ten-day journey from Calicut."[25] And he told the king glorious and amazing things about the Jews of Shingoli.

"Have you heard of Jews who have kings?" the king asked, and the captain replied that there are indeed Jews who are ruled by their own kings. My Jewish servants and the Arabic interpreter who were with me understood the conversation and told me all about it.[26]

After that, I left the king and queen. . . . [There is a break in the text here.] I had not yet left his courtyard with my Jewish servants when the king's brother Afonso,[27] the most respected of his brothers, spoke to me. After summoning the Arabic interpreter to serve as our translator, he discussed my journey and other matters with me. "I will do whatever your brother the king wishes," I assured him. I then returned to my house *in life and in peace*.[28]

From the day that I saw the king and his brothers drinking water even though they dwelled in their own kingdom, I made a firm resolution to drink only water and never wine. The reason: I was in Exile—driven from the East to the West by my love of God, his people, and the land of Israel—and I therefore resolved not to drink wine. From the day I began to drink water, I found that I ate more than I had before at meals at my table and that the water I drank after my fasts was better than wine.

The Signora of Naples had a daughter in Lisbon, who had a son and daughter. She would fast every day and her children would fast on Mondays and Thursdays. She was greatly renowned and, like her mother, she was a philanthropist and a woman of great kindness, blessed may she be before God. The conversos all believed in God, except for one physician who was from Lagos. He came to me and spoke against our religion. I would have struck him had not a converso from Tavira, named Corbélia,[29] grabbed my hand. After that, the physician repented of his deeds.

Difficulties Negotiating with the King and Dom Miguel

The king sent for me while I was with Tobias, David, and Benzion, and 83
so, with them leading the way, I went to him. I entered the palace to find
three rooms filled with people and high-ranking officials, and so I waited
for the king in the third room. When I was finally admitted, the king, in
the presence of about eight servants, was combing his hair.

"Would it please you for us to speak together for an hour?" I asked him.

"I am busy," he answered, "I have many matters to attend to concerning my sister, who is to be married to the emperor, and I want to get them
settled.[30] If you like, you may write down what you request of me. I will
order two scribes to assist you and you can write down for me all your
questions, requests, and whatever else you want."

The king left the room, but I stayed for about another half an hour
during which Dom Miguel and two others approached me.

"Come," they said, "we will write down all your requests."

So we all headed to an upper room and there I began to quarrel with
Dom Miguel, because I did not wish to write down anything in front of
him. I left for my house and remained there until the next day. The king
sent for me again and I went to him with Tobias, David, and Benzion.
This time, we were ushered through a different door into the king's apart-
ments. I was then summoned to the room that the king usually occupied.
I entered alone, while my companions waited outside, but I did not see the
king there. Instead, the room was occupied by Dom Miguel, three high-
ranking officials, and the Arabic interpreter.

Upon seeing Dom Miguel, when I had expected to see the king, I
turned to the Arabic interpreter and exclaimed: "This is not the king!"

"The King has gone to his wife and is sleeping with her," he replied.
"He ordered us to write down everything that you request."

"Did I come to see the king or did I come to see Dom Miguel? If Dom
Miguel remains here with me, I will kill him," I declared.

After that, I started a great argument, refused to write anything down,
and left with my servants. The king's servants tried to prevent me from
leaving by closing the door, but when they saw that I was determined to
break it down, they opened it for me.

My servants and I returned to my house. I had been there only a moment, however, when two servants arrived that the king had sent for

84 me.

"I do not wish to come today," I told them.

They left, only for two others to arrive. "The king orders you to come," these insisted.

"Go in peace," I said, "because, whatever the circumstances, I do not wish to come." And so they too left.

I went riding on my horse accompanied by two conversos and then wandered about with my servants. We had not gone *a bowshot away* (Genesis 21:16) from the house when three more of the king's servants appeared.

"Come before the king," they ordered.

"Go in peace," I repeated, "because, whatever the circumstances, I do not wish to come."

The king's servants returned to him and we rode on over a field and crossed a river. We rode four miles beyond the river and stayed there for about an hour and a half, before returning. When we arrived at the house, we were met by two high-ranking officials and the Arabic interpreter.

"If you desire to come before the king, then do so, because the king is willing to do all that you wish," they said.

"Convey my greetings to the king," I said to the Arabic interpreter.

And to the officials accompanying him, I said: "Today I am unable to come and stand before the king because I am in anguish on account of a fever and all my limbs feel weak. If the king wishes, then tomorrow, after he has eaten, he may summon me to the room in which he stays with the queen and I will come and speak to him." And with that the two high-ranking officials left.

The next morning the king sent for me. When I entered his room with Benzion and the Arabic interpreter, I found him there with the queen. The moment I entered, the king asked me:

"Why is it that, despite my having sent so many messengers for you yesterday, you would not come?"

"I came from the East to the West in order to serve you and because of my love for you," I replied. "And before I reached you, I passed through many Ishmaelite lands, the lands of my enemies, and I also visited Rome.

I have not asked you for silver, gold, precious stones, or pearls. I came only to make your kingdom great, yet you have not given me a day to sit and speak with you and share my thoughts. I have absented myself from my land for many years in order to meet you, yet you will not absent yourself from your affairs for a single day to listen to me."

"Forgive me this time," the king answered. "I have been occupied with much business and could not do a thing on account of my sister, who is to be married to the emperor and become his queen. But I did tell you to 85 write to me with the help of these officials so that I would be apprised of everything."

"I already told you," I insisted, "that if Dom Miguel stands before me, or even if he stands before you, I swear by God and by your own life that I will kill him because he is God's enemy and he is also your enemy and mine. Driven by your enemies' desires, he undid your will by delaying me in Rome. Yesterday I did not want to come to you on account of my anger with Dom Miguel, because anger drives out wisdom. Yesterday my first thought was to come to you and kill him and, for that reason, I did not come. But now, if you please, I am here before you."

"Do you want me to make peace between you and Dom Miguel? He is my servant, he is loyal, and he has my confidence" the king said.

"I do not ever want to make peace with Dom Miguel," I replied.

"Who then would you like to mediate between us in order to arrange all the things that you are asking for?"

"I would be satisfied with any of your servants, whether humble or great, anyone except for Dom Miguel," I answered.

"Write to me then with these two—one is a monk and the other a scribe, and both are distinguished," the king proposed. Then, summoning them, he said: "Tell them all that you want from me and they will write it down because I am now unable to spend time with you because of my affairs. After you have done so, I will be able to understand the situation."

So I went with them to a room and wrote down all that I wanted from the king. I spent half the day with them, going on until night—and I had been fasting for three days and three nights. At nightfall, they went to get a lamp. Then, while they bowed down and jabbered their prayers, I stayed with them and prayed "Hear oh Israel," and completed the evening prayer. After that, while I sat on a chair between them, they wrote down a little more and said: "Sign here."

I signed my name, including my ancestors' names all the way back to King David the son of Jesse. They took the letter and we all went together to the king. I told him that I was tired and weary because I had been fasting for three days and that I wanted to return to my house.

"Go in peace," said the king. But when he saw the letter with the list of kings going back to King David son of Jesse, he asked: "Are all these thirty-two men your forefathers?"

"They are my fathers and the fathers of my fathers," I answered and, with that, I left in peace and returned to my house.

Further Troubles with Reubeni's Entourage

86 There was senseless hatred and slanderous talk among my servants, Tobias, David, and Benzion, who would listen neither to me nor to Solomon Cohen. I did what they wanted and ignored my own desires. I honored Benzion more than my other servants because Daniel da Pisa had said: "My desire is that you put him in charge." I summoned Benzion and privately warned him:

"Beware not to sleep in the same bed as Tobias because I know him to be a scoundrel who drinks too much wine. You too should not drink too much lest you bring sin upon yourself and do something in my house that is against the law."

Although I warned Benzion two or three times about this, he did not listen to me. One night I was on the point of striking him, but he shouted at me and fled. Even once he was outside, he continued to shout at me.

The next day, Benzion went to Santarém without my permission and there he told the conversos villainous things about me, but they rebuked him. They came to me and reported everything he said. I dismissed what they told me as merely reports about the habits of sinful people and so, for the sake of my own honor, I left it to the conversos to handle the matter as they wished.

After Tobias's evildoings with the maidservant, he banded together with David and Benzion. They went to my enemy Dom Miguel and slandered me because I had not said only good things about him. They went to him continually, each and every day, to tell him vile things about me. Dom Miguel was a complete villain and made them his spies. They asked him to write a document with the king's seal that would allow them to leave in safety. Dom Miguel did so and Solomon Cohen and I knew nothing about it. After that, they went on their way. Solomon Cohen, without telling me, went after Benzion and gave him two ducats from his own pocket because he did not want them to leave. I too wanted them to stay with me until I had arranged all my affairs and sent them on their way with great honor in front of all the people, but they did not listen to me. They left for Santarém and I never saw Benzion and Tobias again.

David, however, did return to me and asked for my pardon and for a blessing from God. I showed him my gold seal and said: "Which do you desire more, this seal or ten ducats?"

From the very first, he wanted the seal and so I gave it to him on condition that he swear an oath to take care to do all that I commanded him, for I loved him above all my servants.

"This will be a witness and sign between us," I declared, "that I want you to be my servant all the days of your life because I see that you are 87 humble and God fearing and that you have more decency than all the other servants who attended me on the journey from Rome."

Had he obeyed and remained with me in Portugal, I would have treated him with great honor in front of all Israel but, on Tobias and Benzion's advice, he left with them. "Do not inform your friends of all this," I warned him. He left me and went on his way. Each of them left with the more than thirty ducats that they had collected from Solomon Cohen during the journey from Tavira to Santarém.

Some distinguished conversos visited me at Almeirim. "For God's sake do us a kindness and send these servants away," they begged. "They have no fear of God and we are terrified that they will slander us with some evil accusation to the king. If they have no regard or compassion for you, how much less will they have for us. They commit evil even as you treat them well and please them in everything. Out of respect for you, all the Christians and conversos treat these servants with respect, even though they have no decency. They have even joined your enemy, Dom Miguel, and take counsel with him. How can you trust them when they stay with you?

The best course of action for us all, and the most just, would be for you to dismiss them from your service and let them leave without delay. We will give them provisions for the journey so that they can go on their way. We are superior to them and are even better prepared to do everything you wish."

"It had been my desire to delay them and force them to return to prison," I said, "but given what you have told me, I will dismiss them this very hour."

And so I dismissed them. Now if they wanted to leave, they could, and if they wanted to stay, they could. But I would give them neither my forgiveness nor my authorization, I would just let them do as they wished. These conversos then went to Santarém and gave my servants food and money, upon which they left by sea without my authorization.

Some Moroccan Jews Visit Reubeni

After my servants' departure in the month of Adar 5287 [February or March 1527], five Jews from Safi and Azemmour visited me [Judah of Azemmour, Abraham of Safi, and three others].[31] On the very day they arrived, Solomon Cohen warned me: "Guard yourself against these Jews because I can see that they are villains." But I did not listen to him. I trusted them in good faith and, as he had predicted, they did deceive me. I acquired new clothes for them and put Joseph Cordelha in charge of their expenses. I gave two of them the keys to the clothes chests and dressed them in new garments from head to foot.

Judah of Azemmour and Abraham of Safi served as translators during my meetings with the king, the Christians, and the conversos. They were both knowledgeable in the Holy Tongue and understood what I said. They stayed with me over Passover, causing me great expense because they ate a lot and had a taste for delicacies. Moreover, slander, senseless hatred, and quarrels broke out among them—even worse than those of my previous servants, since those had a better sense of decency. The biggest quarrel and source of contention between Judah and Abraham was over the food and the keys. When they realized that Solomon Cohen had the money and the keys, they wanted to take them from him, and they therefore slandered him to me. I did not believe them, however, because I viewed him as being like an angel of God.

After that, some very distinguished conversos visited me and my new servants told them things about Solomon Cohen that were not decent. These conversos then came to me at night while I was in bed and said: "Send Solomon Cohen back to his land and we will be here to help you. These Jews will be sufficient and they will serve you well. But if you fail to do this, know that we will not come to your aid."

"I cannot send him away until I have time to think about it," I answered.

I took eight days to consider. Great worry and a fever came upon me on account of this, but Solomon Cohen knew nothing of what had happened.

Once these conversos had left, I told Solomon Cohen to write to R. Abraham Benzamerro in Safi. So he wrote a letter, which I took. I also told Judah and Abraham to each write a letter, in good style, to R. Abraham Benzamerro.

"I will check your letters," I said to them, "and if they are better, more accurate, and wiser than the old man's, I will send him away, take you on, and you will serve me."

When I received the letters they had written, I summoned the conversos who had slandered the old man. I addressed Abraham: "Read these three letters to these distinguished conversos—read them in the vernacular in which they were written—so that they may hear them and judge which is the best."   89

Abraham did so and all these conversos judged Solomon Cohen's letter to be better than the other two. I therefore said to them:

"Know and understand that I am an emissary charged by my brother, King Joseph, and his advisors. I came from the East to the West to serve God, may His name be exalted, and to gather Israel from all over and bring them to *a settled land* (Exodus 16:35), to Jerusalem the holy city. When I came to the pope in Rome, God sent me R. Daniel da Pisa, a rich nobleman in Italy, who was more distinguished than all the other Jews. He arranged my dealings with the pope and persuaded him to write all those letters, those to Prester John and the King of Portugal. I left Rome with R. Daniel, traveled to his house in Pisa, and stayed there for seven months until he found a large ship for me. He then gave me this old man and said: 'On account of my love for you, I am giving you this old *kohen*. He will serve you and stay with you in Portugal until the king sends you back to your land in peace. After that, send him back to me in peace.'"

I turned again to these conversos. "What am I to do?" I asked them. "I am on my own and this man is my scribe. He serves me and is commanded by R. Daniel not to leave until I board ship. When I find out what the king plans to do with me, Solomon Cohen will report everything to R. Daniel and, for this reason, I am unable to send him away. He is an old man, seventy years of age. Your claims about him are lies and everything that has been spoken against him was just said in order to take the keys to the money from the old man's hands." Hearing this, the conversos went on their way.

Conversos Arrested at Reubeni's House

After these events, the king had some conversos arrested at my house. In truth, it was not the king himself who had ordered their arrest, rather the order had been made by the king's officials, who had put them in prison. I wrote to the king the moment they were arrested. When he heard about it, he ordered their release, but they remained imprisoned until the next day. So I sent another messenger to the king with a letter and the moment he received it, he said to his officials:

"Did I not order you yesterday to release them?"

They released the conversos and they returned to me. The king then summoned me to the queen's room. I went there with Judah of Azemmour and he summoned the Arabic interpreter.

"I was happy when you first came to offer me aid," the king began, "but I now find that you came to make the conversos Jews again! I have heard that the conversos pray with you and read your books day and night, and that you have set up a synagogue for them."

After hearing what he said, I became angry with him: "I came from the East to the West for one reason alone, to make your kingdom great and to be at your service. Kings should not open their ears to slanderers who do not speak the truth. Everything they have told you is a lie and there is no truth in it at all."

"If this is true and you wish to deal kindly with me," the king replied, "do not do such things from now on."

The king then placated me with kind words because he saw that I was

angry. He spoke to me about my journey and about large and small firearms. He told me that he would give me four gunpowder experts, whom
we could take by ship to our land. I left him and returned to my house.

After all this, the emperor sent a delegation—comprised of people,
horses, and mules too numerous to count—for his bride, the King of Portugal's sister. Among them was his ambassador, who visited my house to
speak with me. He told me that the emperor had heard of my work and
was pleased with it.

"The emperor would like to see you in person," he said.

That ambassador stayed with me for about two hours, with Abraham
and Judah serving as our translators. The duke also came from his land
to Almeirim to see the king, who was a relative of his, and the king sent
many men to greet him.[32] When they met, the king spoke to him about my   91
affairs. The next night, while I was dining, the duke visited me incognito
with four servants. After eating, I invited him in, but he excused himself
and left. Once I went inside, some conversos told me that this man was the
duke and that he had come to visit me incognito to see how I ate.

More Troubles Managing Reubeni's Entourage

The next day the queen left to be married to the emperor, accompanied
by her brother the king, the duke, and many others.[33] I rode with them on
my horse, and a Jewish apostate, who had converted first to the Ishmaelite
religion and then to Christianity, joined me. At the time, however, I knew
nothing of this history. His name was Aldequa and he was from Safi. With
Aldequa leading my horse, I accompanied the queen, the king's sister, for
three parasangs, following which I took leave of them and returned to my
house. I arrived at night and the king returned the next day.

Aldequa, the aforementioned apostate, was a strong and distinguished
man who had a look of decency about him. The Jews, however, said that
he was an apostate and a villain. One night, I summoned Aldequa while
I was on my bed.

"I heard that you converted first to the Ishmaelite religion and then to
Christianity," I said to him. "I believe in you and in your claim that you
want to stay and serve me, yet each morning you leave my house and go
on your way."

Aldequa responded: "I ask that you do me a kindness for the love of Israel but not for my sake, because I have sinned, transgressed, and done wrong.[34] I have committed even greater evil than what people have reported but, with your help, I want to repent and return to the fold. I swear by the Torah of Moses that I wish to repent. If you accept me, and surely God accepts the penitent, I will stay with you until I die and will serve you with all my heart and tend to your horses. Anything you command me I will do."

Then, placing a Bible on his neck, he swore a biblical oath, and stayed at my house.

The Jews were weak and could do nothing for me. Their only strength was in their mouths with which they made demands and requests of me all 92 day. When they came with me to the king, they would cower behind me, afraid and terrified. And they had no decency. One evening, the Arabic interpreter said to me:

"Those Jews who stand behind you have no decency and are not worthy of you. They are arrogant. They do not remove their hats from their heads, neither in my house nor in the king's house, and the gentiles are talking about them."

Every day, the Arabic interpreter would comment on how these Jews, who had lately taken up with me, were despicable on account of their arrogance. Not one of them would wear a baldric over his shoulder. "It is disgraceful for us," they said. I regretted losing my first servants for they had served me honorably. Whenever I was with the king, they had flanked me at my right and at my left, each with his sword at his hip and his hat in his hand. The king's magistrates would tell me that I had driven out my first companions, even though they had been good, and had taken despicable and contemptible ones in their place.

These Jews had given me Aldequa the apostate, who was stronger and more eloquent than them, and he stayed at my house. I rode a horse that was finer than all the king's horses[35] and, each day, Aldequa tended to it and it thrived under his care. He fed and washed it, and cleaned out its droppings, as well as doing all manner of housework. If the Jews went to buy something at the market, Aldequa would go with them and, with the same amount of money, would buy double what they had. Every day they would quarrel and fight with Aldequa and then come to me with slander about him. So I said to them,

"I cannot drive him from my house because he is effective. He provides the horse with the care it needs and sees to household matters, whereas none of you can do all the things he does for me."

The Jews caused me great expense on account of all the conversos and gentiles from Azemmour, Safi, and Fez, that they brought to my house. They would eat and drink, they and their horses, and I would get nothing but their company in exchange! They also started a fight in my house with a converso servant who had come with me from Tavira and who did all the housework and served me better than them. Nonetheless, they continued their condemnations of him, speaking haughtily to me about him, and so, in the end, I was compelled to send him away for their sake.   93

These Jews had come from their country without a letter of safe passage from the King of Portugal and had been arrested upon their arrival in Tavira. They had paid a surety of four hundred ducats in case the king did not grant them safe conduct. The magistrate of Tavira had written to the king regarding their arrival without the letter. As a result, the king summoned me and I appeared before him with Judah and the Arabic interpreter.

"Why is it that Jews have arrived in my land without a letter of safe passage?" he asked me.

"I wrote to tell them to come to me and they came in order to serve me," I answered. "I ask that you, in your exalted glory, write to the magistrate of Tavira to cancel the surety that he received from them and that, for my sake, you give them a letter of safe passage so that they may go about and suffer no injury."

So the king ordered his scribe to write to the magistrate to cancel the surety that they had given him and, as a result, they were able to go about in safety with the seal of the king. Despite all my efforts on their behalf, on that very day, I returned from the palace to my house and was immediately involved in an altercation in which these Jews fought both with me and with Aldequa.

The Circumcision of Diogo Pires (Solomon Molkho)

The king summoned me four times in two days on account of the conversos. "Be wise about what you do with them," he warned me. "And what is
this that I have heard, have you circumcised my scribe?" he added.[36]

"That is not true!" I replied. "Heaven forbid! I did not come here to do
such things. You should not be paying attention to slanderers."

I was in a rage when I spoke with the king. "How can you hear such
falsehood and believe it? Is your accusation of me "wise" behavior? Heaven
forbid that I would do such a thing for I came here only for the sake of my
own business and to serve you."

The king then ceased to speak about this matter and instead spoke
about the voyage of the ships. After that I left him and returned to my
house. I stayed there for four days until he summoned me again and, in
front of Judah and the Arabic interpreter, he said: "I am happy that you
came to offer me aid, but you are destroying my kingdom. All the Christians are reporting that you are making the conversos Jews again. They
say that everyone who visits your house—men, women and children—
94 kisses your hand and, if you are at your table, the sons of the conversos
stand and bow down to you."

I answered the king, but I was angry when I said: "I came from the
East to the West to see you. My door is open to everyone, Christians and
conversos. Indeed, since I am unable to distinguish between Christians
and conversos, I have no choice but to leave my house open to all until you
send me away in peace. But you listen to all the falsehoods that the slanderers tell you—all their words are lies and deception and yet you believe
them."

In response, the king gave me his hand and said, "Do me this kindness,
do not let anyone kiss your hand."

The king then swore that he would give me eight ships in the month of
Nissan [March 1526] with four thousand firearms, both large and small.
And I believed him. I left and returned to my house, where I stayed until
nightfall.

That night, the king's scribe, who had secretly circumcised himself and
had been hiding from the king in the conversos' house,[37] came and spoke
to me. I was furious with him.

"See what you have brought down on us," I said. "Get yourself to Jerusalem and stay far away from the king, lest he burn you at the stake or
kill you."

And so he left me.

This scribe had introduced himself to me when I had first met the king.
He told me that he had dreamed one night that he was being circumcised.

"Do me this kindness. Circumcise me or command Solomon to do so,"
he urged me.

I became angry with him and warned him: "Do not do this at this
time lest you bring danger upon yourself as well as upon us. If the matter
becomes known, they will say that it was I who did it." And I gave him this
advice: "Remain in the king's service until the Holy One Blessed Be He
creates a proper opportunity, because God knows the thoughts of man. At
present, be sure not to do this thing lest you and I and all the conversos be
put in great danger."

He left me and, privately, he performed the circumcision himself.
Since he was a distinguished scribe in the king's service, the king, his officials, and all the Christians and conversos came to know that he had
circumcised himself. He therefore fled and the king, his officials, and all
his servants, claimed that I was the one who had caused him to circumcise
himself, even though I myself had not performed the circumcision.   95

The End of Reubeni's Negotiations with the King of Portugal

The king sent for me when I was not at home, for I had gone across the river
to a villa. When I returned at nightfall, the Arabic interpreter arrived.

"The king summoned you today and this is for the best," he said.

The next day the king again summoned me and I went to him. Whenever he summoned me, he sent his magistrate, mounted on a horse, together with his servants to accompany and guard me. When I visited the
king that day, he said:

"I have much business and cannot send ships with you to the East
either this year or next. If you wish to return to your land, go in peace, for
I grant you leave. Since you came from your land to serve me and give me
aid, I will bless you all my days, but I am unable to send ships with you on
account of the affairs that I must manage in the West. If you wish, you may

go to the emperor and tell him what you desire or you can return to Rome or you can go to Fez. Choose whatever you desire."

I was angry unto death (Jonah 4:9) on account of this. "You swore that you would give me the ships and dispatch them on the first of Nissan [March 25, 1526]. How could you give them to someone else?" I asked the king in great anger. When he responded that he had many obligations in the West, I furiously informed him that I would appeal to the emperor. Two officials, who were intimates of the king, were then present. When I noticed that the king's eyes darkened as he glanced at one of them, I realized that my remarks had angered him, so I said: "It is not my desire to go either to the emperor or to Fez but only to the pope in Rome."

"Good," the king replied, "and you have eight days to think about the matter." I left him and returned to my house.

The queen, the king's wife, sent for me the next day and I visited her, accompanied by Judah.

"Are you satisfied with what my husband the king has done for you?" she asked.

"The king had sworn to give me eight ships," I replied, "but now he 96 has become my adversary. I do not understand the reason he summoned me yesterday to say: 'Return to your land because I do not intend to give you ships.'"

"I know with certainty that the king had wanted to arrange ships for you filled with firearms and *experts in war* (Song of Songs 3:8)," the queen answered. "But then he heard that you had circumcised his scribe and were making the conversos Jews again and conspiring with them against him. It was for this reason that the king's officials and servants advised him to give you nothing and that the king became angry with you."

"This explanation is of benefit both to us and to you!" I exclaimed. "I did not come from my land to do anything to harm the king—heaven forbid! I wanted only to serve and be of use to him. But now my desire is to return to the pope in Rome, long may he live!"

"I wish you well," said the queen.

I took my leave of her and returned to my house. The son that the queen had borne the king was extremely ill.

Yet More Troubles with Reubeni's Entourage

I stayed in my house and some Jews from Fez—R. Jacob the scribe and his five servants—visited me. They stayed with me at my expense for a month, they and their horses, and they were drunken lovers of wine. R. Jacob was a respectable man whom the Christians praised and whom I loved and trusted. Because he was so eloquent, I took him to be a great sage. He asked me for the flag on which the Ten Commandments were written in two rows—the one that the Signora of Naples, *most blessed of women*, had sent to me. He also asked for two gold seals, inscribed with the holy names, that were worth twenty-five gold ducats. So I gave him the flag and the seals. He swore to return to me, come what may, in another month and to bring me a fine white horse, worth two hundred ducats, with silver horse tack so that I could give it as a gift to the pope. He also swore to bring me two good tents as a memento from the Jewish community of Fez. 97

I asked R. Jacob the scribe about Aldequa the apostate, who was staying in my house. He told me that he was from a good family and that he had lamented and regretted his evil deeds and wanted to do all he could to repent. I told R. Jacob that I had not previously believed Aldequa, even though he had declared, "I have sinned, I have transgressed, I have done wrong, and I want to repent," and that I had been afraid that he might sin and steal from me. "But now you have told me this," I said, "I believe your claim that his words are sincere."

"If he stays with you, he will serve you, be there to help you, and will accompany you throughout your journey," R. Jacob assured me. "Moreover, his repentance will be by your hand and its merit will be yours. I know that he comes from a good family and I guarantee that he will do as you desire and will not sin."

Aldequa stood before us. He took a Pentateuch and swore on it to do all that R. Jacob had said he would do and to be loyal to me.

After that, I sent R. Jacob back to his land with his servants and only the five Jews who were there previously remained in my house. One of these was R. Isaac, a young man from Fez who guarded the door. The second was R. Joseph Cordelha, an old man and a complete villain. He had slandered R. Abraham Benzamerro, may God protect and preserve him, to the king, claiming that he had killed a Christian woman. He did this after I had taken him into my house and made him swear upon the Torah that he was under no circumstances to say this. In addition, I had made R. Joseph responsible for the household expenses, with the result that he embezzled more than one hundred ducats. Solomon Cohen wanted to fight with him about the missing money, but I did not want this and instructed him to leave him alone. The third servant was Abraham Pariente of Safi, an old and respected man whom I regarded as loyal. I had sent him to Safi and he had returned with ten ducats worth of wax candles. He also brought us many books and a large shofar. He stayed at my house and was in charge of purchasing wood, wine, chickens, sheep, and all the household necessities, as well as barley for the horse. The two others, Judah and Abraham, were like the biblical Dathan and Abiram, but presented themselves as wise and humble. They were my interpreters when I spoke to the king and the conversos. They were also in charge of my clothes chests, the servants' chests, the tables, beds, and bread box. I did not dismiss them but kept them on only because Solomon Cohen was an old man who was hard of hearing and could understand my words only after they had been repeated several times. I appointed them to speak on my behalf to the king because the king had complained that he could not understand Solomon Cohen's speech. Indeed, it was because all the Christians and conversos who visited me could not understand the old man's speech that I selected Judah and Abraham as interpreters. Although I trusted them and dressed them from head to foot in new clothes, when I checked the clothes chests, I found that many items were missing. They had taken silk garments, a silk turban worth twenty ducats, and another white turban worth five ducats. Although I was missing many things because they had taken them, they constantly quarreled about them with Aldequa, each side accusing the other of taking them.

I bought two black slaves, one twenty years old and the other fifteen, in exchange for a small horse. The older slave was strong and capable of serving me in everything. Aldequa would supervise and give orders to these Kushite slaves. If he left the house even for a day, all my affairs would be in turmoil, because he was the one who oversaw them.

A Meeting with the King and Further Trouble with Reubeni's Entourage
After that the king summoned me and I appeared before him. "What do you plan to do and which road do you want to take?" he asked. "I intend to go to Santarém."

"I want to return to the pope in Rome," I answered. "Please write a letter for me to my brother, King Joseph, that will witness that I reached your kingdom. Also, would you write me another letter to all Christians that I may use as a document of safe passage."

"I will do all that you desire," the king declared.

He summoned his scribe, Antonio Carneiro,[38] and directed him to write these two letters as well as a third ordering the officials in Tavira to pay me three hundred ducats.

"Follow me to Santarém to get the letters," the king instructed me, "and I will send men to accompany you to Tavira."

I left the king and returned to my house. That day, the king and his wife, the queen, left for Santarém to seek a cure for their son who was ill. On the day this son was born in Almeirim [February 24, 1526], I gave three of my garments to the three people who brought me the good news.[39] To the first I gave my golden shawl, worth thirty ducats; to the second, my new red silk overcoat, worth thirty ducats; and to the third, a silk shawl that I had brought from my land and which was worth more than twenty ducats.

I stayed for another three days in Almeirim after the king, his wife, and his son, had departed for Santarém, then left with all my belongings. In Santarém, I stayed at a nice house close to the river and Aldequa managed my household affairs and everything else. Our arrival in Santarém prompted a great quarrel between Aldequa and the Jews [of my entourage], which occurred while I was asleep in bed. After the quarrel, I got up, opened the door, and called for Aldequa, who came to me. He spoke slander about these Jews and I believed him. He said that they had complained that I had shut my door on them. I then became furious with Judah and Abraham, who yelled and shouted over me, making me want to strike them. After that, while I was comfortably in bed, they took "their" belongings, which they had in fact stolen from me, and left on the Sabbath day. They then sent word to me that Aldequa was a slanderer who did

not speak the truth and I replied that I was leaving and no longer wanted
servants. I had done my duty to them, having procured for them a document of safe passage and a letter from the king canceling the surety of four
hundred ducats that they had paid. "Go on your way in peace because I
have work to do," I said.

R. Isaac the door guard came to me and, begging my forgiveness,
asked me to write him a letter because he wanted to travel to Jerusalem.
I wrote a letter, addressed to all Jewish communities, urging them to help
him on his journey. I then gave him money and clothes and sent him away
in peace. Judah and Abraham did not ask for my pardon and did not speak
with me, they just left. Even after they left, they spoke against me, but the
100 conversos stood up to them and threatened to beat them wherever *they
spoke insolently* (Psalms 94:4). In the end, they fled back to their land.

When Joseph Cordelha visited me, I gave him nine ducats and sent
him to ask a converso, who lived fifteen parasangs away from Santarém,
to accompany me to Tavira.[40] Before he left, he stayed in Santarém for
three days, hiding from me, and it was the conversos who told me that he
had not gone. After that he left for wherever he wished to go and I never
saw him again. R. Judah Pariente the elder, of blessed memory, remained
with me.

A Slight on Reubeni's Honor

We stayed in Santarém, where the king's son was sick. I heard a rumor
from the man from whom I had bought my horse that some local Christians had drawn my likeness and were mocking it. When some conversos
heard about this, they challenged them, beat them, and forcibly took away
the drawing. This resulted in the town magistrates arresting two conversos, who sent me a letter requesting that I come to their aid. The moment
I saw it, I went to the king.

"Does it please you that these Christians have drawn my likeness and
mocked me?" I asked. "Some conversos challenged them and seized the
drawing, but the magistrates arrested two of them. If I find favor and kindness in your eyes, write to the magistrates to release them." The king commanded that an order of release be written that very hour.

"I will not leave here until I receive the order in my hand," I told him.

They wrote the order in front of the king, which he signed it in front of me, but laughed as he did so.

"I ask your Excellency to provide me with a servant to deliver this letter so that they release the conversos," I said. The king provided a servant and I sent him with the letter, accompanied by two conversos. They went there and released them.

The king asked me about the flags.

"You have splendid flags," he said, "what do you intend to do with them?"

I told him that they are the standards that the tribes and I use and, when I go to war, I unfurl them in front of the army.

101

"Well and good," the king remarked. Then he asked, "Is it true that you said, in the privacy of your house, that if I gave you a law court for a week, you could rid my land of thieves?"

"Yes, so I said," I replied.

"Who are all these robbers?" he asked me.

"You are already acquainted with them because they are your Ishma-elite slaves," I replied. "That is their nature—to serve you by day and steal from your storehouses by night."

The king laughed, and so too did his officials, because he knew that this was certainly true. After that, I left him.

A Test of Reubeni's Faith

I stayed for two days in my house. Then the cardinal, who was the king's brother, summoned me and I went to his house with the Arabic inter-preter. He treated me with great honor and asked about my flags and my journey. I told him that the flags are my standards and, as for my journey, with God's help, I would go to Rome.

The cardinal then said to me: "If you renounce your religion, I will appoint you as a minister."

"You would make me like the raven that Noah sent from the ark and never returned," I replied. "Would such conduct be fitting for kings? I am the son of a king from the line of King David the son of Jesse. My fathers

did not do this and so how could I, who have come from the East to the
West? Heaven forbid! I came here in order to serve God. I want to earn a
good name on account of the good deed I came to perform and for which I
will be praised throughout the world. How dare you suggest that I commit
such an act? If I were to ask you to renounce your religion, would you be
willing?"

"No," the cardinal answered.

"It is best for you to remain in your religion and I in mine," I said,
"because you say that your religion is true while I say that mine is the true
one—the religion of Moses and Israel."

I was angry with him but, after that, he spoke to me pleasantly, with
the Arabic interpreter serving as our interpreter. I then left and returned
to my house.

The next day the queen sent for me and asked about the flags and
which journey I had decided upon.

102 "The flags are my standards," I replied, "and with God's help, I will
be going to Rome."

At this, the queen rejoiced: "Go and return to your land in peace. The
king has said that he is pleased with you and I heard that he wrote you
letters for the road and also to the pope, long may he live."

I took my leave of her and returned to my house.

By day and by night, conversos visited my house in sorrow at my leaving and their sons would kiss my hand in front of the Christians. Such
gatherings continued until I left Santarém. The Holy One Blessed Be He
saw to it that no conversos suffered injury on my account either at the royal
court or in all the Kingdom of Portugal, praise God. Indeed, the king was
very good. He quarreled with my slanderers and told them not to gossip
any further about the ambassador, who could do as he pleased.

[On April 12, 1526] the king's son died. He did not publicly mourn for
him, however, because his ministers were concerned that to do so would
not be appropriate.[41]

Letters from the King

The Arabic interpreter delivered the letters to me. They were written on paper in a good hand by Antonio Carneiro, who had written good things with integrity and great respect. He had also written a letter stipulating that we be paid three hundred ducats in Tavira. The Arabic interpreter said to me:

"Let us go and bid farewell to the king and receive his permission to leave. I will hold onto the letters until we are with him and will then present them to you in front of him." And so we went together to the king.

I then became angry with the king. "The pope wrote me letters on parchment," I said, "but you, oh king, have written them on paper. I came from the East to the West to serve you. If these letters had been written on parchment, they would remain as a testimony and memento for us and for our children after us, who will thus know that I came to your kingdom."

"Our custom is not to write on parchment and the pope's custom is to write on parchment," the king retorted. "I did for you as was our custom."

"If I have found favor and kindness in your eyes, write them again on parchment," I insisted, "because I want them to be a memento for me."

"We will do this out of our love for you," the king declared.

He ordered the Arabic interpreter to return the letters to Antonio Carneiro, who would rewrite them on parchment. I returned to my house 103 while the Arabic interpreter went to Antonio Carneiro to have the letters rewritten on parchment, but he did not want to write them a second time. When the Arabic interpreter returned to the king with the original letters, Dom Miguel was with him and so the king asked him to rewrite them on parchment. Dom Miguel took all the letters that Antonio Carneiro had written and rewrote them on parchment, but he did not rewrite them with the same great respect with which they had been first written. All this happened because of my anger and, indeed, the elders and King Joseph my brother had warned me against becoming angry. When I had visited R. Yehiel da Pisa's house, his greatly wise and distinguished grandmother, Signora Sarah, *most blessed of women*, advised me: "I see that you are always angry. If you can rid yourself of this anger, you will succeed in your enterprise." She presented me with many books and wrote her warning at the beginning of one of them: "Be neither angry nor rash and you will be wise."[42] But I was unable to conquer my angry impulses and it was my anger at Dom Miguel that had brought me to this point.

The Arabic interpreter had been going like a spy to Dom Miguel to report everything I said to the king and everything I said in my house. For this reason, when he gave me the letters written on parchment, he did not inform me that it had been Dom Miguel who had written them. I asked him about the letter concerning the money that we were to receive in Tavira, and he gave me two sealed letters. Regarding the letter to the magistrate in Tavira, he said: "This is the letter in which the king says you are to receive three hundred ducats."

In fact, it was a letter filled with Dom Miguel's lies, but I was unable to check it because it was sealed. Instead, I believed his words and I took the letters. The person who had sealed it wanted ten ducats for his work, but I instead had the Arabic interpreter pay him seven and a half. I then went with the Arabic interpreter to the king and received permission to leave.

"I am sending the Arabic interpreter to accompany you and be responsible for you until you reach Tavira," the king explained. "I also wrote you a letter ordering them to pay you three hundred ducats. If you need anything, write to me."

Leaving Santarém and Almeirim

I left the king and returned to my house. I wanted to travel that very night but found that the young Kushite slave I had bought had fled. I sent many people to search for him, paying them more than ten ducats. They eventually pulled him out of a large pottery vessel in which he had been hiding. When they returned him to me, I put irons on his legs and severely beat him.

I left Santarém after the afternoon prayer with Solomon Cohen, Judah Pariente, Aldequa the apostate, my two slaves, the Arabic interpreter, and four other officials. All my baggage was loaded on four mules. Once we were beyond the river, the Arabic interpreter took his leave, because he wanted to return to Santarém and sleep there for the night. He said that he would meet me in the morning in Almeirim. That night, my companions and I reached Almeirim and found all the houses open but no one inside. We finally reached a house in which some people were dwelling and stayed there for the night. In the morning, I sent Aldequa to Santarém to recoup the twenty ducats from the maidservant's master. While he was still on that errand, the Arabic interpreter arrived.

"Let's go," he urged me.

"We're waiting for Aldequa," I said.

"Aldequa can follow us."

I loaded the baggage onto the mules and we left. I rode a fine horse from morning until the time of the afternoon prayer, when we reached Coruche, a sprawling town in which there were only a few conversos. We went to the house of a converso, who treated us with great respect.

All the town magistrates came, unfurled our flags, and praised them because they were beautiful and of good workmanship: one was golden and the other was made of white silk. Around the gold flag was a border, 105 a hand span in width. In the middle of the flag there were the two tablets, to each side of which were great lions bearing them in their paws, and the whole design was in gold. The ten commandments were inscribed on the tablets and around the border were the beginning and end verses of Deuteronomy, as well as some verses from the Psalms. The second flag was made of green silk with golden embroidery but with a silver border. There were five other large flags made of silk.

Trouble with Reubeni's Servant Aldequa the Apostate

We stayed in Coruche until nightfall when Aldequa arrived. I rejoiced at his arrival, trusting in him on account of his being well-born. In the morning, we left Coruche and headed for [Mora]. At noon, we reached a forest through which some rivers ran. Since the animals were tired, we unloaded the baggage from them and ate there. In our group, there were six rich conversos. That evening, the Arabic interpreter asked me:

"Which of your servants will present the king's letter to the magistrates of Mora[43] so that they can arrange a good villa for you and order some chickens and everything you need."

"I have no man as good as Aldequa," I replied.

I summoned him and said, "Will you go to Mora to arrange everything?"

"I will go," he answered.

He asked me for a horse and the Arabic interpreter gave him one of his companion's horses. Aldequa had with him my sword, which was worth more than thirty ducats, and a gold belt worth sixteen ducats. He also had ten ducats that he had recovered for me in Santarém from the maidservant's master to whom I had previously sent him. I then gave him the King of Portugal's letter that ordered all the magistrates to treat me with great honor.

Aldequa rode away on that horse. We waited for him for about an hour, then left for Mora. When we reached the town gate, we asked the guards about Aldequa.

"Aldequa has not arrived here. We have not seen him," they informed us.

After that, the Arabic interpreter went to the magistrates and we stayed outside the town, which was very big. All the townspeople came out to see me—many Christians and some conversos. When I learned that the Arabic interpreter had been delayed in appearing before the magistrates, I mounted my horse and went riding with four of the conversos who had accompanied me. We left Mora and rode hither and thither, and all the townspeople—children, women, Christians, officials, monks, and conversos—came out to see us. We then stopped and wandered about on our horses until the Arabic interpreter returned with two magistrates. We went with them to a converso's house, where they arranged a large and beautiful room for me with a bed, table, chair, and lamp. When the town magistrates visited me, I was in great distress on account of the search for Aldequa.

"Deal kindly with me and find me four men to search the road tonight for Aldequa," I said. "I will pay whatever they ask."

The magistrates provided me with four men to whom I promised to pay eight ducats. They left to search for Aldequa before I went for dinner. After eating, I went to sleep, still greatly distressed. In the morning, I got up, washed, and began to pray. When I finished praying, there was Aldequa approaching me alone, his face as black as a crow.

"Where have you been?" I asked him. "Yesterday I sent you with the king's letter to arrange everything with the magistrates of Mora. What happened?"

"I was on my way, riding my horse, when some wicked bandits pelted me with stones," he replied. "I escaped, fleeing all the way back to where we had stayed in Coruche, which I reached at midnight. I then hired a Christian man for one ducat to accompany me on the road back. Once I parted with him, I came here alone. I was on the road yesterday for half the day and then again for the whole night until now. Truly it was God alone who saved me from those bandits, who wanted to kill me."

"Show me the belt that you have and also the money," I demanded. He did so and placed them on the table. I also took back my sword that hung at his waist.

"You have played tricks on me!" I exclaimed. "You swore on the Pentateuch that you wanted to repent and, although all the Jews and Christians 107 told me that you were a robber, I did not listen to them. It was you who stole the slave and hid him because you wanted to sell him. It was you who stole my turban that was worth twenty ducats, just as the Jews told me you had.[44] You also stole my white crown which I had bought for seven ducats, taking it from my bed. Everyone in the house testified that these items were in your hands, yet I did not believe them. 'Do not judge your fellow until you are in his shoes,' I said. But now I see your deeds and understand them. All that they said about you is true. Now go on your way in peace because I no longer want you."

The town magistrates wanted to arrest and punish Aldequa but I said to them, "Do not do anything. For my sake, let him go."

The men I had sent to search for Aldequa returned and, in front of him, I paid them what I had promised.

"Why are you paying them?" Aldequa asked.

"This is all because of you," I retorted. "This is what you have caused me." I then took the king's letter from him.

The baggage had been loaded on the mules and the Arabic interpreter and conversos were already on horseback. I mounted my horse, as did Solomon Cohen, and we left Mora on the road to Évora. Aldequa, however, chased after us and caught up with me while I was riding.

"I served you with all my strength, even though you are a Jew and I am a Christian!" he said.

"You are a dog and the son of a dog!" I replied. "You are neither a Christian nor a Jew nor an Ishmaelite!"

I pointed my sword at him, wanting to kill him, then chased him on my horse as he fled until the Arabic interpreter and the conversos came and begged me to leave him alone.

"I did not let the magistrates arrest him," I said. "I did not want them to harm him even though he caused me great expense and deceived me. But now he wants to accompany me. If he does, I will kill him."

The Arabic interpreter then stood in front of me. "There is no way that you can prevent him from accompanying you," he said. "Anyone can go on the road as he pleases and if Aldequa wants to go to Évora, let him go."

Journey through Évora, Beja, Almodôvar, Loulé, and Tavira

We traveled on until we reached Évora and lodged at the same converso's house at which we had stayed on our first visit to the town. We stayed there 108 on the Sabbath and on Sunday. Corbélia, the converso who knew the Holy Tongue, joined me. He had served me from the day I arrived in Tavira until I reached the King of Portugal, and from then until today. And he possessed firearms.

After that, the Arabic interpreter said to me, "The road from Évora to Beja is a bad one and you will need to hire people to accompany you because of the bandits along the way." He would never have said this had Aldequa not been speaking with him, day and night, although at that time I knew nothing of this. "I recommend taking Aldequa with us," he continued, "because he is a brave and capable man and you will need such men on the road."

"Let him come and lead the way," I said.

We left Évora the next day and all the townspeople came to see me off. The conversos were greatly saddened and wept at our departure. We left the town and traveled until we reached Beja. There we entered a converso's house, but it was not like the previous one—they arranged beds and a table and everything else for us. Many conversos visited me that night. They were afraid and wept.

"Trust in the Lord forever[45] for you will be blessed to see the rebuilding of Jerusalem," I comforted them. "Do not fear. I did not visit the king this time to take you and bring you to Jerusalem. Before you can come, we must first fight great wars in Jerusalem so that our land will be ours and we can offer the sacrifice.[46] Only after that will we return to bring you to *an inhabited land* (Exodus 16:35). This time, however, I came only to bring you the good news that salvation is near at hand."

On Tuesday, we left Beja and, at nighttime, reached a village in which there were some conversos. We entered a converso's house and they arranged beds and all that we needed. In the morning we left and came to Almodôvar, a beautiful place with many conversos. We visited a converso's house and then went to the town magistrates. Everywhere we went, we unfurled our flags and people praised them.

On Thursday, we reached Loulé, a beautiful place and a big town. We 109 lodged at a converso's house, where all the magistrates visited me. They treated us with great honor and wanted to see the flags.

"If you want anything, just give the order," they said, "because we will serve you in all your needs."

And they did indeed give us help. We stayed there the whole of Friday, and on the Sabbath, and on Sunday.

Aldequa returned to his work and heavy service, but I was afraid of him. Some Jews arrived from Azemmour—Solomon Cohen (or Levi)[47] and Isaac, his son-in-law—and joined us. Isaac was from Safi and had gone to see the king. [A passage is likely missing from the manuscript.]

I sent Corbélia to the magistrate in Tavira with the king's letter to arrange a house for me there. On Monday we left Loulé and many people, including the converso we had been staying with, accompanied us. Then Corbélia met us and I asked him about the house.

"I arranged a nice villa for you that is better than all the others," he assured me.

We reached Tavira and lodged at that villa. It was beautiful and had many rooms. The chief magistrate visited me and arranged beds and everything we needed.

"If you need anything," he said, "send word and I will see to everything." Then he went home.

The Arabic interpreter stayed with me and we slept through the night. In the morning, he asked me for permission to leave because he wanted to return to the king. In Évora, I had bought him a horse for thirty-five ducats and in Tavira I had given him eight ducats, the gold belt that I had

110   entrusted with Aldequa, and two golden robes. I bade him farewell and he
left, swearing to apprise the king of all my needs. We had not received the
three hundred ducats that the king had ordered to be paid to us because
Dom Miguel had lied and contradicted the king's order when he wrote the
letter. The Arabic interpreter was aware of all this because he had been my
translator with the king. I believed everything that the Arabic interpreter
said to me and he had assured me as he left: "On your behalf, I will tell the
king everything exactly as it happened."

I remained with Aldequa at my house in Tavira. When I had arrived
in Tavira, I had met five Jews who came from Fez and Azemmour. They
had not come out to see me on the road but came only on the day after I
arrived. They had great pride. They stayed in Tavira for about six days
and came to my house to eat and drink with us. For seventeen ducats, I
bought a burnous cloak from one of them as a gift for Antonio Carneiro.

Solomon Levi, a young man from Safi with many relatives among the
conversos of Tavira, came to stay with me. So too did a distinguished
converso who had followed me from Santarém. He was a fine tailor and
he would dress me. Another old man also joined. In total, about eight conversos stayed at my house in Tavira.

It was at that time that R. Moses Cohen visited me with letters from
King Joseph and his elders regarding the journey that I would take.

Every day, from morning until evening, my house was filled with
people, both conversos and Christians. Later, those five Maghrebi Jews
went on their way to the king.

Writing to the King of Portugal

After we left Tavira, I thought it would be a good idea to send the king my
horse and all its tack as a gift and to send the burnous to Antonio Carneiro. But who would undertake this task and deliver the gift? I decided to
send Cristofolo, a converso staying in my house, who was loyal and gentle-
hearted, but weak. Then Aldequa came to me.

"For this task, no one but me will be able to impress both you and the
king," he informed me. "If you intend to send this horse to the king, you
will need a man who is both strong and shrewd. This emissary will have to
111   keep watch until the king leaves his house to hunt in the field. He will then

need to be brave enough to bring the horse to the king and declare, 'This is a gift for you from the Jewish ambassador,' and deliver the letter to him. And now I say to you, I am at your command if you wish it and will do all that you command me."

"I want someone who can help me but I am worried on account of your prior misdeeds," I replied. "Go with Cristofolo, with whom I will entrust everything, because I will not entrust anything of mine to you. If you go and help him along the road, then you may present the king with the horse as you have sworn. If you accomplish this, I will always be there to help you."

I then wrote a letter to the king: "I have not found a ship on which to depart and so I am staying in Tavira. I do not know what to do. I am sending you a gift: my horse and all its tack. Would you find me one of your ships? And please note that I have not received the three hundred ducats that you said would be paid to me in Tavira on your behalf."

I placed the horse with all its tack, the burnous, and the letter to the king in the care of Cristofolo and wrote two letters to Antonio Carneiro. I then instructed Aldequa to accompany him. I gave Cristofolo ten ducats for their expenses, including the horse's expenses, and ordered them not to ride the horse. Privately, I instructed Cristofolo to be strong and to give the burnous to Antonio Carneiro. I told him not to trust Aldequa and to let Aldequa go to the king only in his company. Then I sent them off from Tavira and they went on their way to the king.

Troubles with Reubeni's Entourage Involve the Authorities

After they left, the young Kushite slave fled from my house, but the older one remained and he was a complete villain. When he went to the market, he would strike the Christians' slaves and so some Christians came to me complaining, "Your slave sinned against us." He would also pick fights with them over their prostitutes. Then one day this big Kushite slave threw himself on the converso tailor who was staying with me and tried to kill him while he was sitting at the table. I was inside the house and, hearing voices, I went out to see what was happening and saw the slave striking the converso. I immediately ordered that he be bound with ropes. Once they had tied his hands and feet, I grabbed a large stick and beat him on

112 the head with it until it broke. I then got another stick and beat him some
more. Having broken both sticks, I said to the converso: "Give him one
hundred lashes."

Once we were finished, his flesh was all swollen. We put him in iron
shackles and locked him up in the house, where he stayed for ten days. I
then brought him out and dressed him and he became a worthy and valiant slave who was very fond of me. He returned to doing all the housework
as he had before and I made peace between him and the tailor.

Solomon Levi, a young, handsome, and strong man who spoke Arabic,
stayed at my house. I gave him my new coat and a colorful cloak with black
velvet edges—these were new clothes worth fifteen ducats that I had had
made for me. He put them on and passed through the market on his way
to visit the home of his converso relatives. Some slanderers saw him as he
went from house to house, flirting with the women.[48] This angered them
and they reported him to the town magistrate, who was an evil man. They
said that no one in the Kingdom of Portugal wore silk garments—neither
Christians, Jews, nor conversos—and that the king had imposed a fine of
fifty ducats on anyone who did so.[49] They then imprisoned Solomon Levi
for wearing my silk garments. When I heard about this, I told Solomon
Cohen to appeal to my dear friend the chief magistrate and so they
released Solomon Levi after a surety, gathered by his converso relatives,
had been paid.

Before this incident with Solomon Levi, I had sent my friend, the good
chief magistrate, a gift of fine garments, but he had not wanted to accept
them. He then visited my house with his secretary and said: "If you want
to honor and assist me, do a favor for this secretary of mine."

He did not ask for clothes or anything else but asked that this secretary
be made superintendent over all my servants. That secretary, who was a
complete villain, then approached me.

"If you please, for the sake your honor, have a garment made for me
that will be a memento for me always," he said.

So I said to Solomon Cohen, "Please go and find a handsome black
garment," and off he went to find one. I also took fourteen ducats from
Solomon and gave them to that secretary. When my friend, the chief magistrate, heard about this, he again visited my house.

"Why did you do this?" he asked. "Why did you give the secretary a 113 garment of such value?"

"I bestowed this honor on him only in order to honor you," I replied.

Then that magistrate said to me: "I did not tell you to get him such clothes as you have given him." And with that, he left to go home.

My friend the magistrate used to arrange things for me and guide me in everything, just as a father would a son, and he always treated me with great kindness. One day, I visited his home without warning and found it filled with people to whom he was administering justice. When he saw me, he dropped everything. He came to me and sent everyone else away. There was no one left in his house but us—me, the magistrate, and Solomon Cohen, who was our interpreter—and we were ushered into his bedroom. I got out twenty ducats and said,

"For the sake of my love, accept this gift of twenty ducats. I have heard that the king has sent for you to appear before him, so take this for the expenses on the road."

"I won't take a penny from you," he said and swore by his God that he would not do so. When it became clear that he would not accept the money, I said to him: "I have a suit of armor, made of iron and complete from head to foot. It has protection for both fingers and toes and a helmet, covering head and neck, such that no one can see anything of you except your eyes. I bought it for thirty ducats. Accept it as a gift because I would like to send it to you."

"If the king hears about this he will kill me. Never in my life have I accepted a gift." But then he added, "I have heard that you have two beautiful swords."

"Yes," I replied, "I have them here. If you, for the sake of my love for you, will accept one of them as well as the suit of armor, I will send them to you and they will be a memento of our mighty and awe-inspiring love."

"On account of your love, I will accept everything," he declared. "Send them with Solomon Levi and a friend of mine will meet him tonight."

I returned to my house in peace and, in the evening, I sent Solomon Levi to him with the armor and the two swords.

"Tell him that he may take whichever of the two swords he prefers and return the other to me," I said.

He took the better one. I had bought the suit of armor and sword for fifteen ducats, but in my land they were worth more than a hundred ducats. Solomon Levi returned with the other sword. I then wrote a letter to the king and gave it to my friend the magistrate, who took it with him when he went to the king. The arrest of Solomon Levi occurred only after my
114 friend, the magistrate, left Tavira.

After that, R. Abraham Rut, an old Jew from Safi, came to ingratiate himself with the King of Portugal so that he would appoint him head of the Jews.[50] When he arrived in Tavira, he and two of his companions visited my house and spoke with me. He was the most pious of all the Jews in the kingdom. Although he allowed his companions to eat at our table, he himself would not do so.[51] He stayed in Tavira for about eight days before going to the king.

R. Jacob Sofer of Fez then arrived because he was unable to return to Fez. Since he had departed from Lisbon, which was afflicted by plague, they had not allowed him to disembark either in Azemmour or Safi and now, although he was close to Tavira, they would not allow him to enter the town. I rode to him on a mule, followed by all the townspeople. We met in an orchard and I spoke with him there from a distance.

"Did you reach Fez?" I asked.

He told me that he had not, but that he had sent the flag, seals, and letters there. "I want to travel to Fez and return to you in another month," he added. He went on his way and I returned to my house. He never returned to me.

Eight days after the departure of my friend, the chief magistrate, another magistrate replaced him. The new one was a complete villain and a friend of Dom Miguel. The very day he arrived, he sent for Corbélia, Solomon Levi, and Solomon Cohen.

"Why is the Jewish ambassador still staying here?" he asked them. "The king granted him permission to stay for just two months, but he has stayed for close to four. He can only be staying here for the purpose of making the conversos Jews again, given that they are at his house day and night."

"That is not true," Corbélia replied, "he is staying only because he is awaiting an answer from the king."

"Tell your converso friends to be smart and to refrain from entering the ambassador's house," the magistrate warned Corbélia. He also instructed the people who were with him to give this order to the conversos. Corbélia, 115 Solomon Cohen, and Solomon Levi reported all of this to me.

We had a neighbor who was evil, both to God and to all creation, and who was a friend of Dom Miguel. He would write every week to the king and Dom Miguel about what we said and what we did and he reported to Dom Miguel about the conversos who came to see me. This led me to decide to send a messenger, in haste, to the king with a letter. So I wrote the letter and Solomon Levi agreed to take it.

In the meantime, Cristofolo returned without a letter from the king, but with one from the Arabic interpreter and another from a converso from Santarém. These informed me of what Aldequa the apostate had done. He had stolen the burnous from Cristofolo, which he then wore, and had taken the letters from him. He had also stolen all the tack from the horse. Cristofolo appealed to the Arabic interpreter for help and together they had searched throughout the town for Aldequa, but had found neither him nor the horse. They pursued him and discovered him in the woods, where he had been hiding the horse, because he had wanted to travel to Lisbon to sell it. The Arabic interpreter took the horse from him, now bare without its tack, and left with Cristofolo. Aldequa fled and went on his way. They gave the horse as it was to the king, who greatly rejoiced at receiving it but wrote nothing to me in reply. Although he said to the Arabic interpreter, "I will write and do for him what he desires," he did not do so and Cristofolo returned to me empty-handed.

The moment that Cristofolo returned, I instructed Solomon Levi to travel to the king and gave him ten ducats for his expenses.

"I want Cristofolo to accompany me," he said.

I agreed, gave him my beautiful sword that was worth thirty ducats, and said to the two of them: "You can see how matters stand with me, so please return quickly."

I gave them two letters: one for the king and the other for Antonio Carneiro. I also ordered Solomon Levi to recover the burnous from Aldequa. Then Solomon Levi and Cristofolo went together to the king.

Every day the new magistrate would make false accusations against

conversos. "You all want to become Jews again," he said. This filled the
conversos with dread. He also ordered people to investigate the conversos
116 with regard to whether or not they had visited my house. But the Holy One
Blessed Be He dealt kindly with them and with me and he was not able to
harm them.

Expelled from Portugal

One morning the new magistrate and his entire entourage arrived at my
house while I was still asleep in bed because I had been reading all night and
had only fallen asleep in the morning. Solomon Cohen came to alert me.

"The accursed magistrate is out there in the main room," he said.

"Call Corbélia," I replied.

When Corbélia came, I said: "Tell the magistrate to sit and wait until
I get dressed and can meet with him."

Once I had washed and the tailor had dressed me, I went to the magistrate. In his hand was a letter from the king which he read to me:

"The moment this letter reaches you, send for the ambassador. If there
is a ship in Tavira, let him depart on it. If there is not, you yourself must
accompany him to Lagos and find a ship for him with all haste. Do not
delay."

Not believing that the magistrate had read the letter correctly, I asked
him to give it to me and he did so. Corbélia read it to me, translating it
into the Holy Tongue. When he had finished, the villainous magistrate
spoke up:

"Now do you believe my words? I do not do this on my own whim but
at the king's command. See to whatever business you need to complete
while I return to my home for an hour. I will send you five mules and a
horse for you to ride." Then, seeing my Kushite slave, he asked him, "Are
you an Ishmaelite or a Christian?"

"I am a Christian," the slave replied.

Upon hearing those words, the magistrate took the slave from my
house and left. I did not utter a word of protest.

We organized our baggage. Anything that we could not take, we gave
to Corbélia. I also gave him a silk garment that had been given to me by
R. Yehiel da Pisa, for he had served me from the day I had first arrived

in this region. I summoned Birantina and his wife, at whose house I had 117
stayed and who had treated me with great honor. I gave him a beautiful
sword and his wife six gold rings and a diamond set in gold, which together
were worth twenty ducats. In addition, I gave her a beautiful new blouse
with pearls, worth ten ducats, and three bolts of silk, also worth ten ducats.
I gave them all this in thanks for their kindness and for the expenses they
had incurred during our first stay in Tavira—and they had never asked
me for a thing!

The magistrate sent mules to carry our baggage and a very bad horse
for me. Not wanting to ride it, I walked on foot to his house that was in
a nearby town. Hearing that I was walking on foot and did not want the
horse, he gave me the horse that he himself rode and mounted a mule.
That day, the conversos—men, women, and children—mourned and
wept. We left Tavira at midday and the accursed magistrate accompanied
us with his entire entourage, including the slave that he had taken from
me. Corbélia came with the old converso, the converso tailor who dressed
me, and Solomon Cohen.

Faro, Vila Nova, and Lagos

We reached Faro that night. There the magistrate decided that we had
to lodge at a house belonging to a Christian and not to a converso. The
Christian householder was an honorable man and he arranged a beautiful
room for us with all that we needed. We stayed there until morning. While
I was reciting the morning prayer, the magistrate sent Corbélia to me with
the message that we should stay at the house until he returned from a trip
to Lagos, where he had gone to arrange a ship for us. The magistrate then
left, taking my Kushite slave with him. We stayed at that Christian's house
for about eight days. Many conversos from Tavira visited me there. When
they inquired how I was, I replied: "Do not fear for me. Be strong and wise
in your own deeds. God is with me. He has guided me in performing this
commandment and has chosen a good path for me."

The magistrate returned from Lagos and sent for Corbélia.

"Go to Lagos," he ordered him, "because there is a ship there heading
for Livorno. I instructed the magistrates to arrange everything for you and
I will follow."

It was Corbélia who reported all of this to me after he got back from
118 the magistrate.

We left immediately with all our baggage in the middle of a heavy rain-
fall. Corbélia, the old man, the tailor, and some conversos all accompanied
me. We left Faro and, by nighttime, reached a village on the Mediterranean coast. We found an inn near the town gate, unloaded our baggage,
and let the horses rest. After about half an hour, two distinguished magistrates and some village notables came to meet me.

"Come with us, we have prepared a beautiful villa for you!" they said.

So we went with them, leaving our baggage at the inn. We arrived at
the villa, which was indeed beautiful. They had set up a table for us there.
Solomon Cohen laid it for me and we ate. Then, while he returned to the
inn to retrieve the baggage, they prepared a nice bed for me. Corbélia,
the tailor, and I slept at the villa and the old converso slept at the inn
with Solomon Cohen. In the morning, I got up, washed, put on clothes,
and prayed. While I was still in an inside room, all the village people—
including women, children, and the magistrates—came into the large out-
door room. When I had finished praying, I went out to greet them.

"We want to see the flags," they said.

"Show them," I instructed Solomon Cohen and Corbélia.

They brought the flags and spread them out. And how greatly the
people praised them!

After that, they fetched the horses and I rode out of the village with all
the village people following. We reached a great and mighty river.[52] We
paid the mule owners, who loaded our baggage onto a boat and then left.

We sailed on that boat to Vila Nova [de Portimão], a large town by the
river. There they unloaded our baggage and we all went ashore. All the
townspeople—including women, children, and the magistrates—came to
see me. The absolutely villainous magistrate had written to the magistrates of Vila Nova and Lagos with this order:

"Do not host him in a house belonging to conversos, but only in the
house of a Christian. Keep your eyes on the conversos to make sure that
they do not approach him or attempt to meet with him in secret."

As a result, the town magistrate arrived and sent his servants to take us
to a Christian-owned inn outside of the town. Although we did not enter

the town, all the townspeople followed us to the inn and brought our bag- 119
gage there. Four conversos from Vila Nova came to see me but I had to tell
them to go in peace on account of that villain.

We stayed at the inn on Thursday night. During the night, while I was
asleep, the magistrates searched the inn to see if any conversos were there.
I would have had no idea that they had been there had not Corbélia and
Solomon Cohen informed me after they left. Had I known they were there
to search me, I would have given them a beating, but I heard nothing and
that was for the best. In the morning, the magistrates brought mules and a
horse for me to ride. We left Vila Nova and went to Lagos. Again, all the
magistrates and townspeople—including women and children—came out
to meet me.

At Lagos, they escorted us with our baggage to the house of a Christian.
All the magistrates came there and wanted to see the flags. When I showed
them, they praised them greatly with the result that all the officials and
notables came to see them. The magistrates then said: "See this letter from
the villainous magistrate. It prohibits conversos from meeting with you."

"I have no interest in either conversos or Christians," I informed them.
"Indeed, I do not distinguish between them at all. If they come, they come;
if they return, they return. I will not summon them but neither will I prevent them from coming."

After that, the magistrates went on their way.

Ordered to Leave Portugal

On our eighth day there, some magistrates visited me. "Depart on this
ship from Biscay[53] that is leaving tomorrow," they ordered.

"I will think it over and give you a response at noon," I answered.

Both Christians and conversos then came to me. "Under no circumstances should you go on that ship because its crew is bloodthirsty," they
advised me.

When the magistrates returned, I said, "I do not wish to travel on that
ship under any circumstances."

"You will travel on it even against your will," they retorted.

"Under no circumstances," I insisted. The magistrates left in a fury 120
and Corbélia went with them. When he returned, he said:

"I have received permission from the magistrates for you to ride with me in all haste to meet with the villainous magistrate. He is now in the village in which we stayed on the coast, midway through our journey."

So I left the house and they gave me a horse. Corbélia and I rode off, he on his horse and I on mine. We rode quickly from Lagos for a distance of two parasangs. While I was talking to Corbélia, I saw that the magistrates were pursuing us with a party of more than one hundred men, so we waited until they reached us. They spoke angrily with Corbélia and so too did he with them, because his heart was like that of a lion. But I laughed to myself for I knew this to be an act of God. I had no desire to meet the chief magistrate and had only gone because that was what Corbélia and my servants had wanted. It was I who had given in to them. When Corbélia and the magistrates had finished arguing, I asked him, "What were you saying to them and why have they come here?"

"They chased after us to say, 'Return with us and depart on that ship no matter what.'"

"That's a good thing, let's go," I replied, and we returned with them, my heart joyous at my return. Corbélia was afraid of the magistrates. He trembled and was terrified because they had said to him: "You are the one who is responsible for everything because the ambassador does everything that you say. Now we want to arrest you and put you in prison."

After Corbélia told me these things, I reassured him: "Do not be afraid and do not fear because I will redeem you with everything I have."

We were escorted back to Lagos by the magistrates. There they forbade Corbélia from entering my house, but I had neither heard nor understood their order. Therefore, when I entered the house to find two magistrates there, I asked them where Corbélia was.

"He is in another house," they answered.

I sent messenger after messenger to get him, but he did not come. After that, taking the two magistrates by the hand, I left the house with them.

"Show me the house where Corbélia is," I said.

They showed me and we entered, only to find that he had left for another one. However, when Corbélia heard that I had been to see him, he immediately came to me and I made peace between him and the magistrates.

"I am all alone because I do not know your language," I explained to them. "Solomon Cohen is a deaf, old man whose speech you cannot understand, but Corbélia knows my language and you can understand him. He has served me from the time I first arrived in Portugal until this very day, including when I was with the king. I pay him a salary every month—he does not work for me for free." 121

Corbélia then returned with me to my house. That day I spent fifteen ducats to buy him a new coat, robe, and pants. I also gave him a new long-sword worth ten ducats—and all the magistrates witnessed this.

A Letter from the King

The magistrates then again decided that, no matter what, I had to leave the next day on that same ship from Biscay. That night, Cristofolo returned from the king with a letter. It said:

> I gave you permission to stay for two months but you stayed for four. You stayed in order to make the conversos Jews again. Every week I receive letters from the magistrates of Tavira and so I know all about your activities with the conversos. I had already noticed everything you were doing in front of me and behind my back, but I did not want to hurt you because you told me that you had come here only on account of your love for me and for my benefit. This is why I did not listen to anyone who spoke against you and I told you to go in peace and to return to your land. But now, as soon as this letter reaches you, go in peace without delay.

That same night Cristofolo arrived with Judah Pariente of Safi, who gave me ten ducats and some wax candles. He also delivered a letter written by the Arabic interpreter which said:

> It was Dom Miguel who was responsible for all of this and the king knew nothing of it. The king signed that letter without knowing what was written in it. This is the King of Portugal's way of doing things: everything that is in the hands of the king is also in the hands of Dom Miguel, who is the mover and shaker.[54] It was he who sent the villainous magistrate and he sent him solely to deal with you. The king has shown you great kindness, has done you no harm, and has not believed the accusations against you, yet Dom

Miguel speaks against you to the king day and night. I could do nothing for you because Dom Miguel is always with him. Also, Antonio Carneiro did not want to write another letter demanding the three hundred ducats that you did not receive. I told the king about it, but he gave me no response. When he received the horse, he said good things to me about you, but then Dom Miguel arrived and persuaded him to change his mind and I was 122 powerless to do anything about it. So go on your way in peace and do not delay, for there are many slanderers who testify against you to the king and to Dom Miguel. Every week I receive letters to the king from Tavira against you and I have indeed seen the king angry with you. This is my advice: leave and do not delay. You are wise and you know what you must do.

Cristofolo delivered a third letter from Solomon Levi.[55] He wrote that despite doing everything in his power on my behalf, speaking with the king many times and gifting him my sword, he had received no response. He had spoken to Antonio Carneiro, who also gave no response, and he had a great argument with Dom Miguel. He had then sought out Aldequa the apostate but could not get a penny out of him, neither for the horse tack, that he had already sold, nor for the burnous. [Solomon Levi's letter concluded]:

Some conversos in Coruche reported that from the very first time you sent Aldequa to Mora, he had wanted to steal everything and travel to Lisbon to sell the horse. They said that he would have done so had they not compelled him to return to Mora. They were the reason that he had returned. I was thus unable to recover anything from Aldequa. I sent Cristofolo quickly back to you so that you can determine what to do while I remain with the king to await his answer.

After Solomon Levi left Tavira, his converso relatives came to tell me that they had paid a guarantee on his behalf—a fine of fifty ducats—and had made an agreement with the magistrate. They told me that it was better to settle the matter with the magistrate without involving the king and asked me to contribute ten ducats towards the fine, which I did.

Finding a Ship and Departing from Portugal

That night, while Corbélia the converso was with me, I read those three letters. I slept until morning and then went to the chief magistrate's house with Corbélia and Solomon Cohen.

"I want to leave," I assured him, "but I know that the ship on which you wish me to leave is filled with bloodthirsty people. All the Christians have advised me against boarding it. It would not please the king if you handed me over to murderous and treacherous men, who have always been our enemies. Would you do me a great kindness, for the love of God and for the love of the King of Portugal, and find a better ship? Let its crew be from this town so that we can travel in safety."

So they contacted another shipowner and, for two hundred gold ducats, arranged for him to take us to Livorno. This shipowner, who was 123 from Lagos, was an honorable and upright man from a good family. In any event, I had no other option, as the magistrates had declared, "This man is excellent. We will neither seek out nor approve of any other."

At midday I returned to my house, where I was visited by the town magistrates. "Pay two hundred ducats for the cost of the trip," they said.

"I will give you one hundred ducats here," I replied, "and another hundred in Livorno."

But the magistrates were not satisfied. "Pay two hundred ducats now because the shipowner needs to make all the necessary repairs," they demanded.

"Go and return later this afternoon," I replied.

Corbélia then arrived. He informed me that he knew of a converso with an even better ship, equipped with firearms, who would charge 150 ducats. But when the magistrates returned, I had to agree to taking their ship and no other. I paid them the two hundred ducats and they wrote a letter of commitment for the shipowner. It stipulated that he was to convey me to Livorno and return with sworn testimonies that I had reached there safely. If he failed to return with written testimony, he had to pay the king a fine of ten thousand liras.

I went to inspect the ship and found that the cabin was in ruins. I wanted them to fix it, so I paid another ten ducats for planks, boards, and nails. We stayed eight more days while they repaired the ship and cabin.

I then decided to send Judah Pariente quickly to the king to inform him about all of this and about the Kushite slave that the villainous magistrate had taken from me. I gave him some money, dressed him yet again in new clothes, and then hurriedly sent him off on a horse. Meanwhile, we arranged the food for our voyage. At noon, after they had completed the repairs of the ship and cabin, they announced that the villainous magistrate had arrived. When I heard this, I immediately boarded the ship before he could order me to depart and I had them load the baggage. Before I boarded, I gave authorizations to all the conversos who had served me in the house to go on their way. They were all weeping. I gave Cristofolo an authorization to leave but I did not know where he would go. Corbélia accompanied me onto the ship and arranged all the baggage in a large cabin, which also had a bed for Solomon Cohen. He then set up my cabin nicely before returning to town.

124

The villainous magistrate boarded the ship with Corbélia and ten of his servants. His other servants waited on the shore along with all the townspeople. They searched throughout the entire ship to check if I had any conversos with me. They opened all my chests and rifled through my baggage to see if I had weapons and, in particular, if I had any firearms. Thank God they found nothing but a single sword, the last that remained of all my swords, and they did not find a single converso. After the search, the villainous magistrate came with Corbélia to my cabin door and asked for my pardon.

"I did this only on account of the written order of the king," he said and showed me the letter, which was in Dom Miguel's hand.

"Tell the magistrate," I said to Corbélia, "that *as the Lord lives who has redeemed me from all adversity*,[56] if he had been alone with me and my four servants, he would never have left this ship. I would have taken him with me to the desert of Habor to the court of my brother, King Joseph."

The magistrate left. I gave Corbélia two more ducats for travel provisions and sent him on his way. We then sailed away from Lagos, but docked nearby, so that Solomon Cohen could return there that night with the shipowner. I sent him with the rent payment to the old converso at whose house we had stayed in Lagos, because I had not been able to see him before I left. I also gave him money to purchase provisions for the voyage. He bought various things and returned that same night.

After departing from Lagos in the middle of the night, we sailed for two days. I had been fasting for three days and three nights. From the day I had left Pisa for Portugal, I had never eaten by day, only by night. In addition, I had completed six fasts during which I neither ate nor drank anything, and each had lasted six days and six nights. I had also completed a fast of forty consecutive days, three days of which had lasted through both day and night, during which I had eaten no bread and drunk no water. Similarly, when I had previously been aboard ship, I had fasted for forty days, three of which had lasted through both day and night, with neither eating nor drinking. On all the other days, I had fasted from morning until evening. Despite all of this, I remained well and strong, praise God, and my body required nothing of me. On each day of the trip, I prayed from morning until evening.

A Theft Aboard Ship and Terror at Sea

My ship docked by the coast close to Tavira—about four parasangs from the border of the emperor's kingdom. It remained at anchor for twelve days in order to load a merchant's cargo of fish that was to be delivered to Valencia.

Corbélia came to see me twice. The first time he came alone and the second with his brother. Before Corbélia's second visit, Immanuel, a Christian boy who had done many tasks for us in Lagos, visited me. He had been a frequent companion of Solomon Cohen. He had served him, washed the dishes, delivered water, and set the table. He had also slept near his bed. Solomon Cohen had about fifty ducats. I had asked him to store his money with mine but he refused and instead sewed it into two pockets in his stockings. One night Immanuel, while taking off Solomon Cohen's stockings, had seen the money. He broke open a pocket containing twelve ducats and stole them, putting in their place a single silver coin, and then returned to his duties. Solomon Cohen did not notice any of this.

After that, Corbélia and his brother came to spend the night with us and slept in Solomon Cohen's cabin. Solomon Cohen wanted to give two

ducats to Corbélia's brother as alms, so he searched his stockings. When
he did not find the money, he turned to Corbélia's brother and said: "You
stole the money from my bed last night while you were staying with me."
A great argument ensued between Solomon Cohen and Corbélia and his
brother. I called to Corbélia and asked: "What's all this shouting and yell-
ing I hear? Who is responsible?"

He told me that Solomon Cohen suspected his brother of stealing
money from his stockings. I summoned Solomon Cohen.

"Didn't I tell you to remove the money from your stockings and store
it with mine," I reprimanded him. "It is because you did not listen to me
that all of this happened."

I then summoned the shipowner. "Immanuel has the money," I informed him. "I know that it was he who committed this vile deed. Search
him because it is an affront to you that he committed this theft on your
126 ship."

The shipowner spoke with both Immanuel and Corbélia, and Immanuel admitted to stealing the money, which was now in the town. The shipowner went with him to get it and Immanuel gave him six ducats, two
of which the shipowner took for himself. From the remainder, Solomon
Cohen gave Corbélia's brother the two ducats he had promised him. The
thief then went on his way and we sent Corbélia and his brother back to
their home in peace.

After Corbélia left, Cristofolo visited me on the ship. The shipowner
grumbled that the villainous magistrate had ordered him not to let anyone
board, regardless of whether they were Christians or conversos, but because I treated him with respect, he let Cristofolo meet with me.

On Thursday we sailed away with a good wind, keeping close to the
coast. The good wind lasted for three days until midnight on Thursday.
The ship on which we were sailing had two small ships accompanying
it, but none of our ships had any firearms. We were like sitting ducks.
On Thursday at midnight, a Portuguese ship approached. The crew,
taking them to be pirates, let out cries of great dismay and tied our fleet
together. The shipowner then came to me with the news that the pirates
were Ishmaelites.

"I will stay in my cabin until they come to me and the Holy One

Blessed Be He will show me the right way," I declared. "I am not afraid because I trust in the *God of my salvation* (Psalms 27:9). I fear no man, not even
pirates. If they come to my cabin, I will know that the Holy One Blessed
Be He sent them there for my benefit and for the benefit of all Israel, for
everywhere I go I trust in God."

We stayed put, with the boats tied together and their sails lowered. I
remained in my cabin, praying until morning, at which point they discovered that the approaching ship was in fact part of the King of Portugal's
fleet.

SPAIN

That Friday, we set sail with a treacherous wind that placed us in great
127 danger throughout the day, driving us against our will towards the shores
of Almería, which is in the emperor's territory. We anchored nearby for the
Sabbath, then, on Sunday, we drew into the Almería harbor and remained
there until noon because of the strong winds at sea. The town magistrate
and his attendants boarded our ship and the magistrate visited me while I
was busy writing. I called Solomon Cohen and the magistrate said to him,

"I have come to arrest you all because no Jew is allowed to travel to the
emperor's territory without his permission."

In response, I presented him with the papal bull as well as the King of
Portugal's letter. The magistrate read them before returning them to me.

"Keep these documents with you and come with me," he said. "We will
write all of this down in detail and whatever the emperor tells us we will do."

"This is from God," I replied.

I was happy as Solomon Cohen and I left the ship, feeling neither fear
nor dread. We left all our baggage on the ship because I thought that Solomon Cohen would return for it that very night. We disembarked from
our ship into one of their small boats and went through Almería to the
home of the magistrate who had arrested us. We entered his apartment
on the upper floor of the villa. It had four rooms, each with a door. The
magistrate appointed someone to guard the door to the room in which
we stayed, day and night. As for the shipowner, he was jailed. I said to the
magistrate in whose house I was staying, "Please release the shipowner
and let him stay with us," and he did so.

The bed they had prepared for me that night was the one in which
the magistrate's wife used to sleep. I said to him: "I would like to send my
companion, Solomon Cohen, to guard my baggage on the ship so that
people do not steal it."

The magistrate, however, did not let me send him and so we went to sleep. We stayed in the magistrate's house and our baggage and clothes remained on the ship.

The shipowner now stayed in the house with the magistrate, but he ate and drank with us. One morning the magistrate said to me, "Send for the baggage which you have on the ship and leave nothing behind."

"Even before you said this, I had already decided to send for everything," I replied. "Would you send two of your men to the ship with Solomon Cohen so that they can collect my baggage for him?" 128

The magistrate agreed, dispatching two of his men. They discovered that the crew of the ship from which we had disembarked that previous night had stolen a black silk turban and twenty-five ducats. They gave what was left back to Solomon Cohen.

After that, we took an inventory of our clothes and of the five flags, of great fame and renown, that I had made. Two of them were inscribed with the following words: *The Finger of God* (Exodus 8:15) and *God's Torah is Complete* (Psalms 19:8).[1] As for the three remaining flags, made from new white silk, I fashioned them to serve as a testimony and reminder for all who saw them, including my brother, King Joseph, the elders, and all the tribes of Israel. I inscribed the first with the name of the prince, the illustrious R. Daniel da Pisa, my friend, long may his lineage last. I inscribed the second with the name of his cousin, R. Yehiel da Pisa, may God protect and preserve him, in whose house I had stayed for six months. I inscribed the third with the name of R. Abraham Benzamerro of Safi. These three large and beautiful flags of white silk will serve as a reminder for my brother, King Joseph, his advisors, and all Jews who see and hear, that it was on account of my love of God and love of them that I did all of this for the generations to come.[2] The flags will be a memento for the tribes and for all those of Israel who, with the help of God, redeemed me with their money and persons. May their reward be great and may God be with them, Selah!

As for the two old flags I received from the Christians in Italy, I kept them in whichever cabin of the ship I slept. I dedicated the silver one to my brother, King Joseph, because there is silver in his desert kingdom of Habor and he is presented with silver every day. I dedicated the gold one 129 to myself—David the son of King Solomon, a righteous man of blessed memory—because, with God's help, I will acquire the Kingdom of Sheba, which will provide the gold needed for rebuilding the Temple. I stored these flags in a case, as King Joseph and the elders had commanded me, so that I would be able to display them when I reached the border of his kingdom.

The magistrate compiled a list of my gold seals, our silver bowls, and money. There was nothing we had that he did not note down. They sent a messenger to the emperor on the second day of my arrest. Our baggage stayed with us and they treated us with great honor.

On the evening of the third day, I decided to send a messenger to the emperor. I summoned the magistrate and proposed this to him.

"Go ahead," he agreed, "It is a good idea and I will find you a reliable man."

That night, with Solomon Cohen's help, I wrote a letter to the emperor and his wife, the queen. In the morning, the magistrate asked me: "Do you wish me to find a messenger for you?"

"Yes, send for one," I replied.

He summoned a strong man, who promised to travel to the emperor and return with his reply in eight days.

"It would be best for you to write two letters: one to the emperor and the other to his wife, the queen," the magistrate advised.

He said this because I had told him that the queen had met me with her brother, the King of Portugal, and that I had accompanied her on her way to Spain for a distance of three parasangs. For this reason, the magistrate personally wrote down my letter to the queen, explaining that I had come from her brother, the King of Portugal, and that the wind had brought me to Almería, where I had been arrested.

I sent the messenger to the emperor and his wife with all the credentials I had received from the pope and the King of Portugal, and I paid him ten ducats before he left. That evening, the magistrate announced that he would visit the emperor and the queen and so I gave him four more letters. On Tuesday, he left Almería for Granada, while Solomon Cohen, Cristofolo, and I remained at his house. This magistrate was very distinguished and was of Israelite lineage, although he played the stranger to us and even the Christians knew nothing of it. He treated us with much kindness and great honor. In the presence of the shipowner, he had asked me: "Would you like us to remove the ship's sail and bring it here so that the ship will remain docked as long as you wish?"

At this, the shipowner loudly protested: "I'm staying here with you. If you want to put me in irons, go ahead, but do not remove the sails from the ship!"

Until then I had no idea that they were planning a hasty departure. I said to the shipowner, "I want you to return all the money I paid you—the two hundred ducats to convey me to Livorno—because you have taken me only as far as Almería."

"I will return one hundred and you will let me go on my way," he replied.

"Hand it over this very hour," I ordered.

But when the shipowner's servants heard that the magistrate wanted to remove the ship's sails, they immediately set sail, departing with a good wind. So I put the shipowner in leg irons and sent him to prison.[3]

The magistrate treated us with great honor and the town notables called on us every day. Many Ishmaelites, who had become Christians, also came. An important Ishmaelite official visited, who spoke with me at length.

"For what reason did you leave your land and what is it that you seek from the Christians?" he asked.

He was very wise and shared with me his various calculations and astrological predictions. He had deduced that the end of the kingdoms of the Christians and Ishmaelites had arrived: within three years, the Kingdom of Edom would be in the hands of the King of Israel in Jerusalem and all the nations of the world would return to a single faith. He told me great, mighty, and awesome things, but I did not want to give him any response.

The town bishop sent a gift to my house. When I then visited his home to pay my respects, he again gave me a gift. That bishop was both the most distinguished person in the town and the town's chief justice, so I sent Solomon Cohen to present him with a nice gift.

131

The town of Almería was almost entirely in ruins—less than a tenth of it remained standing. This was the result of a powerful earthquake that had struck five years ago, toppling houses onto people and killing them.[4] On the day it struck, a voice was heard and everyone who heard it understood that it emanated from Jerusalem. The voice was heard throughout the town, but no one could see who was speaking.

We stayed in Almería awaiting an answer from the emperor. Twelve days later, our messenger returned with a letter from the emperor and a signed "bull." This "bull" ordered the entire kingdom to permit us to travel by sea or by land and to do us no harm. It ordered them to treat us with honor, supply us with accommodation at our own expense, and provide us with everything that we might need on the road as we traveled through his kingdom. The messenger whom I had sent told me that, when he arrived, the emperor and the queen were together. [A passage is likely missing from the manuscript.[5]]

People greatly feared for [the magistrate's wife] and believed that she would die, God forbid. However, she gave birth to a daughter, thank God. When I went to see her, I gave her many gifts because we were all staying in the same house and she was in bed.

Before leaving Lagos, I spent more than thirty ducats on sweet foods and delicacies of all kinds to take with us to Livorno—these alone filled four crates and we still had other baggage packed with all kinds of good things. Everything was sent to that magistrate's house in Almería. I had been fasting for three days and three nights when the messenger whom I had sent in great haste to the emperor returned. I bought a good, large mule from the magistrate in Almería for twenty-four ducats and acquired four more to carry all my baggage. I then had the shipowner released from prison.

Journey through Sorbas, Purchena, Lorca, Albudeite, and Cartagena
We left Almería. Solomon Cohen went ahead, departing before the afternoon prayer to accompany our baggage, while I visited the town bishop. The bishop was asleep, but I waited for him to wake up because he had wanted to send some men to serve me. When he awoke, I told him that I did not want him to send anyone, explaining, "I do not wish to trouble you." I thanked him and left. The town magistrate arrived with ten servants to accompany me, because it was nearly nighttime and I was alone. I left Almería and the magistrate accompanied me for one and a half parasangs.

Then, fearing that they would shut the town gates, he returned with his entourage, but left two men with me because it was nighttime. I went on with those two and it was still nighttime when we reached an inn that was situated in an orchard. There were many people at that inn because it was right by the road. We stayed there for the night and, in the morning, we left: I, Solomon Cohen, the muleteers, the shipowner, and Cristofolo, who had accompanied us on foot.

That night we reached Sorbas, which had been an Ishmaelite town. We met its "Christians" and all of them, young and old, knew how to speak Arabic. They were all very poor. We slept at an inn from night until morning. The next day was Christmas eve for the Christians [1526]. The muleteers told me that they wanted to stay and celebrate their holiday at the inn, so I gave in and we stayed. The town magistrate, a distinguished man, visited me.

"If you want anything, just give the word and I will see to it," he said.

I bought a sheep and many chickens for the muleteers so that they could eat their fill. The townspeople had been Ishmaelites and many came to kiss my hand, greatly rejoicing at my presence.

After that, I summoned the town magistrate to consult with him about the shipowner, because I was greatly afraid that he would flee. I had put him in irons and had paid three ducats for a mule to carry him to Cartagena.

"Do you want a strong man to guard him?" the magistrate asked me.

"Yes," I replied, "find one and I will pay his wage."

So the magistrate found me a good, strong, young man and instructed him: "If the shipowner escapes, you will be obligated to pay two hundred ducats, so guard him very carefully."   133

On the morning after Christmas, we left Sorbas with that young man guarding the shipowner all the way. He was right behind him even when he went to take care of his needs. That night we arrived at Purchena, a town of Ishmaelites who had converted to Christianity, and we slept there. In the morning, we set out and reached Lorca, which is a large town, and we stayed there with the young man still guarding the shipowner.

On Friday morning we set out for Albudeite,[6] a place of baths and hot springs, and stayed there at an inn over the Sabbath. On Sunday we set out again. When we approached Cartagena, I sent the young man and the two muleteers ahead to find us a nice and spacious lodging. They returned, reporting that they had found a beautiful villa, and together we entered the town and lodged there. The villa was indeed beautiful, but it belonged to a harlot. They set up a table for us and Solomon Cohen was about to unpack our crates in order to lay it, when the harlot landlady thrust herself between him and the crates.

"Keep your eyes open, guard our baggage, and do not leave it unattended," I warned him. "I can tell that this woman is utterly wicked and is planning something evil because she sells herself every day."

While I was speaking, the wicked woman slipped into my bedroom, stole the red woolen blanket from my bed, passed it out the window to her maidservant, and left. The blanket was worth fifteen ducats. When Solomon Cohen entered the room after she left, he noticed that it was missing. He exchanged angry words with her and yelled at the Ishmaelite [guard of the shipowner] and at the servants.[7] I was then praying but, after finishing, I summoned Solomon.

"What's the matter with you?" I asked.

"The red woolen blanket has been stolen and I suspect the Ishmaelite
134 guard," he replied.

"He didn't take it, it was the wicked woman who did so," I told him, but Solomon Cohen and the Ishmaelite nonetheless continued to argue. I then summoned two town magistrates.

"Get my blanket from this woman immediately," I ordered, and they did so.

After that, the table was set and we ate. Many important people came to the house to see me that evening and they stayed until morning.

Arrested and Then Released by the Inquisition

The young guard continued to keep watch on the shipowner. The next day, the shipowner attempted to escape while I was supervising him and so I had him put in prison. The magistrates visited and I showed them the letters and bulls from the emperor, the pope, and the King of Portugal, as well as my other letters. When they saw the emperor's letter that ordered them to treat me with great honor, all the town notables came to see me without exception, great and small.

That afternoon, a magistrate arrived while I was with the other magistrates.

"I want to arrest these Jews because they are not allowed to be in our land," he announced.

I showed him the emperor's letter, which he read. He wanted to seize it from me, but I grabbed it from his hand and held onto it.

This magistrate then produced a letter from the Grand Inquisitor of the Emperor, who was in Murcia, which ordered our arrest, come what may. All the town magistrates came to my aid, but he would accept none of their arguments. He announced that he would write to the inquisitor in Murcia, requesting that he instruct him on what to do with "these Jews." So he wrote to the inquisitor, "I have in my hands a letter from the Emperor and a letter from the Pope," and so on at length.

Without my knowing it, this magistrate decided to imprison us in the house in which we were staying and he stationed two guards outside. When Solomon Cohen, with my permission, was about to leave to get something at the market, he discovered that the door was locked and guarded outside. When he informed me of this, I became *angry unto death* (Jonah 4:9). I had got up to open the door, searching for something with which to break it, when Cristofolo interjected, "There is another door through which you can exit, do not break this one." He showed it to me and I left, while the guards were still with the magistrate at the entrance to the house. There were many Ishmaelites in that town. When I went out, the magistrate approached me, along with many other people.

"Do you see how this magistrate transgresses the orders of both the emperor and the pope," I declared. "The emperor commanded everyone in his kingdom to treat me with honor, whether I travel by land or sea, but this man locked me in that house and wanted to arrest me, even though I had the emperor's letter in my very hand. Even if it costs me two hundred ducats, I will send a messenger to the emperor with a letter describing all that this magistrate has done to me. We will see how this turns out."

In response, that magistrate sent by the inquisitor in Murcia said: "I will not lock any of you in but stay in your house and two of my servants will stay with you until I receive a reply from the inquisitor tomorrow. I can do nothing for you, whether great or small, except by his command."

When I heard this, I could do nothing but return to the house. I said to that magistrate, "Please permit Solomon Cohen to go to the market to buy what is needed. I will stay at the house and your servants will stay with me." And this was done.

That night, the magistrate came to my house and slept on the ground with his servants. He would not let them sleep on the beds so as to better keep an eye on us. Though they were greatly agitated, I remained calm. Solomon Cohen and I slept soundly in our beds, fearing nothing from them. In the morning, the messenger whom the magistrate had sent to Murcia returned with a letter from the inquisitor that permitted us to stay.[8]

SOLOMON COHEN'S ADDENDUM

[This short text by David Reubeni's companion,
Solomon Cohen, is appended to the manuscript.]

This is a list of the expenditures that I, Solomon Cohen,[1] made on behalf of our master, the commander of the army, R. David.

Here I, Solomon Cohen the son of R. Abraham Cohen of Prato (may the memory of the righteous be a blessing), will write down all the expenditures that I made on behalf of our master, the commander of the army, R. David, the son of King Solomon (may the memory of the righteous be a blessing) of the desert of Habor, since 18 Tevet 5286 [January 13, 1526], 136 the day on which I took charge of the accounts from Benzion of Correggio, may God protect and preserve him. On the journey from Tavira to Almeirim,[2] [Benzion] spent a sum amounting to more than eighty ducats.

The expenditures that I made from 18 Tevet 5286 [January 13, 1526] until we were shipwrecked on 15 Iyyar [April 26, 1527]—some fourteen and a half months—totaled 2,200 ducats. This sum includes expenses in Almeirim, Santarém, Tavira (on our return), hiring mules, and expenses in Lagos, on the coast, in Almería, and in renting ships. It excludes the 2,000 ducats that the Lord of Clermont[3] seized when he arrested us on the island [near] Cap d'Agde. It also excludes the money I paid in Portugal to the king's servants and for the horse that I sent to the king as a gift, which amounted to 2,000 ducats.

The commander of the army, David the son of King Solomon, entrusted all his clothing and belongings to me. And I, Solomon Cohen, list them here as he had commanded me so that this will be remembered for all the generations.

[A detailed list of items follows.]

Here I, Solomon Cohen the son of R. Abraham Cohen of Prato will 143 write down all the things that the Lord of Clermont took from our master, commander of the army of Israel, David the son of King Solomon of the desert of Habor on 15 Iyyar 5287 [April 26, 1527]. I do this so that it may be a memento, a witness, and a keepsake for all generations.

[I sent] twenty gold ducats to the Lord of Clermont on Tuesday, 14 Iyyar 5287 [April 25, 1527] in the care of Gabriele Bulla, the owner of our ship. He went to him from the aforementioned island upon which our ship had been wrecked. I sent him to Cap d'Agde to the Lord of Clermont to obtain a safe passage, because I had heard of all the things that he had done. So I sent Gabriele Bulla to the aforementioned lord with all the bulls, letters, and permits that I had received from the pope, long may he live, the King of Portugal, and the emperor. And the Lord of Clermont thus received the letters and twenty ducats from Gabriele Bulla.

On Tuesday, 15 Iyyar 5287 [April 26, 1527], the aforementioned lord and his officials journeyed to us on the island from Cap d'Agde, a distance of four miles. He returned our ship's owner to us, then he and his party remained on the beach while his attendants arrested us and seized everything we had. All that they took from us is noted below. There was nothing we had that they did not take and all of these things were those that I had rescued from the boat before it sank and placed in our barchetta. We had arrived at the island with those things and there they arrested us and seized everything we had.

I, Solomon Cohen of Prato, may God protect and preserve me, made a list of all these things so that it may be a witness and memento of the commander of the army, our master, David the son of King Solomon.

[A detailed list of items follows.]

148   In total, the value of what the Lord of Clermont and his servants seized, enumerated above, equaled 1,708 ducats. This amount excludes the four large gold seals, my handsome sword, my genealogical book,[4] and the silver fork. These were enumerated here but their value was not appraised. Together these [latter] items were worth 1,573 ducats.

I, Solomon Cohen of Prato, wrote down all of this with my own hand because it was I who made all these expenditures and I did so because I managed all the affairs of our leader and master, the commander of the army, David the son of King Solomon (may the memory of the righteous be a blessing) of the desert of Habor. I wrote all this down on 24 Av 5287

[August 1, 1527] so that it may be a memento for the generations.

Finished and completed, praise be the Everlasting God, Amen. Be strong!

[Description of the redemption of David Reubeni.]

The Lord of Clermont further received the sum of 600 ducats for the redemption of our master, the commander of the army, David the son of King Solomon, from the Jewish communities of Avignon, Carpentras, and environs. David, the commander of the army, had begged these Jews for this sum and had then paid it to the Lord of Clermont.

This amount does not include what was taken from him at Cap d'Agde, noted above, which was valued at 2,173 gold ducats. This amount also excludes the great expenses that the Jews incurred to send an emissary to Rome to request that the remaining ransom be cancelled. Indeed, the Lord of Clermont had asked for such great sums that I was forced to sell myself into slavery in order to pay a further sum of 900 ducats.

Finished and completed, praise be the Everlasting God, Amen. Be strong!

NOTES

Introduction

1. David Reubeni, *The Story of David Reubeni* (in Hebrew), ed. Aaron Aescoly (Jerusalem: Mossad Bialik, 1993), 76. Cf. Amos 7:14. Here and elsewhere, biblical quotations are given in italics.

2. Although in biblical times and even into the early Middle Ages the term *kushi* referred specifically to Nubians, by Reubeni's time, it had become a general term for "Black people." Jonathan Schorsch, *Jews and Blacks in the Early Modern World* (New York: Cambridge University Press, 2014), 116–17.

3. According to 1 Chronicles 5:26, Habor was the place to which the Reubenites, the Gadites, and the half-tribe of Manasseh were exiled. Cf. 2 Kings 17:6 and 18:11. Although Reubeni claimed that this desert was in Arabia, the Bible itself locates it in Assyria. Zvi Ben-Dor Benite, *The Ten Lost Tribes: A World History* (New York: Oxford University Press, 2013), 37.

4. For views that Reubeni did indeed travel to the Funj Sultanate, see Gabriel Warburg, "A Note on David Ha-Reuveni's Visit to the Funj Sultan in 1523," *Sudan Studies* 34 (2006), 20–31; and Sigmar Hillelson, "David Reubeni, An Early Visitor to Sennar," *Sudan Notes and Records* 26 (1933), 55–66. For a view that he did not travel there, see Moti Benmelech, "History, Politics, and Messianism: David Ha-Reuveni's Origin and Mission," *AJS Review* 35 (2011), 58.

5. On the Funj Sultanate, see A.C.S. Peacock, "The Ottomans and the Funj Sultanate in the Sixteenth and Seventeenth Centuries," *Bulletin of the School of Oriental and African Studies* 75 (2012), 90–92.

6. On his life, see Abraham David, "Towards a History of Abraham Castro in the Light of Genizah Documents" (in Hebrew), *Michael* 9 (1985), 147–62.

7. Reubeni, *Story of David Reubeni*, 19.

8. Azriel Shohat, "Notes on the David Reubeni Affair" (in Hebrew), *Zion* 35 (1970), 100.

9. Abraham David, "Gaza as a Trade Center between Egypt and the Land of Israel in the 16th Century" (in Hebrew), *Mahanayim* 2 (1992), 184–91.

10. Reubeni, *Story of David Reubeni*, 29–31.

11. Reubeni, *Story of David Reubeni*, 29–30.

12. Carlos Caracciolo, "Natural Disasters and the European Printed News Network," in *News Networks in Early Modern Europe*, ed. Joad Raymond and Noah Moxham (Leiden: Brill, 2016), 756–66.

13. Cornell Fleischer, "A Mediterranean Apocalypse: Prophecies of Empire in the Fifteenth and Sixteenth Centuries," *Journal of the Economic and Social History of the Orient* 61 (2018), 21.

14. Jean Delumeau, *Sin and Fear: The Emergence of a Western Guilt Culture, 13th–18th Centuries* (New York: St. Martin's Press, 1991), 206.

15. Reubeni notes that he left Alexandria for Venice on December 2, 1523. He does not mention the date of his arrival in Venice, but travel between Venice and Alexandria in the early sixteenth century by ship has been estimated by one scholar to have taken an average of 65 days, and perhaps even longer during the difficult December weather. We can thus assume that Reubeni arrived in Venice in late January or perhaps even in early February of 1524. Pierre Sardella, *Nouvelles et spéculations à Venise au début du XVIe siècle* (Paris: A Colin, 1948), 56–64. On ambassadors and their gifts, see Catherine Fletcher, "'Those Who Give Are Not All Generous': The World of Gifts," in *Diplomacy in Renaissance Rome: The Rise of the Resident Ambassador* (Cambridge: Cambridge University Press, 2015), 145–67.

16. On Moses dal Castellazzo, see Paul Kaplan, "Jewish Artists and Images of Black Africans in Renaissance Venice," in *Multicultural Europe and Cultural Exchange in the Middle Ages and Renaissance*, ed. James Helfers (Turnholt: Brepols, 2005), 67–90. On Simon ben Asher Meshullam, see David Jacoby, "New Evidence on Jewish Bankers in Venice and the Venetian Terraferma (c. 1450–1550)," in *The Mediterranean and the Jews: Banking, Finance and International Trade (XVI–XVIII Centuries)*, ed. Ariel Toaff and Simon Schwarzfuchs (Ramat-Gan: Bar Ilan University Press, 1989), 151–78.

17. Ottavia Niccoli, *Prophecy and People in Renaissance Italy*, tr. Lydia Cochrane (Princeton: Princeton University Press, 1990), 141.

18. The term *sheharhor* (blackish), a biblical hapax legomenon, is ambiguous. Scholars since Abraham Ibn Ezra (Commentary on the *Song of Songs* 1:6) have debated whether its effect is to diminish or intensify blackness. It is unclear how Farissol, who used the term only once, understood it. As Jonathan Schorsch has noted, Farissol, despite citing reports of Jews living in Abyssinia, seems to have drawn a sharp distinction between Jews and Blacks (*shehorim*). It is perhaps for this reason that he preferred to describe Reubeni as "blackish" rather than "black" (*shahor*). See Schorsch, *Jews and Blacks in the Early Modern World*, 117–18 and 124.

19. Letter written by Daniel da Pisa (d. 1527), in Umberto Cassuto, "Sulla famiglia da Pisa," *Rivista Israelitica* 7 (1910), 149; Abraham Farissol (d. 1526), *Iggeret Orhot 'Olam* (Venice: Giovanni di Gara, 1586), 17 and 103; and Gedaliah ibn Yahya (d. 1587), *Sefer Shalshelet ha-Kabbalah* (Venice: Giovanni di Gara, 1587), 103. For Diogo Mendes's statement, see Herman Prins Salomon and Aron di Leone Leoni, "Mendes, Benveniste, de Luna, Micas, Nasci: The State of the Art (1532–1558)," *Jewish Quarterly Review* 88 (1998), 184.

20. Marino Sanuto, *I Diarii di Marino Sanuto* (Venice: Visentini, 1899), 54:148–49 and Francisco Álvares, *The Prester John of the Indies: A True Relation of the Lands of the Prester John, Being the Narrative of the Portuguese Embassy to Ethiopia in 1520* (London: Routledge, 2016).

21. Much fruitless effort has been expended to pinpoint Reubeni's origins, which scholars have placed across the Old World. For the claim that Reubeni was of Indian origin, see Ervin Birnbaum, "David Reubeni's Indian Origin," *Historia Judaica* 20 (1958), 3–30; for an Abyssinian origin, see Umberto Cassuto, "Who Was David Reubeni?" (in Hebrew), *Tarbiz* 32 (1963), 346–47; for a Yemeni origin, see Shohat, "Notes on the David Reubeni Affair," 109. For the claim that Reubeni was an Ashkenazi,

Yiddish-speaking, Jew, see Aaron Aescoly, "David Reubeni's Language" (in Hebrew), in Reubeni, *Story of David Reubeni*, 195–96. For the claim that he was Sephardic and Hispanic-speaking, see Abraham Yahuda, "David Reubeni: His Origin, Language and Identity" (in Hebrew), *ha-Tekufah* 35 (1950), 599–25. For the suggestion that Reubeni might not have been Jewish, see José Alberto Rodrigues da Silva Tavim, "David Reubeni: um 'embaixador' inusitado (1525–1526)," in *D. João III e o Império: Actas do Congresso Internacional comemorativo do seu nascimento*, ed. Roberto Carneiro and Artur Teodoro de Matos (Lisbon: Centro de História de Além-Mar, 2004), 712–13.

22. Andrew Kurt, "The Search for Prester John: A Projected Crusade and the Eroding Prestige of Ethiopian Kings, c.1200–c.1540," *Journal of Medieval History* 39 (2013), 297–320; and Adam Knobler, *Mythology and Diplomacy in the Age of Exploration* (Leiden: Brill, 2017), 30–56.

23. Moti Benmelech, "Back to the Future: The Ten Tribes and Messianic Hopes in Jewish Society during the Early Modern Age," in *Peoples of the Apocalypse: Eschatological Beliefs and Political Scenarios*, ed. Wolfram Brandes, Felicitas Schmieder, and Rebekka Voß (Berlin: De Gruyter, 2016), 193–210.

24. Fabrizio Lelli, "The Role of Early Renaissance Geographical Discoveries in Yohanan Alemanno's Messianic Thought," in *Hebraic Aspects of the Renaissance*, ed. Ilana Zinguer, Abraham Melamed, and Zur Shalev (Leiden: Brill, 2011), 196–97.

25. Miriam Eliav-Feldon, *Renaissance Impostors and Proofs of Identity* (New York: Palgrave Macmillan, 2012), 94.

26. Ariel Toaff, "Il Messia Negro," in *Mostri giudei: l'immaginario ebraico dal Medioevo alla prima età moderna* (Bologna: Il Mulino, 1996), 49–63. Cf. Menachem Waldman, *Beyond the Rivers of Ethiopia: The Jews of Ethiopia and the Jewish People* (in Hebrew) (Tel Aviv: Misrad ha-Bitahon, 1989), 54–56.

27. Stefanie Siegmund, *The Medici State and the Ghetto of Florence: The Construction of an Early Modern Jewish Community* (Stanford: Stanford University Press, 2006), 355–56.

28. Bernard Cooperman, "Licenses, Cartels, and Kehila: Jewish Moneylending and the Struggle against Restraint of Trade in Early Modern Rome," in *Purchasing Power: The Economics of Modern Jewish History*, ed. Rebecca Kobrin and Adam Teller (Philadelphia: University of Pennsylvania Press, 2015), 32–33; and Attilio Milano, "I capitoli di Daniel da Pisa e la comunità di Roma," *La rassegna mensile di Israel* 10 (1935), 324–38 and 409–26.

29. Umberto Cassuto, *La famiglia da Pisa: estratto dalla Rivista Israelitica, anni V–VIII* (Florence: Galletti & Cassuto, 1910).

30. David Kaufmann, "La famille de Yehiel de Pise," *Revue des études juives* 26 (1893): 83–110; David Kaufmann, "Notes sur l'histoire de la famille 'de Pise,'" *Revue des études juives* 29 (1894): 142–47; David Kaufmann, "La famille de Pise," *Revue des études juives* 31 (1895): 62–73; Cassuto, "La famiglia da Pisa," passim; Michele Luzzati, *La casa dell'Ebreo* (Pisa: Nistri-Lischi, 1985); and Lelli, "The Role of Early Renaissance Geographical Discoveries in Yohanan Alemanno's Messianic Thought," 195–96.

31. Reubeni, *Story of David Reubeni*, 47. Cf. Saverio Campanini, "Un intellettuale ebreo del Rinascimento: 'Ovadyah Sforno a Bologna e i suoi rapporti con i cristiani," in *Verso l'epilogo di una convivenza gli ebrei a Bologna nel XVI secolo*, ed. Maria Giuseppina Muzzarelli (Florence: Firenze Giuntina, 1996), 103–4.

32. Reubeni, *Story of David Reubeni*, 46.

33. Reubeni, *Story of David Reubeni*, 41. On the conversos of Rome, see James Nelson Novoa, *Being the Nação in the Eternal City: New Christian Lives in Sixteenth-Century Rome* (Peterborough: Baywolf Press, 2014).

34. Reubeni, *Story of David Reubeni*, 44.

35. On Benvenida Abravanel, see Renata Segre, "Sephardic Refugees in Ferrara: Two Notable Families," in *Crisis and Creativity in the Sephardic World, 1391–1648*, ed. Benjamin Gampel (New York: Columbia University Press, 1997), 164–85; and Samuel Margulies, "La famiglia Abravanel in Italia," *Rivista Israelitica* 3 (1906), 97–107 and 147–54.

36. Reubeni, *Story of David Reubeni*, 57, 100–101, and 104–5.

37. Howard Adelman, "The Educational and Literary Activities of Jewish Women in Italy during the Renaissance and the Catholic Restoration," in *Shlomo Simonsohn Jubilee Volume*, ed. Daniel Carpi (Tel Aviv: Tel Aviv University, 1993), 9–23.

38. Reubeni, *Story of David Reubeni*, 37.

39. Reubeni, *Story of David Reubeni*, 53 and 55.

40. Reubeni, *Story of David Reubeni*, 43.

41. There was considerable reason to fear that Iberia's anti-Jewish policies might spread throughout Italy. Ferdinand of Aragon, who had expelled the Jews from Spain in 1492, had attempted to institute similar policies in his lands in southern Italy. Although, ultimately, this effort was not successful, there were several attempts to expel the Jews from this area over the course of the sixteenth century. Ferdinand was succeeded by his grandson, Charles V, the Holy Roman Emperor, who continued these policies, allowed them to spread to many areas of his empire, and made several attempts to expand his empire into Italy. Later in the sixteenth century, such policies led to the expulsion of the Jews of Milan by Charles V's son, Philip II of Spain. See Flora Cassen, "The Last Spanish Expulsion in Europe: Milan 1565–1597," *AJS Review* 38 (2014), 59–88; Céline Dauverd, "Viceroys, Jews, and Conversos," in *Church and State in Spanish Italy: Rituals and Legitimacy in the Kingdom of Naples* (Cambridge: Cambridge University Press, 2021), 64–91; and Kenneth Stow, "Stigma, Acceptance, and the End to Liminality: Jews and Christians in Early Modern Italy," in *At the Margins: Minority Groups in Premodern Italy*, ed. Stephen Milner (Minneapolis: University of Minnesota Press, 2005), 71–92.

42. François Secret, *Les Kabbalistes chrétiens de la Renaissance* (Paris: Dunod, 1964), 120; and Marjorie Reeves, "Cardinal Egidio of Viterbo: A Prophetic Interpretation of History," in *Prophetic Rome in the High Renaissance Period* (Oxford: Oxford University Press, 1992), 91–109. Cf. Moshe Idel, "Egidio da Viterbo and R. Abraham Abulafia's Writings" (in Hebrew), *Italia* 2 (1981), 48–50.

43. John O'Malley, *Giles of Viterbo on Church and Reform* (Leiden: Brill, 1968), 67–99.

44. Eliav-Feldon, *Renaissance Impostors and Proofs of Identity*, 77. Reubeni was not the first messianic figure to become a subject of interest for Christians. For other examples, see David Ruderman, "Hope against Hope: Jewish and Christian Messianic Expectations in the Late Middle Ages," in *Exile and Diaspora: Studies in the History of the Jewish People Presented to Professor Haim Beinart*, ed. A. Mirsky, A. Grossman, and Y. Kaplan (Jerusalem: Ben-Zvi Institute, 1991), 195.

45. Natalie Zemon Davis, *Trickster Travels: A Sixteenth-Century Muslim between Worlds* (New York: Hill and Wang, 2006), 76–77.

46. Gérard Weil, *Élie Lévita: humaniste et massorète (1469–1549)* (Leiden: Brill, 1963), 210.

47. Robert Knecht, *Francis I* (Cambridge: Cambridge University Press, 1984), 69–70.

48. Letter written by Daniel da Pisa, in Cassuto, "Sulla famiglia da Pisa," 149.

49. For the pope's letter of introduction to Dawit II, see Appendix B in Reubeni *Story of David Reubeni*, 175–78.

50. Letter from Clement VII to João III, in Reubeni, *Story of David Reubeni*, 173–75.

51. See, e.g., Susan Schreiner, *Are You Alone Wise? The Search for Certainty in the Early Modern Era* (Oxford: Oxford University Press, 2011).

52. Eliav-Feldon, *Renaissance Impostors and Proofs of Identity*, 96.

53. Eliav-Feldon, *Renaissance Impostors and Proofs of Identity*, 68–74; Valentin Groebner, *Who Are You? Identification, Deception, and Surveillance in Early Modern Europe* (Brooklyn: Zone Books, 2007), 171–222; and Kate Lowe, "'Representing' Africa: Ambassadors and Princes from Christian Africa to Renaissance Italy and Portugal, 1402–1608," *Transactions of the Royal Historical Society* 17 (2007), 101–28.

54. Reubeni, *Story of David Reubeni*, 51. On Ismael da Rieti, see Shlomo Simonsohn, "On the History of the Rieti Banking Family in Tuscany," *Festschrift in Honor of Dr. George S. Wise*, ed. Haim Ben-Shahar (Tel Aviv: Tel Aviv University, 1981), 301–15.

55. On the location of this house, see Michele Luzzatti, "Per la storia degli ebrei italiani nel Rinascimento: Matrimonii e apostasia di Clemenza di Vitale da Pisa," in *Studi sul Medioevo cristiano offerti a Raffaello Morghen* (Rome: Istituto storico italiano per il Medio Evo, 1974), 433 and 439.

56. Reubeni, *Story of David Reubeni*, 56. For examples of other pre-modern Italian rabbis who visited churches, see Marc Shapiro, "May One Enter a Church? An Unpublished Responsum of Rabbi Eliezer Berkovits" (in Hebrew), *Milin Havivin* 4 (2008–2010), 44. Cecil Roth writes that when Michelangelo was working on his sculpture of Moses (c. 1513–1515) in the Church of San Pietro in Vincoli, "Roman Jews suppressed their traditional inhibitions and went on pilgrimage on Saturday afternoons to gaze upon their Lawgiver's marble features." Cecil Roth, *History of the Jews of Italy* (Philadelphia: Jewish Publication Society, 1946), 195.

57. Cf. Ecclesiastes 7:9.

58. Uberto Motta, *Castiglione e il mito di Urbino: studi sull'elaborazione del 'Cortegiano'* (Milan: Vita e Pensiero, 2003), 385–444; and Ana Isabel Buescu, "D. João III e D. Miguel da Silva, bispo de Viseu: novas razões para um ódio velho," *Revista de história da sociedade e da cultura* 10 (2010), 141–68.

59. Tavim, "David Reubeni: um 'embaixador' inusitado," 690.

60. Mark D. Meyerson, "Religious Change, Regionalism, and Royal Power in the Spain of Fernando and Isabel," in *Iberia and the Mediterranean World of the Middle Ages*, vol. 1 (Leiden: Brill, 1995), 99 and 111. On changes to converso life in Spain before and after 1492, see Renée Levine Melammed, "Judaizing Women in Castile: A Look at Their Lives Before and After 1492," in *Religion in the Age of Exploration: The Case of Spain and New Spain*, ed. Bryan LeBeau and Menachem Mor (Omaha: Creighton University Press, 1996), 28–29. Melammed describes the lives of crypto-Jewish women in this period as "a living hell."

61. François Soyer, *The Persecution of the Jews and Muslims of Portugal: King Manuel I*

and the End of Religious Tolerance (1496–7) (Leiden: Brill, 2007), 219, 224, and 285. For other explanations of the differences between Spanish and Portuguese conversos, see Yosef Yerushalmi, *From Spanish Court to Italian Ghetto: Isaac Cardoso: A Study in Seventeenth-Century Marranism and Jewish Apologetics* (Seattle: University of Washington Press, 1981), 3–8; and Miriam Bodian, *Hebrews of the Portuguese Nation: Conversos and Community in Early Modern Amsterdam* (Bloomington: Indiana University Press, 2001), 12.

62. Yerushalmi, *From Spanish Court to Italian Ghetto*, 305. The theme is also extensively referenced in Inquisition documents. See also, Renée Levine Melammed, *Heretics or Daughters of Israel? The Crypto-Jewish Women of Castile* (New York: Oxford University Press, 1999), 45ff.

63. Goldish, "Patterns in Converso Messianism," in *Jewish Messianism in the Early Modern World*, ed. Matt Goldish and Richard Popkin (Dordrecht: Kluwer, 2001), 42.

64. Joseph Hacker, "Links between Spanish Jewry and Palestine, 1391–1492," in *Vision and Conflict in the Holy Land*, ed. Richard Cohen (Jerusalem: Yad Ben-Zvi, 1985), 119.

65. Carlos Carrete Parrondo, "Judeoconversos andaluces y expectativas mesiánicas," in Carlos Barros, *Guimerans, Xudeus e Conversos na Historica* (Santiago de Compostela: La Editorial de la Historia, 1994), 1:325–37; Carlos Carrete Parrondo, "Idealismo y realidad: notas sobre la noción de Jerusalem entre los judeoconversos castellanos," *El Olivo* 20 (1996), 7–11; and Carlos Carrete Parrondo, "Movimientos mesiánicos en las juderías de Castilla," in *Las tres culturas en la Corona de Castilla y los Sefardíes* (Salamanca: Junta de Castilla y León, 1990), 65–69, esp. 68–69.

66. Haim Beinart, "The Conversos of Chillón and Siruela and the Prophecies of Mari Gómez and Inés, the Daughter of Juan Esteban" (in Hebrew), *Zion* 48 (1983), 241–72, and Melammed, *Heretics or Daughters of Israel?*, 45ff.

67. Melamed, *Heretics or Daughters of Israel?*, 61.

68. David Gitlitz, *Secrecy and Deceit: The Religion of the Crypto-Jews* (Philadelphia: Jewish Publication Society, 1996), 104.

69. Carlos Carrete and Yolanda Moreno, "Movimiento mesiánico hispano-portugués: Badajoz 1525," in *Homenaje al Prof. Fernando Díaz Esteban*, ed. María Victoria Spottorno Díaz-Caro, Ángel Sáenz-Badillos, and Gregorio del Olmo Lete (Madrid: Consejo Superior de Investigaciones Científicas, 1992), 65–68; and Mercedes García-Arenal, "'Un réconfort pour ceux qui sont dans l'attent': Prophéte et millénarisme dans la péninsule Ibérique et au Maghreb (XVIe–XVIIe siècles)," *Revue de l'histoire des religions* 220 (2003), 467–68.

70. Reubeni, *Story of David Reubeni*, 90 and 124.

71. Giuseppe Marcocci, "A fundação da Inquisição em Portugal: um novo olhar," *Lusitania Sacra* 23 (2011), 25–26. Cf. "Letter from Doctor Selaya to D. João III, March 30, 1528," in *As Gavetas da Torre do Tombo*, ed. António da Silva Rego (Lisbon: Centro de Estudos Históricos Ultramarinos, 1960), 164–66.

72. Reubeni, *Story of David Reubeni*, 91.

73. Reubeni, *Story of David Reubeni*, 40.

74. For examples, see Reubeni, *Story of David Reubeni*, 72, 74, and 112.

75. For a thorough treatment of this issue, see José Alberto Rodrigues da Silva Tavim, *Os judeus na expansão portuguesa em Marrocos durante o século XVI: origens e actividades duma comunidade* (Braga: APPACDM Distrital, 1997), passim. For a discussion in English, see Yosef Yerushalmi, "Professing Jews in Post-Expulsion Spain and Portugal,"

in *Salo Wittmayer Baron Jubilee Volume*, ed. Saul Lieberman (Jerusalem: American Academy for Jewish Research, 1974), 2:1023–58.

76. Joseph Chetrit, "The Secret of David Hareuveni According to a Hebrew Poem from Morocco" (in Hebrew), *Tarbiz* 60 (1991), 237–63.

77. Sanjay Subrahmanyam, "Turning the Stones Over: Sixteenth-Century Millenarianism from the Tagus to the Ganges," *Indian Economic and Social History Review* 40 (2003), 155; and Luís Filipe Thomaz, "L'idée impériale manueline," in *La Découverte, le Portugal et l'Europe*, ed. Jean Aubin (Paris: Fondation Calouste Gulbenkian, 1990), 35–103.

78. Sanjay Subrahmanyam, *The Career and Legend of Vasco da Gama* (Cambridge: Cambridge University Press, 1997), 54–57; and Carole Myscofski, "Messianic Themes in Portuguese and Brazilian Literature in the Sixteenth and Seventeenth Centuries," *Luso-Brazilian Review* 28 (1991), 79.

79. Reubeni, *Story of David Reubeni*, 62.

80. Reubeni, *Story of David Reubeni*, 83–84.

81. Reubeni, *The Story of David Reubeni*, 35.

82. Subrahmanyam, "Turning the Stones Over," 132.

83. Andreu Martínez d'Alòs-Moner, "Conquistadores, Mercenaries, and Missionaries: The Failed Portuguese Dominion of the Red Sea," *Northeast African Studies* 12 (2012), 1–28.

84. Reubeni, *Story of David Reubeni*, 65. Reubeni's failure to secure ships may also have been the result of a tacit Portuguese acknowledgment of Ottoman naval dominance in the Red Sea and a corresponding geographic shift of Portuguese imperialist activities away from that area. Martínez d'Alòs-Moner, "Conquistadores, Mercenaries, and Missionaries," 6–7.

85. Reubeni, *Story of David Reubeni*, 94.

86. Reubeni, *Story of David Reubeni*, 102–03; Tavim, "David Reubeni: um 'embaixador' inusitado," 703; and Elias Lipiner, *O Sapateiro de Trancoso e o Alfaiate de Setúbal* (Rio de Janeiro: Imago Editora, 1993), 147.

87. Reubeni, *Story of David Reubeni*, 103.

88. Simonsohn suggests that the "Lord of Clermont" might be Francis William of Clerman, who was cardinal bishop of Tusculum and the papal legate in Avignon. Shlomo Simonsohn, *The Apostolic See and the Jews: History* (Toronto: Pontifical Institute for Medieval Studies, 1990), 91.

89. See "Solomon Cohen's Addendum" (in Hebrew), in Reubeni, *Story of David Reubeni*, 143 and 148; and Sanuto, *I diarii di Marino Sanuto*, 54:145–48.

90. Ariel Toaff, "Gli ebrei a Roma," in *Storia d'Italia, Annali 11, Gli ebrei in Italia*, vol. 1, *Dall'alto Medioevo all'età dei ghetti*, ed. Corrado Vivanti (Turin: Einuadi, 1996), 151–52; Anna Esposito and Manuel Vaquero Piñeiro, "Rome during the Sack: Chronicles and Testimonies from an Occupied City," in *The Pontificate of Clement VII: History, Politics, Culture*, ed. Kenneth Gouwens and Sheryl Reiss (Abingdon: Routledge, 2016), 125–42; and Anne Reynolds, "The Papal Court in Exile: Clement VII in Orvieto, 1527–28," in *The Pontificate of Clement VII*, 143–64.

91. On this incident, see Shlomo Simonsohn, "David Reubeni's Second Mission in Italy" (in Hebrew), *Zion* 26 (1961), 198–207.

92. David Kaufmann, "Azriel b. Salomon Dayiena et la seconde intervention de David Reubéni en Italie," *Revue des études juives* 30 (1895), 304–09. According to Si-

monsohn, Dienna's letter dates to 1530; according to Baron, 1532. Simonsohn, "David Reubeni's Second Mission in Italy," 200–202; and Salo Wittmayer Baron, *A Social and Religious History of the Jews* (New York: Columbia University Press, 1969), 13:365n57. It is difficult to know whether Dienna's assessment of the size of Reubeni's following is accurate. Joseph Ha-Cohen (d. 1578), writing decades after Reubeni's death, claimed that most Italian Jews refused to help Reubeni because they were reluctant to leave their wives and children and risk death in war. It is possible, however, that Ha-Cohen was writing with wishful hindsight. Joseph Ha-Cohen, *The Vale of Tears (Emek Habacha)* (The Hague: Martinius Nijhoff, 1971), 77.

93. Tavim, "David Reubeni: um 'embaixador' inusitado," 706.

94. Jerome R. Barnes, "Giovanni Battista Ramusio and the History of Discoveries" (Ph.D. diss., University of Texas at Arlington, 2007), 14–34.

95. Sanuto, *I diarii di Marino Sanuto*, 54:148.

96. On these events, see Solomon Molkho, *The Collected Writings of Solomon Molkho* (in Hebrew), ed. Zev Golan (Jerusalem: Ze'ev Golan, 2019), 115–19; Reubeni, *Story of David Reubeni*, 94; and Moti Benmelech, *Solomon Molkho: The Life and Death of Messiah Ben Joseph* (in Hebrew) (Jerusalem: Ben Zvi Institute, 2016), 146–51.

97. Benmelech, *Solomon Molkho*, 123–27. On the many rabbis who were impressed with Molkho's learning, see Moshe Idel, *Messianic Mystics* (New Haven: Yale University Press, 2008), 145–46; and R. J. Zwi Werblowsky, *Joseph Karo: Lawyer and Mystic* (Philadelphia: Jewish Publication Society, 1980), 98–99.

98. On Molkho's concept of the Messiah, see Benmelech, *Solomon Molkho*, 187–228.

99. Benmelech, *Solomon Molkho*, 261; and Moshe Idel, "Solomon Molkho as a Magician" (in Hebrew), *Sefunot* 18 (1985): 193–219.

100. Benmelech, *Solomon Molkho*, 252. Cf. Sanuto, *I diarii di Marino Sanuto*, 54:145–52.

101. François Secret, "Notes sur les Hébraïsants Chrétiens," *Revue des études juives* 123 (1964), 142–45.

102. George Parker, "Messianic Visions in the Spanish Monarchy, 1516–1598," *Calíope: Journal of the Society for Renaissance and Baroque Hispanic Poetry* 8 (2002), 6–7. Also see, Rebecca Boone, "Empire and Medieval Simulacrum: A Political Project of Mercurino di Gattinara, Grand Chancellor of Charles V," *Sixteenth Century Journal* 42 (2011), 1027–49.

103. Edward Peters, *Inquisition* (Berkeley: University of California Press, 1989), 102.

104. On these events, see Chava Fraenkel-Goldschmidt, *The Historical Writings of Joseph of Rosheim*, tr. Naomi Schendowich (Leiden: Brill, 2006), 188–98; and Selma Stern, *Josel of Rosheim, Commander of Jewry in the Holy Roman Empire of the German Nation*, tr. Gertrude Hirschler (Philadelphia: Jewish Publication Society, 1965), 132–35. For Hebrew-language primary sources, see David Gans, *Sefer Tsemah David*, ed. M. Breuer (Jerusalem: Magnes Press, 1983), 138–39; Azariah de' Rossi, *The Light of the Eyes*, tr. Joanna Weinberg (New Haven: Yale University Press, 2001), 261–62; and Avraham David, Leon Weinberger, and Dena Ordan, *A Hebrew Chronicle from Prague, c. 1615* (Tuscaloosa: University of Alabama Press, 2012), 37–38.

105. Fraenkel-Goldschmidt, *Historical Writings of Joseph of Rosheim*, 323–24.

106. Antonio Rodríguez Moñino, "Les judaïsants à Badajoz de 1493 à 1599," *Revue des études juives* 115 (1957), 73–86.

107. Reubeni, *Story of David Reubeni*, 84; and Letter from Clement VII to João

III, in Reubeni, *Story of David Reubeni*, 173–78. Reubeni was not the first to present Christian rulers with the possibility of a non-Christian ally against the Muslims. For decades rumors had circulated about the existence of such an ally in the east who was known as the "grand khan." Indeed, in 1492, Christopher Columbus had justified his famous voyage to the Spanish monarchs as a quest to make contact with him. Thirty years later, Reubeni's offer of allyship must have seemed to his audiences as a realization of such hopes. Christopher Columbus, *The Diario of Christopher Columbus's First Voyage to America (1492–1493)*, transcribed and translated by Oliver Dunn and James E. Kelley, Jr. (Norman: University of Oklahoma Press, 1991), 16–17; and Knobler, *Mythology and Diplomacy in the Age of Exploration*, 70–79.

108. Letter written by Daniel da Pisa, in Reubeni, *Story of David Reubeni*, 151.

109. Yosef Yerushalmi, "Messianic Impulses in Joseph Ha-Kohen," in *Jewish Thought in the Sixteenth Century*, ed. Bernard Cooperman (Cambridge: Harvard University Press, 1983), 485; and Shohat, "Notes on the David Reubeni Affair," 96–116.

110. Benmelech, "History, Politics, and Messianism," 42–56; and Moshe Idel, "On Mishmarot and Messianism in Jerusalem in the Early Sixteenth Century" (in Hebrew), *Shalem* 5 (1987), 83–90.

111. Abraham ben Eli'ezer Halevi, "Nevu'at ha-Yeled," in *Sheloshah ma'amre ge'ulah*, ed. Amnon Gros (Jerusalem: Amnon Gros, 2000), 75–76.

112. Fleischer, "Mediterranean Apocalypse," 79.

113. Isaiah Tishby, "Acute Apocalyptic Messianism," in *Essential Papers on Messianic Movements and Personalities in Jewish History*, ed. Marc Saperstein (New York: New York University Press, 1992), 281. For other examples of Jews embracing Islamic victories over Christendom in this period, see Mercedes García-Arenal and Gerard Wiegers, *A Man of Three Worlds: Samuel Pallache, a Moroccan Jew in Catholic and Protestant Europe*, tr. Martin Beagles (Baltimore: Johns Hopkins University Press, 2003), 23.

114. Tishby, "Acute Apocalyptic Messianism," 282.

115. Yitzhak Baer, *A History of the Jews in Christian Spain* (Philadelphia: Jewish Publication Society, 1978), 2:347. For further examples, see Baer, "The Messianic Movement in Spain in the Period of the Exile" (in Hebrew), *Zion* 5 (1933), 61–77; Jacqueline Genot-Bismuth, "Le mythe de l'Orient dans l'eschatologie des Juifs d'Espagne à l'époque des conversions forcées et de l'expulsion," *Annales* 45 (1990), 819–38; and Mark Myerson, "Seeking the Messiah: Converso Messianism in Post-1453 Valencia," in *The Conversos and Moriscos in Late Medieval Spain and Beyond*, ed. Kevin Ingram (Leiden: Brill, 2009), 1:51–82.

116. Reubeni, *Story of David Reubeni*, 132. The idea of Muslim followers of Jewish messianic claimants is attested elsewhere in Jewish history, both predating and postdating David Reubeni. See, for example, Bat-Zion Eraqi Klorman, "Jewish and Muslim Messianism in Yemen," *International Journal of Middle East Studies* 22 (1990), especially 223n2.

117. Reubeni, *Story of David Reubeni*, 75. Reubeni had a similarly positive encounter with a Muslim dignitary who was visiting Spain, see *Story of David Reubeni*, 130.

118. Esther Benbassa and Aron Rodrigue, *Sephardi Jewry: A History of the Judeo-Spanish Community: 14th–20th Centuries* (Berkeley: University of California Press, 2000), 7–9. As these authors indicate, the same rulers who encouraged Jewish migration to their territory did also subject Jews to significant restrictions that stemmed from concerns over maintaining Islamic norms.

119. Shohat, "Notes on the David Reubeni Affair," 103.

120. On this, see Alanna Cooper, "Conceptualizing Diaspora: Tales of Jewish Travelers in Search of the Lost Tribes," *AJS Review* 30 (2006), 103–6.

121. Samuel Schwartz, "O Sionismo no reinado de D. João III," *Ver e Crer* 11 (1946), 101–15; Cecil Roth, "A Zionist Experiment in the XVIth Century," *Midstream* 9 (1963), 76–81; Martin Jacobs, "David ha-Re'uveni: ein 'zionistisches Experiment' im Kontext der europäischen Expansion des 16. Jahrhunderts?" in *An der Schwelle zur Moderne: Juden in der Renaissance*, eds. Giuseppe Veltri and Annette Winkelmann (Leiden: Brill, 2002), 191–206; and Carsten Schliwski, "Der Messias als Staatsmann und Diplomat," *Zeitschrift für Religions- und Geistesgeschichte* 68 (2016), 183–89.

122. Even as far west as Germany, there is evidence of Jewish interest in Reubeni and his army, see Sandor Scheiber and Lajos Tardy, "L'écho de la première manifestation de David Reubeni dans les brochures de colportage allemandes de l'époque," *Revue des études juives* 132 (1973), 595–601.

123. Werblowsky, *Joseph Karo: Lawyer and Mystic*, 98–99.

124. Matt Goldish, "Jews and Habsburgs in Prague and Regensburg: On the Political and Cultural Significance of Solomon Molkho's Relics," in *Jewish Culture in Early Modern Europe*, ed. Richard Cohen, Natalie Dohrmann, Adam Shear, and Elchanan Reiner (Pittsburgh: University of Pittsburgh Press, 2014), 28–38; and Elisheva Carlebach, "The Sabbatian Posture of German Jewry," *Jerusalem Studies in Jewish Thought* 17 (2001), 14–18.

125. Isaac Aqrish, *Kol mevaser* (Offenbach, 1720), 43. Referred to in Aaron Aescoly, "Introduction," in Reubeni, *Story of David Reubeni*, 63.

126. See, for example, Aescoly, "David Reubeni's Language," in Reubeni, *Story of David Reubeni*, 195–220. Notwithstanding the difficulties of paleographical analysis of a manuscript that exists only in a nineteenth-century facsimile, it has been noted that the style of its Hebrew script is consistent with that used in sixteenth-century Italy. This suggests that the facsimile may well have been made from a manuscript that had been written while Reubeni was still alive. Isaiah Sonne, "Bibliotheca Historiographica Hebraica," *Jewish Quarterly Review* 34 (1943), 244.

127. Haim Beinart, "The Converso Community in Sixteenth- and Seventeenth-Century Spain," in *The Sephardi Heritage*, ed. R. Barnett (London: Valentine Mitchell, 1971), 477.

128. Miriam Bodian, *Dying in the Law of Moses: Crypto-Jewish Martyrdom in the Iberian World* (Bloomington: Indiana University Press, 2000), 158–59. For the documents, see Kenneth Brown, *De la cárcel inquisitorial a la sinagoga de Amsterdam (edición y estudio del "Romance a Lope de Vera" de Antonio Enríquez Gómez)* (Toledo: Consejería de Cultura de Castilla, 2007), 375–78.

129. Bodian, *Dying in the Law of Moses*, 244.

130. Leopold Zunz, "Geographische Literatur der Juden von den ältesten Zeiten bis zum Jahre 1841," *Gesammelte Schriften* (Berlin: Louis Goischel Verlagsbuchhandlung, 1875), 179–82; and Ismar Schorsch, *Leopold Zunz: Creativity in Adversity* (Philadelphia: University of Pennsylvania Press, 2017), 76–77.

131. Adolph Neubauer, *Medieval Jewish Chronicles and Chronological Notes* (Oxford: Oxford University Press, 1895), 2:xii–xiii; and Aescoly, "David Reubeni's Language," 210–12.

132. Heinrich Graetz, *History of the Jews* (Philadelphia: Jewish Publication Society, 1897), 4:504.

133. Adolf Poznański, "The Wisdom of Israel" (in Hebrew), *Ha-Tsefirah*, no. 167 (August 7, 1896), 810–11.

134. Israel Zinberg, *A History of Jewish Literature*, vol. 5, *The Jewish Center of Culture in the Ottoman Empire* (Cincinnati: Hebrew Union College Press, 1974), 29.

135. Yitzhak Baer, review (in Hebrew) of David Reubeni, *The Story of David Reubeni*, edited by Aaron Aescoly, *Kiryat Sefer* 17 (1940), 312.

136. Max Brod, *Reubeni: Prince of the Jews*, tr. Hannah Waller (London: Knopf, 1929). For a list of literary and journalistic works about Reubeni during this period, see the preface to the 1927 Yiddish translation of Reubeni's diary: David Reubeni, *Der seyfer hazikhroynes*, tr. Elijah Jacob Goldschmidt (Vilna: Farlag Tamar, 1927), i–iii.

137. Yaacov Shavit, "Realism and Messianism in Zionism and the Yishuv," in *Studies in Contemporary Jewry*, vol. 7, *Jews and Messianism in the Modern Era*, ed. Jonathan Frankel (New York: Oxford University Press, 1991), 120; Melissa Weininger, "An Ethical Zionist: Jesus in A. A. Kabak's *Bemish'ol hatsar*," *Prooftexts* 32 (2012), 23; and Aharon Abraham Kabak, *Solomon Molkho* (in Hebrew) (London: Ha-Olam, 1927), 3:259 and 317–18. The *Encyclopedia Judaica* declared Reubeni to be "a man of imagination and political courage," echoing the value that Theodor Herzl placed on *Staatsmut* (political courage) for the Jews, a quality he had claimed that they had lost since their exile. *Encyclopedia Judaica*, 9:1436, s.v. "Jerusalem."

138. Harriet Murav, *David Bergelson's Strange New World* (Bloomington: Indiana University Press, 2019), 279 and 295–96.

Chapter 1

1. As noted in the Introduction, according to 1 Chronicles 5:26, Habor was the place to which "the Reubenites, the Gadites, and the half-tribe of Manasseh" were exiled. Cf. 2 Kings 18:11. Although Reubeni claimed that it was located in Arabia, it is usually thought to have been in Assyria. Zvi Ben-Dor Benite, *The Ten Lost Tribes: A World History* (New York: Oxford University Press, 2013), 37.

2. On these medical techniques, see Peter Pormann and Emilie Savage-Smith, *Medieval Islamic Medicine* (Washington, DC: Georgetown University Press, 2007), 121.

3. Mentioned in the Bible, Kush was an ancient kingdom located in Nubia, a region that today embraces parts of southern Egypt and northern Sudan.

4. Located in central Sudan, Soba was the capital of the medieval Nubian Kingdom of Alwa. Reubeni spells the word "Soba" the same way that "Sheba" is spelled in Hebrew. His intention is to lead the reader to connect his journey in Africa with the legends surrounding the Kingdom of Sheba that are referenced in the Bible and in Jewish literature.

5. Hillelson suggests that this town is Lul or Lulu. Sigmar Hillelson, "David Reubeni, An Early Visitor to Sennar," *Sudan Notes and Records* 26 (1933), 57.

6. This passage seems to contradict Reubeni's statement in the paragraph above that huts were indeed built for the slaves who accompanied the king on such journeys.

7. Literally: "with chapter headings alone." Here, Reubeni uses this phrase, which is common in mystical works, without mystical connotations.

8. I.e., at the time when signs of dawn first begin to become visible.

9. The evidence for a missing section is that Reubeni never mentions Abu Kamil having left, and yet it appears that Reubeni must now make a long journey to him. Further, Reubeni requests to see the minister of the treasury but, for no clear reason, the king instead directs a messenger to take him to Obadiah, a neighboring ruler.

10. According to Hillelson, this is perhaps "the earliest reference to the well-known Ga'liyin tribe, whose traditional *dar* extends from the Shabluka cataract to the Atbara." Hillelson, "David Reubeni, An Early Visitor to Sennar," 61.

11. It appears that Amram, here and below, is an alternate spelling for Amara.

12. This mountain cannot be identified.

Chapter 2

1. This passage was intended to indicate Reubeni's adherence to Jewish dietary law. Reubeni was prepared to eat bread prepared by gentiles, but not cheese that might contain rennet from non-kosher meat.

2. Reubeni's formulation draws on the Mishnah, Avot 4:2.

3. The text here is corrupt.

4. Reubeni is referring to the Jewish daily prayers for agriculture, which change according to the time of the year.

5. Cf. Genesis 45:3.

6. Pamela Berger, *The Crescent on the Temple: The Dome of the Rock as Image of the Ancient Jewish Sanctuary* (Leiden: Brill, 2012), 241.

7. When Reubeni visited, this building was indeed split between the Franciscans and Muslims. In the following year the Franciscans were expelled by order of Sultan Suleyman. Denys Pringle, *The Churches of the Crusader Kingdom of Jerusalem* (Cambridge: Cambridge University Press, 2007), 3:270–71.

8. I.e., Isaac ha-Kohen Solal, the last nagid of Egyptian Jewry, who left Egypt for Jerusalem in 1517 after the Ottoman conquest.

9. It is noteworthy that Joseph, Reubeni's first follower, was from Naples. Controlled by Spain, Naples had a large population of both local Jews and conversos who had fled Iberia. A decade earlier, Naples had narrowly escaped the imposition of the Inquisition and an accompanying decree that ordered the expulsion of its Jews. Céline Dauverd, "Viceroys, Jews, and Conversos," in *Church and State in Spanish Italy: Rituals and Legitimacy in the Kingdom of Naples* (Cambridge: Cambridge University Press, 2021), 64–91.

Chapter 3

1. On Moses dal Castellazzo, see Paul Kaplan, "Jewish Artists and Images of Black Africans in Renaissance Venice," in *Multicultural Europe and Cultural Exchange in the Middle Ages and Renaissance*, ed. James Helfers (Turnholt: Brepols, 2005), 67–90.

2. R. Hiyya Meir served as a judge in Venice and assisted in the publication of the Bomberg Talmud. Ilona Steimann, "Jewish Scribes and Christian Patrons: The Hebraica Collection of Johann Jakob Fugger," *Renaissance Quarterly* 70 (2017), 1242.

3. R. Simon ben Asher Meshullam was a member of a prominent family of Venetian bankers; see David Jacoby, "New Evidence on Jewish Bankers in Venice and the Venetian Terraferma (c. 1450–1550)," in *The Mediterranean and the Jews: Banking, Finance and International Trade (XVI–XVIII Centuries)*, ed. Ariel Toaff and Simon Schwarzfuchs (Ramat-Gan: Bar Ilan University Press, 1989), 168.

4. Moses Nissim Foligno of Pesaro was an important banker. Howard Adelman, *Women and Jewish Marriage Negotiations in Early Modern Italy: For Love and Money* (Abingdon: Routledge, 2018), 186–87.

5. It is not clear to what custom Reubeni is referring.

6. By contrast, Reubeni's contemporary, Abraham Farissol, describes Reubeni riding a mule, not a horse, into the Vatican. Abraham Farissol, *Iggeret Orhot 'Olam* (Venice: Giovanni di Gara, 1586), 17.

7. For further information on this important humanist, see the Introduction to this book.

8. Aescoly identifies this figure as Joseph Hagri, who was known to have served as a Hebrew tutor to Cardinal Egidio. Aaron Aescoly, "Introduction," in David Reubeni, *Story of David Reubeni* (in Hebrew), ed. Aaron Aescoly (Jerusalem: Mossad Bialik, 1993), 105.

9. On Joseph Tsarfati, see Dan Almagor, "Joseph ben Samuel Tsarfati: Annotated Bibliography," *Italia* 12 (1996), 53–113.

10. The blessing of the redeemer is recited after deliverance from danger, including after the completion of a dangerous journey.

11. On the figure of Prester John, see the Introduction.

12. For references to Judah Gattegno, see Norman Roth, *The Bible and Jews in Medieval Spain* (Abingdon: Taylor and Francis, 2021), 151.

13. On the Abudarham family, see *Encyclopedia Judaica*, 2nd ed., s.v. "Abudarham."

14. Reubeni notes this because it is a marker of piety on par with what would have been expected for a man.

15. This phrase, that Reubeni denotes with an acronym, occurs several times in his diary. It is drawn from Deborah's praise of Jael in Judges.

16. Kenneth Stow, *The Jews in Rome (1536–1551)* (Leiden: Brill, 1995), 112.

17. The manuscript reads, "who had accompanied me from Crete." Since Reubeni first met Joseph in Alexandria, I have corrected the name to Alexandria, as suggested by Aescoly.

18. On the conversos of Rome, see James Nelson Novoa, *Being the Nação in the Eternal City: New Christian Lives in Sixteenth-Century Rome* (Peterborough: Baywolf Press, 2014).

19. On Daniel da Pisa, who was at that time the de facto head of the Jews of Rome, see the Introduction.

20. Reading *datarius* for *ratieri*. Cf. Eduard Biberfeld, *Der Reisebericht des David Rëubêni* (Berlin: Druck von H. Itzkowski, 1892), 7n97. Biberfeld's work contains the Hebrew text and a German translation of about half of Reubeni's diary.

21. Although Reubeni uses the term in rabbinic law that denotes a person for whom there is definitive proof that he was born of a forbidden union, *mamzer vadai*, its use here is casually derogatory rather than legal.

22. Reubeni spells this name "Latin," a corruption of "Alatino." The Alatino family were a well-established Italian Jewish family, many of whom practiced medicine. See Cecil Roth, *Jews in the Renaissance* (Philadelphia: Jewish Publication Society, 1959), 82–85.

23. This is likely a reference to the lazarettos of Italy, the plague hospitals in which people were detained for quarantine. Linda Clark and Carole Rawcliffe, *The Fifteenth Century*, vol. 12, *Society in an Age of Plague* (Woodbridge: Boydell and Brewer, 2013), 163–64.

24. *Hatan Torah* is the title for the individual honored with reciting the final blessing at the end of the yearly Torah reading cycle. Also, reading "my house" for "his house" to fit the context.

25. On Obadiah Sforno, see Saverio Campanini, "Un intellettuale ebreo del Rinascimento: 'Ovadyah Sforno a Bologna e i suoi rapporti con i cristiani," in *Verso l'epilogo di una convivenza gli ebrei a Bologna nel XVI secolo*, ed. Maria Giuseppina Muzzarelli (Florence: Firenze Giuntina, 1996), 103–04.

26. On the possible identity of Judah Ascoli, see Joseph Davis, *Eliezer Eilburg: The Ten Questions and Memoir of a Renaissance Jewish Skeptic* (Cincinnati: Hebrew Union College Press, 2018), 224.

27. Cf. 1 Chronicles 28:20.

28. On the term musician *(menagen)*, see David Ruderman, *The World of a Renaissance Jew: The Life and Thought of Abraham ben Mordecai Farissol* (Cincinnati: Hebrew Union College Press, 1981), 19.

29. I.e., Fra' Philippe de Villiers de L'Isle-Adam, the grand master of the Knights Hospitaller (d. 1534). When Reubeni met him, Rhodes had fallen to the Ottomans and the Knights had moved to Malta. See Carmelina Gugliuzzo, "Building a Sense of Belonging: The Foundation of Valletta in Malta," in *Foundation, Dedication and Consecration in Early Modern Europe*, ed. Maarten Delbeke and Minou Schraven (Leiden: Brill, 2012), 212–13.

30. R. Yehiel and R. Moses are likely the names of local Jews. It is not likely that R. Yehiel here refers to R. Yehiel da Pisa or that R. Moses refers to R. Moses Abudarham.

31. Perhaps R. Joseph had two houses, one in Viterbo and the other in Bolsena. His first wife's sons perhaps stayed with his mother in Viterbo and his second wife's sons in Bolsena. Alternatively, perhaps "him" refers to the son of R. Joseph with whom they stayed.

32. On Ismael da Rieti, see Shlomo Simonsohn, "On the History of the Rieti Banking Family in Tuscany," *Festschrift in Honor of Dr. George S. Wise* (Tel Aviv: Tel Aviv University, 1981), 301–15.

33. On the location of this house, see Michele Luzzatti, "Per la storia degli ebrei italiani nel Rinascimento. Matrimonii e apostasia di Clemenza di Vitale da Pisa," in *Studi sul Medioevo cristiano offerti a Raffaello Morghen* (Rome: Istituto storico italiano per il Medio Evo, 1974), 433 and 439.

34. The word *duda'im* was often used in the medieval period, following the Talmud, to signify violets. *Babylonian Talmud*, Sanhedrin 99b.

35. My translation of this sentence is an admittedly creative attempt to make sense of a flawed text.

36. Reubeni uses the word *to'evah* to refer to a church. The building in question was likely the Leaning Tower of Pisa.

37. I.e., Benvenida Abravanel. On this accomplished businesswoman and philanthropist, see Renata Segre, "Sephardic Refugees in Ferrara: Two Notable Families," in *Crisis and Creativity in the Sephardic World, 1391–1648*, ed. Benjamin Gampel (New York: Columbia University Press, 1997), 164–85.

38. Cf. Ecclesiastes 7:9.

39. Ana Buescu, who has studied the stormy relations between Dom Miguel and King João III, notes that Dom Miguel's recall was ordered by King João III and was

against Dom Miguel's wishes. Ana Buescu, "D. João III e D. Miguel da Silva, bispo de Viseu: novas razões para um ódio velho," *Revista de história da sociedade e da cultura* 10 (2010), 152. On the work of Dom Martin (Martinho de Portugal) as ambassador to Rome, see Raphael Barroso, "Práticas diplomáticas e disputas políticas na correspondência entre D. João III e seus embaixadores em Roma (1521–1557)," *Revista Hydra* 4 (2019), 255–60.

40. Aescoly's edition is in error here and my translation is therefore in accordance with Adolph Neubauer's edition of Reubeni's diary. Adolph Neubauer, *Medieval Jewish Chronicles and Chronological Notes* (Oxford: Oxford University Press, 1895), 2:168. Cf. Biberfeld, *Der Reisebericht des David Rëubêni*, 46.

41. The text reads ק״ב (102), but ק״ב and ק״ס (120) are easily confused and I have therefore opted for the rounder sum.

Chapter 4

1. Reading קאדיצי for קאליצי.

2. There appears to be a problem with the manuscript. Almería is over 400 km away from Cádiz. Moreover, it is not clear why Reubeni would have, without comment, disembarked in Spain after just noting that the local officials had prohibited him from doing so and were planning his arrest.

3. The original letter from the king survives; it is reprinted in Elias Lipiner, *O Sapateiro de Trancoso e o Alfaiate de Setúbal* (Rio de Janeiro: Imago Editora, 1993), 147.

4. The king was indeed staying in Almeirim because of the plague; see José Alberto Rodrigues da Silva Tavim, "David Reubeni: um 'embaixador' inusitado (1525–1526)," in *D. João III e o Império: Actas do Congresso Internacional comemorativo do seu nascimento* (Lisbon: Centro de História de Além-Mar, 2004), 691.

5. Reubeni appears to be referring to the order of King João II to remove Jewish children from their parents and send them to the island of São Tomé. He mistakenly understands the island to be located in the Mediterranean, a short distance away from Portugal. Maria José Pimenta Ferro Tavares, *Judaísmo e inquisição: estudos* (Lisbon: Editorial Presença, 1987), 24; and Robert Garfield, "Crypto-Judaism on an African Island: Reality and Fantasy on São Tomé from the 16th to the 20th Centuries," *Journal of Spanish, Portuguese, and Italian Crypto Jews* 2 (2010), 61–76.

6. The Portuguese controlled Hormuz from 1507 to 1622. Dejanirah Couto and Rui Manuel Loureiro, eds., *Revisiting Hormuz: Portuguese Interactions in the Persian Gulf Region in the Early Modern Period* (Wiesbaden: Harrassowitz, 2008).

7. In some parts of Italy, there were laws to discourage servants from leaving their employers before their contracted term of service had expired. Unless they had documentation proving the mutuality of the decision to end the contract, any new employer could face a fine for hiring them. It seems likely that it is this document that Tobias seeks from Reubeni and which Reubeni refers to as an "authorization" *(reshut)*. Dennis Romano, "The Regulation of Domestic Service in Renaissance Venice," *Sixteenth Century Journal* 22 (1991), 663.

8. Cf. Deuteronomy 21:11.

9. Literally, "revert" or "return you to being a Jew."

10. Reubeni is referencing Deuteronomy 21:10–13, which details the laws pertaining to marrying a woman who has been taken captive in war.

11. This phrase is taken from the Yom Kippur penitential liturgy.

12. Reading עמך for עמי.

13. Reubeni is referring to a series of devastating famines in the Maghreb that occurred between 1521 and 1524. His report that some Muslims sold their children as slaves to Christians, and especially to the Portuguese, in a desperate bid to keep them alive is corroborated by other contemporary sources. Eloy Martín-Corrales, *Muslims in Spain, 1492–1814: Living and Negotiating in the Land of the Infidel* (Leiden: Brill, 2021), 192.

14. The name given in the manuscript, מעיר, is corrupt. My rendering of al-Mughira is a beſt conjecture.

15. Mercedes García-Arenal, "Un réconfort pour ceux qui sont dans l'attente," *Revue de l'histoire des religions* 220 (2003), 469. On Abraham Benzamerro, see José Alberto Rodrigues da Silva Tavim, "Abraão Benzamerro, 'Judeu de sinal', sem sinal, entre o Norte de África e o Reino de Portugal," *Mare Liberum* 6 (1993), 115–41.

16. Reading אותי for אותו.

17. This name is perhaps a reference to Isaiah 11:1: "A shoot (*hoter*) shall grow from the stump of Jesse."

18. As mentioned, Hormuz was then under Portuguese occupation. On relations between Portugal and Hormuz, see Salih Ozbaran, "The Ottoman Turks and the Portuguese in the Persian Gulf, 1534–1581," in *The Ottoman Response to European Expansion: Studies in Ottoman-Portuguese Relations in the Indian Ocean and Ottoman Administration in the Arab Lands during the Sixteenth Century* (Istanbul: Isis Press, 1994), 123.

19. When he met Reubeni, Joseph Cordelha was chief rabbi of Azemmour, a position appointed by the Portuguese king. He eventually converted to Christianity and testified on behalf of the Inquisition. For his biography, see José Alberto Rodrigues da Silva Tavim, *Os judeus na expansão portuguesa em Marrocos durante o século XVI* (Braga: APPACDM Distrital, 1997), 218–24.

20. I.e., the Sa'di ruler, Mahammad al-Shaykh b. Muhammad al-Mahdi (r. 1517–1557). Clifford Bosworth, *The New Islamic Dynasties* (New York: Columbia University Press, 1996), 50.

21. See Chetrit's note on the reading of the word *al-Sus*. Joseph Chetrit, "The Secret of David Hareuveni According to a Hebrew Poem from Morocco" (in Hebrew), *Tarbiz* 60 (1991), 239 n.19.

22. A *kohen* is a descendant of the biblical priestly class. Although kohanim lost most of their prerogatives with the destruction of the second Temple, they continued to occupy some ritual functions.

23. On the phenomenon of converso children fasting, see Yitzhak Baer, *A History of the Jews in Christian Spain* (Philadelphia: Jewish Publication Society, 1978), 2:358.

24. Reubeni is indicating that the animal was not slaughtered in the way prescribed by Jewish law.

25. Shingoli is the name of a town in the district of Maharashtra which had a large Jewish population.

26. I.e., although Reubeni was present, he did not understand the conversation and required a translation.

27. I.e., Afonso de Portugal (1509–1540).

28. This is a quotation from the Jewish daily evening prayer.

29. It is unclear what name קרבלייאה represents. It is possible that it is a nickname that Reubeni uses to shield this converso's identity. Lea Sestieri renders it "Carvalho," although this does not seem plausible to me. Lea Sestieri, *David Reubeni: un ebreo d'Arabia in missione segreta nell'Europa del '500* (Genoa: Marietti, 1991), 175.

30. Reubeni refers to the preparations for the wedding of Isabella of Portugal (d. 1539) to her first cousin, Charles V.

31. Although Judaism had been banned in Portugal since 1497, Jews from Portugal's North African territories, because of their importance to imperial rule there, were sometimes permitted to travel as Jews in Portugal. See the Introduction.

32. The identity of this duke is unclear.

33. Isabella of Portugal left for her wedding on January 30, 1526; see Claudia Möller Recondo and Isidoro Jiménez, "Carlos V e Isabel: Imperatorum Itinera," *Investigaciones históricas: Época moderna y contemporánea* 40 (2020), 186–87. The wedding took place on March 10, 1526.

34. This phrase is taken from the Yom Kippur penitential liturgy.

35. I have transposed this line from the beginning of this paragraph.

36. The reference is to Diogo Pires, who later renamed himself Solomon Molkho. See the Introduction.

37. Perhaps "the conversos' house" refers to a building that conversos were using as a synagogue.

38. On Antonio Carneiro, see Ana Buescu, *D. João III: 1502–1557* (Lisbon: Temas e Debates, 2008), 224 and 264–65.

39. Reubeni is referring to the birth of Prince Afonso, the son of the king and Catherine of Austria.

40. This sentence refers to both a "Judah Cordelha" and a "Joseph Cordelha." This is clearly a manuscript error and I have corrected "Judah" to "Joseph."

41. This sentence is difficult to interpret. Afonso, the king's son, died in infancy on April 12, 1526. The reticence about mourning the death was likely a reflection of cultural practices surrounding neonatal death. Perhaps the ministers believed that the child had not been baptized and were thus reluctant to facilitate a ritual of public mourning. Cf. Ana Buescu, *Catarina de Áustria (1507–1578)* (Lisbon: A Esfera dos Livros, 2007), 184.

42. See David Reubeni, *The Story of David Reubeni* (in Hebrew), ed. Aaron Aescoly (Jerusalem: Mossad Bialik, 1993), 57.

43. Tavim, "David Reubeni: um 'embaixador' inusitado," 702n89.

44. I have corrected the text as suggested by Aescoly.

45. Cf. Isaiah 26:4.

46. Reading בתחילה for בתפילה.

47. The text is corrupt and conflates two names: Solomon Levi and Solomon Cohen. I have preserved both in the translation.

48. Literally, "some slanderers at the house of the conversos." I have omitted the phrase because it is likely a dittography.

49. On the laws against wearing silk, see Francisco Bethencourt, "Sumptuary Laws in Portugal and Its Empire from the Fourteenth to the Eighteenth Century," in *The Right to Dress: Sumptuary Laws in a Global Perspective, c. 1200–1800* (Cambridge: Cambridge University Press, 2019), 279–80.

50. Tavim, *Os judeus na expansão portuguesa em Marrocos*, 202–10.

51. Reubeni is indicating that R. Abraham Rut had reservations about whether the food that Reubeni served was properly kosher.

52. I.e., the Arade river.

53. Or alternatively, *boscaioli*, "woodcutters."

54. Here, Reubeni echoes the biblical language used to describe David's leadership during the reign of King Saul (2 Samuel 5:2).

55. I have rearranged the order of the following text, as it appears to be jumbled due to a scribal error.

56. Cf. 2 Samuel 4:9.

Chapter 5

1. In Exodus 8:15, Pharaoh's court magicians recognize the plague of lice as being not merely the product of Moses and Aaron's talent, but of divine intervention, "the finger of God." In the *Passover Haggadah*, Rabbi Yose the Galilean attributes all ten plagues, by means of which the Israelites were liberated from Egypt, to one finger of God. By using this phrase, Reubeni may be emphasizing that he is but a representative of a divine mission. The phrase "God's Torah is complete" is likely intended as a polemical rejoinder to the Christian charge that the Hebrew Bible (the Christian Old Testament) is lacking without the New Testament to complete it, and to the Muslim charge that the current Hebrew Bible is a corrupt version of the original revelation.

2. Cf. Isaiah 51:8.

3. Reubeni adds the sentence: "I was thinking of going up to the emperor." As it appears disconnected from the context, it might indicate a further gap in the manuscript.

4. A massive earthquake leveled most of Almería in 1522. César Olivera Serrano, *La actividad sísmica en el reino de Granada (1487–1531)* (Madrid: C. Olivera Serrano, 1995), 39–44.

5. A marginal note in the manuscript says a page is likely missing here.

6. I tentatively identify this village as Albudeite (Reubeni has אלבגייט). This village is not directly on Reubeni's route to Cartagena, but it is located near some hot springs.

7. Here and below, Reubeni refers to Ishmaelites living in Spain. Since Islam had been outlawed in Spain since 1502, Reubeni is apparently referring to those Moriscos (Iberian Muslim forced converts to Christianity and their descendants) who continued to observe Islamic rituals in secret.

8. It is possible that the diary continued but that these pages are missing from the manuscript.

Appendix

1. For speculation on the identity of Solomon Cohen, see Élodie Attia, *Les manuscrits de Raphaël de Prato: une bibliothèque privée juive italienne du 16ᵉ siècle* (Berlin: Institut für Judaistik, 2012), 25–26.

2. The text reads "almarina" but, based on context, it appears that the author was referring to Almeirim.

3. On the Lord of Clermont, see the Introduction to this book.

4. On the phenomenon of Italian Jews keeping such genealogical records, see Julia Lieberman, "Childhood and Family among the Western Sephardim in the Seventeenth Century," *Sephardi Family Life in the Early Modern Diaspora* (Waltham: Brandeis University Press, 2011), 144.

INDEX

Abravanel, Benvenida, 8, 83, 108, 123
Abravanel, Isaac, 25
Abudarham family, 66, 67
Abyssinia, 56, 10–11, 168n18
Afonso de Portugal, Cardinal (brother of João III), 108, 127–28
Alatino, Moses, 71–72
Albudeite, 159
Alexandria, 3, 54–58, 68, 83
Alkabets, Shlomo, 21
Almeirim, 91, 93, 95–125, 130, 163
Almería, 18, 88, 154–58, 163
Amara Dunqas, King, 2, 31, 32, 33, 38, 39
Amram, King. *See* Amara Dunqas, King
apocalypticism. *See* millennialism
Aqrish, Isaac, 27
Arabic interpreter, the, 105–110, 116–21, 127–36, 141, 147–48
Arabic language: letter in, 104–5; Reubeni speaking, xiii, 1, 8, 10, 95–96; proper names, 43, 46; speakers, 60, 66, 77, 81, 93, 98, 138, 159. *See also* Arabic interpreter, the
Ascoli, Judah, 74
Ashkenazi, R. Joseph, 60, 62, 72, 179n8
Assua River, 31
astrology, 94, 157
Avignon, 19, 165

Beja, 90, 134–35
Benzamerro, Abraham, 101, 103, 105, 115, 123, 155
Bergelson, David, 29
Black skin, 1, 5–7, 32, 93, 101, 105, 124, 167n2. *See also* Kushites
Bolsena, 78, 80
Brod, Max, 28–29

Cádiz, 12, 87–88
Cairo, 2, 9, 40, 43–47, 55
Candia, 58
cannibalism, 2, 33, 94
Cap d'Agde, 163–65
Carneiro, Antonio, 125, 129, 136–37, 141, 148
Carpentras, 19, 165
Cartagena, 18, 159–60
Castelnuovo di Porto, 60
Catherine of Austria (queen of Portugal), 93, 108, 110, 122, 125, 128
Cave of the Patriarchs, 3, 48–50
Charles V, Holy Roman Emperor: Reubeni's relations with, 1, 18, 22, 24, 117, 122, 158; political relations of, 4, 10, 22–23, 62, 87; Jews and, 9, 170n41; Isabella of Portugal and, 109, 111, 117, 158; letters from, 160–61, 164; messengers sent to, 156; territory of, 151, 154
Christian Hebraism, 9
churches, 3, 53, 83, 171n56
circumcision, 6, 17, 21, 120–22
Clement VII, Pope, 1, 2, 7–12, 15, 18–21, 24; Daniel da Pisa and, 68–70, 73–74; gift-giving and, 86, 123; king of Portugal and, 96; letters from, 18, 74, 84, 87–88, 115, 129, 154, 156, 160–61, 164; letters to, 128; officials of, 68–70, 72, 74–75; plans to meet, 31, 55, 59–62, 122, 125; Reubeni's interactions with, 62–63, 70, 72, 75, 84, 96, 115; Reubeni's opponents and, 71, 76
Clermont, Lord of, 18–19, 163–65, 173n88

Cohen, Solomon (of Prato), 106, 130,
    133, 140–45, 149–50, 154–62; accu-
    sations against, 115–16; appointment
    of, 86; as interpreter, 95, 124, 139,
    147, 154; as manager of Reubeni's en-
    tourage, 100, 112–16, 138; as money
    manager, 91, 97–98, 113, 116, 124,
    150–52; as writer 18, 115, 163–65
conversion or return to Judaism, 22,
    98–101, 118, 120–22, 140. *See also*
    conversos, accusations of Judaization.
conversion to Christianity, 117, 127–28,
    182n19
conversos, passim; accusations of Juda-
    ization, 17, 68, 115, 120–22, 140–42,
    147; arrested, 116, 126, 133–34; as
    hosts, 88, 90, 93–94, 131–32, 134–
    35, 143; converso children fasting,
    106, 108
Cordelha, Joseph, 104, 114, 123, 126
Coruche, 131, 133, 148
Crete. *See* Candia
cupping 31, 64
dal Castellazzo, Moses, 5, 58, 59

Damietta, 3, 8, 54–55
da Pisa, Daniel, 5, 7, 10, 12, 19, 24, 83–
    85, 155; as appointer of Reubeni's
    servants, 76–77, 79, 82, 115–16; as
    Reubeni's financial backer, 72–73,
    80, 84, 86, 91; as Reubeni's liaison
    with the pope, 68–70, 74–75, 84;
    Dom Miguel and, 75–76; Reubeni's
    dispute with, 72–74
da Pisa, Leora, 78–82, 85
da Pisa, Signora Sarah, 12, 18, 78–84,
    129
da Pisa, Yehiel, 7, 12, 77–86, 129, 142,
    155
da Rieti, Ismael, 12, 78
da Silva, Dom Miguel, 12, 17–18, in
    Rome, 68, 71–72, 75–76, 78–80, 84;
    in Portugal 91–93, 95–97, 109, 111–
    13, 129–30, 136, 140–41, 147–48,
    150
Dawit II, Emperor of Abyssinia, 6, 10–
    11. *See also* Prester John

de Castro, Abraham, 2, 44–45
de Varthema, Ludovico de, 6
Dienna, Abraham ben Solomon, 20
di Viterbo, Cardinal Egidio, 9–10, 19,
    60, 62–63, 68
Dome of the Rock, 3, 51–52
Dongola, 38, 39
dreams, 21, 38, 45, 121

enslaved people, 2, 15; enslavement,
    101, 165; in Africa 31–47; Kushite (in
    Africa), 43, 46–47, 167n2; Kushite (in
    Portugal), 101, 124, 130, 133, 137–38,
    142–43, 150; Muslim, 101, 106, 127.
    See also maidservants
Esteban, Inés, 14
Évora, 90, 100, 133–35

famine, 101
Farissol, Abraham, 5
Faro, 143–44
fasting: by Benvenida Abravanel's
    family, 83, 108; by converso
    children, 106, 108; by Reubeni at
    sea, 58, 151; by Reubeni in Africa,
    32, 34–35, 39, 43; by Reubeni in
    Italy 5, 58–59, 62–63, 79–80, 85;
    by Reubeni in Palestine 51–52, 63;
    by Reubeni in Portugal 93–94, 108,
    111–12, 151, 158; by Reubeni in
    Spain, 158
Federigo, Marquis of Mantua, 19–20
Ferdinand of Aragon, 13, 22
Fez, 101–4, 106, 119, 122–23, 136, 140
Florence, 80, 82–86
Foligno, R. Moses, 59–60
Foundation Stone, the, 51–52
Francis I, King of France, 4, 10, 19, 22,
    62, 77
Funj Sultanate, 2. *See also* Amara
    Dunqas, King

Gattegno, Judah, 65, 67
Gaza, 3, 8, 47–48, 53–55
Ghetto of Venice, 59–60
Girga, 40, 43
Graetz, Heinrich, 28

Granada, 156
graves, 3, 35, 48–50, 52–53

Hagri, Joseph. *See* Ashkenazi, R. Joseph
Halevi, Abraham ben Eliezer, 24–25
Hebrew: as language of Reubeni's diary,
    xiii, xiv, 28; Egidio di Viterbo and,
    9–10; inscription in, 54; interpreters
    of, 68, 95, 114, 134, 142; Reubeni
    speaking, 1, 44, 58; Solomon Molkho
    and, 21–22
Hebron, 3, 48–51
Herzl, Theodor, 27–28
Hormuz, 94, 104

Ibn Forno, David, 67
Ibn Yahya, Gedaliah, 5
India, 9, 103, 108
Inquisition, 9, 22; conversos and, 5,
    12–13, 15, 25; Reubeni and, 1, 18,
    24, 27, 29, 161–62; Solomon Molkho
    and, 21
Isabella of Castille, 13, 22
Isabella of Portugal (wife of Charles V),
    18, 111, 117, 156, 157
Israel, land of, 1, 14, 24–26, 90, 102–3,
    108. *See also* Jerusalem *and* Palestine

Jeddah, 2, 10, 17, 24, 31
Jerusalem: Christian conquest of, 16,
    22; directions to, 44–45; 63, 73, 78;
    Jewish attitudes to, 12, 54, 78; Jewish
    conquest of, 16, 20, 26, 64–65, 102–
    3, 115, 134, 157; Jewish travel to, 84,
    121, 126; Reubeni's dedication to, 73;
    Reubeni in, 3, 9, 51–53, 63, 83; voice
    emanating from, 158
Jerusalemites, 54, 70, 83
Jewish dietary law, 44, 58, 140
João I, King of Portugal, 93
João III, King of Portugal, 1, 16–18; in-
    vitation to Reubeni, 87–89; letters of,
    119, 125–35, 142, 147, 154, 160, 164;
    pope and, 10, 15, 62, 75–76; Reubeni
    and, 79–80, 84–97, 100–42, 147–50,
    153, 156, 163. *See also* Dom Miguel
Josel of Rosheim, 22

Kabbalah and kabbalists: Christians
    and, 9; in Egypt, 3, 55, 57; in Italy,
    7, 12, 68; Reubeni and, 1, 90, 103;
    Solomon Molkho and, 21, 27
Karo, Joseph, 21, 27
Kush, land of, 31–37, 102, 105
Kushites, *see under* enslaved people

Lagos, 108, 142–51, 158, 163
Leaning Tower of Pisa, 12, 83
Lemlein, Asher, 25
Leo Africanus, 9–10
Levita, Elijah, 9–10
Lisbon, 21, 91, 108, 140–41, 148
Livorno, 18, 84–86, 143, 149, 157–58
Llerena, 15, 24
Lorca, 159
Loulé, 135

Maghrebi Jews. *See* Moroccan Jews
maidservants, 97–101, 112, 131, 160. *See*
    enslaved people
Maimonides, Moses, 26
Mantua, 19–20, 24
Manuel I, King of Portugal, 13, 16,
    103
marriage, Jewish, 15, 78; royal, 18, 109,
    111, 117
Martin, Dom (Martinho de Portugal),
    84
Massawa, 39
matchmaking, 71, 84, 98–99
Mecca, 6, 24, 33–35
Mehmet II (Ottoman sultan), 25
Meir, R. Hiyya, 59
Meshullam, Simon ben Asher, 5, 59, 79
messianism and messiahs, Reubeni and,
    1–2, 6, 12, 16, 20, 26–29, 103; con-
    versos and, 13–14; Jewish views on,
    6, 25. *See also* Molkho, Solomon
millennialism: Egidio di Viterbo and, 9;
    Reubeni and, 24–26, 64–65, 102–3,
    115, 134–35, 156
Molkho, Solomon, 17, 21–22, 24, 27–28,
    120–22; world politics and, 4, 6,
    16–17, 157
Mora, 131–33, 148

Moriscos. *See* Muslim converts to Christianity,

Moroccan Jews, 101, 103, 105–6; in Italy, 65; in Portugal, 16, 104–6, 114–20, 123–26, 130–41, 147–48, 150

Mount Zion, 52–53

Muhammad, Islamic prophet, 34, 40, 56–57; descendants of 2, 31–35, 38, 41, 46–52, 56, 104

Murcia, 18, 161–62

music, 8, 76, 80, 82, 86, 104, 107

Muslim converts to Christianity, 95, 127, 159, 160

Naples, 3, 55, 68, 83, 108, 123

Nile River, 2, 32, 37–40, 43, 102, 105

Ottoman Empire, 1, 4, 6, 10, 17, 21–26, 51. *See also* Turks

Palestine, 3, 8, 25, 47–55. *See also* Israel, land of *and* Jerusalem

Pesaro, 59–60

Pires, Diogo. *See* Molkho, Solomon

Pisa, 12, 75–76, 78–86, 115, 151

plague, 19, 65–66, 72, 85, 91, 101, 140

Poznański, Adolf, 28

Prague, 27

Prester John, 5, 6, 62, 70, 75, 115. *See also* Dawit II, Emperor of Abyssinia

prophets and prophecy, 5, 25; Reubeni and, 1, 103; converso prophets, 14; Solomon Molkho and, 21. *See also* Muhammad, Islamic prophet

prostitutes, 137, 160

Purchena, 159

Purim, holiday of, 48, 60

Queen of Portugal. *See* Catherine of Austria

Ramusio, Giovanni Battista, 5, 20

Red Sea, 2, 17, 31

Reformation, 4

Regensburg, 21–22

Rome, 3–12, 17, 19–21, 25, 60–77; messengers sent to, 79, 84, 165; plans to return to, 100, 122, 125, 127–28; recollections of, 83, 91, 96–97, 110–11, 113, 115; reports from, 85; Reubeni's servants return to, 79–80, 86; traveling to, 52–53, 55, 57, 59–60. *See also* sack of Rome

Ronciglione, 77

Rut, Abraham, 140

sack of Rome, 4, 9, 19

Sambatyon River, 105

Santarém, 93–99, 112–14, 125–32, 136, 141, 163

São Tomé, 93, 181n5

Sennar, 37

sexual relations and coercion, 33, 98–99, 101, 112. *See also* maidservants *and* prostitutes

Sforno, Obadiah, 7, 74

Shabbetai Tsvi, 27

Sheba, Kingdom of. *See* Soba, Kingdom of

sickness: of Reubeni, 8, 31, 63–67; of others, 19, 39, 45, 57–58, 85, 122, 125–26. *See also* plague

Siena, 12, 78

Soba, Kingdom of, 31–39, 102, 105

Sorbas, 159

Suakin, 31

Suleyman the Magnificent, 4, 43

synagogues: in Egypt, 3, 56–57; in Italy, 60, 65, 67, 73, 81; in Palestine, 53–54; in Portugal, 116

Tavira, 88–90, 134–43, 151; officials of, 119, 125, 129–30, 147–48; people joining Reubeni in, 91–92, 94, 104, 108, 119, 134; travel to and from, 79, 88, 126, 163

Temple, the, 48, 50–53, 102, 156

Tribes, Lost Israelite, 1, 6, 31, 40, 102, 105, 127, 155

Tsarfati, R. Joseph, 60, 63–67, 71, 77, 84–85

Turks, 43, 46–47, 52, 55, 57, 81–82. *See also* Ottoman Empire

Venice, 2–5, 19–21, 25, 58–59, 63; Cardinal of, 71–72; traveling to, 53, 55, 57
Vila Nova, 144–45
Viterbo, 68, 77–78, 80

women, 1, 8, 15; in crowds, 60, 62, 88, 90, 120, 132, 143–45; Italy, 8, 12, 64–67, 71, 77–85, 123, 129; Converso, 14, 88, 91, 93, 108, 143; Africa, 32–36, 39; Spain, 154, 158; in Palestine, 53; in Portugal, 92, 101, 109, 111, 117, 138; in Egypt, 46, 55, 57; as queens, 13, 18, 32–36, 93, 108–9, 122, 125, 156. *See also* maidservants *and* prostitutes

Zionism, 27–29
Zunz, Leopold, 28

STANFORD STUDIES IN JEWISH HISTORY AND CULTURE

David Biale and Sarah Abrevaya Stein, Editors

This series features novel approaches to examining the Jewish past in the form of innovative work that brings the field into productive dialogue with the newest scholarly concepts and methods. Open to a range of disciplinary and interdisciplinary approaches, from history to cultural studies, this series publishes exceptional scholarship balanced by an accessible tone, illustrating histories of difference and addressing issues of current urgency. Books in this list push the boundaries of Jewish Studies and speak compellingly to a wide audience of scholars and students.

Dina Porat, *Nakam: The Holocaust Survivors Who Sought Full-Scale Revenge*
2022

Christian Bailey, *German Jews in Love: A History*
2022

Matthias B. Lehmann, *The Baron: Maurice de Hirsch and the Jewish Nineteenth Century*
2022

Liora R. Halperin, *The Oldest Guard: Forging the Zionist Settler Past*
2021

Samuel J. Spinner, *Jewish Primitivism*
2021

Sonia Gollance, *It Could Lead to Dancing: Mixed-Sex Dancing and Jewish Modernity*
2021

Julia Elsky, *Writing Occupation: Jewish Émigré Voices in Wartime France*
2020

Alma Rachel Heckman, *The Sultan's Communists:
Moroccan Jews and the Politics of Belonging*
2020

Golan Y. Moskowitz, *Queer Jewish Sendak: A Wild Visionary in Context*
2020

Devi Mays, *Forging Ties, Forging Passports: Migration and the Modern Sephardi Diaspora*
2020

Clémence Boulouque, *Another Modernity: Elia Benamozegh's Jewish Universalism*
2020

Dalia Kandiyoti, *The Converso's Return: Conversion and Sephardi History in Contemporary Literature and Culture*
2020

Natan M. Meir, *Stepchildren of the Shtetl: The Destitute, Disabled, and Mad of Jewish Eastern Europe, 1800-1939*
2020

Marc Volovici, *German as a Jewish Problem: The Language Politics of Jewish Nationalism*
2020

Dina Danon, *The Jews of Ottoman Izmir: A Modern History*
2019

Omri Asscher, *Reading Israel, Reading America: The Politics of Translation Between Jews*
2019

Yael Zerubavel, *Desert in the Promised Land*
2018

Sunny S. Yudkoff, *Tubercular Capital: Illness and the Conditions of Modern Jewish Writing*
2018

Sarah Wobick-Segev, *Homes Away from Home: Jewish Belonging in Twentieth-Century Paris, Berlin, and St. Petersburg*
2018

Eddy Portnoy, *Bad Rabbi: And Other Strange but True Stories from the Yiddish Press*
2017

Jeffrey Shandler, *Holocaust Memory in the Digital Age: Survivors' Stories and New Media Practices*
2017

Joshua Schreier, *The Merchants of Oran: A Jewish Port at the Dawn of Empire*
2017

Alan Mintz, *Ancestral Tales: Reading the Buczacz Stories of S. Y. Agnon*
2017

Ellie R. Schainker, *Confessions of the Shtetl: Converts from Judaism in Imperial Russia, 1817–1906*
2016

For a complete listing of titles in this series, visit the
Stanford University Press website, www.sup.org.

Lightning Source UK Ltd.
Milton Keynes UK
UKHW010608060123
414924UK00001B/88